PENGUIN

MEDIEVAL WRITINGS (

ELISABETH VAN HOUTS is a Fellow and lecturer in Medieval History at Emmanuel College, Cambridge, with particular interests in the Anglo-Norman period, Latin historiography and the role of women in medieval society. Her books include *The Gesta Normannorum Ducum of William of Jumièges, Orderic Vitalis and Robert of Torigni* (1992–5); *Memory and Gender in Medieval Europe 900–1200* (1999); *History and Family Traditions in England and the Continent, 100–1200* (1999); *Medieval Memories: Men, Women and the Past 700–1300* (2001); and *The Normans in Europe* (2000). She is currently preparing a book on the lay experience of medieval marriage.

PATRICIA SKINNER was Reader in Medieval History at the University of Southampton and now combines her continuing writing career with supporting researchers at the University of Portsmouth. She has published extensively on the social and gender history of medieval Italy, as well as editing books on Anglo-Jewish medieval history and medieval historiography. She is currently writing a book about Amalfi in the middle ages.

Medieval Writings on Secular Women

Translated and with an Introduction by
PATRICIA SKINNER *and* ELISABETH VAN HOUTS

PENGUIN BOOKS

PENGUIN BOOKS

Published by the Penguin Group
Penguin Books Ltd, 80 Strand, London WC2R ORL, England
Penguin Group (USA) Inc., 375 Hudson Street, New York, New York 10014, USA
Penguin Group (Canada), 90 Eglinton Avenue East, Suite 700, Toronto, Ontario,
Canada M4P 2Y3 (a division of Pearson Penguin Canada Inc.)
Penguin Ireland, 25 St Stephen's Green, Dublin 2, Ireland (a division of Penguin Books Ltd)
Penguin Group (Australia), 250 Camberwell Road, Camberwell, Victoria 3124, Australia
(a division of Pearson Australia Group Pty Ltd)
Penguin Books India Pvt Ltd, 11 Community Centre, Panchsheel Park, New Delhi – 110 017, India
Penguin Group (NZ), 67 Apollo Drive, Rosedale, Auckland 0632, New Zealand
(a division of Pearson New Zealand Ltd)
Penguin Books (South Africa) (Pty) Ltd, 24 Sturdee Avenue, Rosebank, Johannesburg 2196, South Africa

Penguin Books Ltd, Registered Offices: 80 Strand, London WC2R ORL, England

www.penguin.com

First published 2011
004

Copyright © Patricia Skinner and Elisabeth van Houts, 2011

Set in 10.25/12.25pt PostScript Adobe Sabon
Typeset by Jouve (UK), Milton Keynes
Printed in Great Britain by Clays Ltd, Elcograf S.p.A.

ISBN: 978-0-141-43991-4

www.greenpenguin.co.uk

Penguin Books is committed to a sustainable
future for our business, our readers and our planet.
This book is made from Forest Stewardship
Council™ certified paper.

Contents

Chapter 2: Girls and Young Women

Chapter 3: Married Women and Mothers

Chapter 4: Widows

Chapter 5: Older Women and Death

      Guînes, Flanders, 2 July 1177   267

132. Benefactors of the Hôtel-Dieu, Listed for
      Commemoration, Beauvais, 1292   268

133. 'Competitive' Commemoration after the Death of
      Queen Matilda II, England, 1118   270

134. Letter to Einhard Commiserating on the Death of
      his Wife, Imma, 836   272

135. Guisanda's Will Disputed, Bari, 1021   273

136. The Will of Eva Peche Disputed, Cambridge,
      1286   275

137. Beneficiary of a Will, Crete, 1301   276

138. Commemoration Stone Erected by Helmgöt
      for his Deceased Wife, Odendis, Sweden, Tenth
      to Eleventh Centuries   277

139. The Will of Æthelgifu, England, Tenth Century   277

      Notes   285
      Bibliography   295

Acknowledgements

This book was conceived just after the second-millennium celebrations when the then editor of Penguin Classics, Laura Barber, suggested a twin volume to the *Medieval Writings on Female Spirituality* by Elisabeth Spearing. Both of us were immediately enthusiastic, because we realized that between us we could span a good selection of writings on secular women from the north and south of Europe. At the same time, we were apprehensive, in that as medievalists we were not trained Latinists (or for that matter translators of other medieval vernacular languages), so translating texts from scratch would be a daunting task. Any sense of burden, however, was soon lightened somewhat when we hit on the idea of using the female life cycle as a guiding principle. The speed with which we collected texts soon made it clear that by translating sections at a time we could manage to fit the workload into our busy professional and personal lives.

We are immensely grateful to a number of friends, colleagues and organizations for their generous permission to use their translations: Dr T. Hunt for text 2, Professor Monserrat Cabre for text 4, Professor James Montgomery for text 29, Professor Sir John Baker for text 69, Dr Keiko Nowacka for text 44, Lucy McKitterick for texts 87 and 89, Dr Rosalind Love for her share in text 133 and Dr Julia Crick for text 139. The Selden Society gave us permission to use translations of texts 38, 47 and 115 and Manchester University Press for text 78; the University of California Press originally published excerpts 13 and 22 and the Jewish Historical Society of England text 34. We thank all of them for their kind cooperation. Unpublished texts were most kindly made available for us to translate by Professor Jonathan Rose (text 69) and Dr Paul Brand (text 92). We benefited enormously from the advice on technical language (legal vocabulary) given by Professor Sir John Baker. Mrs Johanna Dale shared her expertise on images of medieval women with us, which allowed us to select the splendid picture of sage-collectors from the fourteenth-century Viennese *Tacuinum sanitatis codex Vindobonensis*, which is used for the front cover of our volume; we are indebted to her for her advice.

The editors and staff at Penguin have been an endless source of advice and support. In particular we owe a great deal to the encouragement of Alexis Kirchbaum and Rachel Love. Above all, we owe an immense debt to the care taken by Louisa Watson, our meticulous copy-editor.

Finally we should both like to thank our families and friends, who have lived with this project and provided valuable support and feedback since its inception.

Introduction

Since research into medieval women's lives started in earnest nearly half a century ago, and has taken its place within academic curricula for at least the last forty years, one may wonder why it is that a new source book on the subject is required.[1] The simple answer is that whilst there are plenty of source books detailing medieval women's activities, their focus has been on prominent women, women in power, or those who are well documented through their religious activity. Medieval secular women on the ground have been explored in limited geographical and chronological contexts (most notably in late medieval England, where the source base allows for often quite extensive recording of laywomen's lives),[2] but have rarely been examined in a comparative work.

This collection aims to juxtapose materials from various regions and periods in the Middle Ages. The earliest material presented dates to the ninth century, the latest, to the fifteenth. Geographically, the sources relate mainly to western Europe, with a rather higher proportion of southern European texts than is the norm for this type of collection. Inevitably, in a collaboration of this type, the regional bias of the sources unapologetically reflects the research interests of the two editors, but this is far from a parochial collection. We have grouped texts to enable comparisons across time and place to be made, and to provoke discussion about the validity of such comparisons. This does not imply that our purpose is to revive the old idea of a universality of experience among women, nor to suggest that a similar practice or custom in two separate parts of medieval Europe was as a result of one region influencing another (more likely these would be regions sharing a common legal culture stemming from the extensive Roman conquests and, where Rome had not penetrated, the later influence of Christianization). Simply put, this collection seeks to break down barriers: women's lives have often been studied along regional lines, and only more recent work has been ambitious enough to take a theme and study it across cultures. We hope that these extracts will provide more ideas for such comparison.

ORGANIZING PRINCIPLE:
WOMEN'S LIFE CYCLE

As well as the wide chronological and geographical span of our sources, they are also diverse in their typology, an issue which will be discussed in detail below. The major question which arose when we were compiling the collection was how to organize such a variety of material. In fact this diversity offered its own answer, as many sources were, ultimately, concerned with specific stages in the female life cycle, and thus provided a series of markers along the life journey which lent themselves to use as organizing milestones.

As a scheme, the life cycle is one that reflects current interests in women's and gender history. The seventeenth annual conference of the Women's History Network in Glasgow in 2008 was themed 'Gender and Generations: Women and Life Cycles', and covered all periods, not just the Middle Ages. Despite differences in class, religion, race, locality or time, women's life stages appear to provide a common thread that can be used to test those variables (although it is by no means unproblematic, as we shall see). To cite just one example, which will be elaborated on within the section on marriage below, it has long been known that the age of marriage for girls in elite households might be earlier than for those of lower social rank, but that northern Europe differed from southern Europe in this regard. Some women might therefore be widowed very early in their lives, and/or remarry several times. By placing sources about widows from different contexts alongside each other in this volume, we can see how these variances worked on the ground.

In fact it is rare to find explicit reference to numerical ages in order to pinpoint exactly the issue of regional or temporal difference, but other indicators, such as the appearance of surviving parents and/or grandparents, can also give us clues as to the age of the protagonists in our sources. The problem lies in determining exactly what we mean by the 'life cycle'. It would be too easy to assume that the life course provides a sort of anchor, a universal shared experience, which unites women, whatever their race or class. Nothing could be further from the truth – in fact the life course provided the excuse for cultures to differentiate between different groups of women. The ways in which this appropriation of life stages happened – and how they are recorded in the sources – can be loosely termed 'biological', 'legal' and 'imagined', and they radically shape our view of secular women's lives in the Middle Ages.

The control of marriage and childbirth means that the 'biological' life cycle inevitably intersects with the 'legal' one. Using the term 'biological' is not without its own problems, for if women's history over the past four decades has taught us anything, it is that the physical, biological body and its 'natural' events, such as menarche (the onset of periods) and menopause, are never understood as purely natural phenomena, but are invested in all cultures with positive and negative meanings which affects the way in which a person is viewed and treated by her community.[3] This was just as applicable in the medieval period: we might cite as examples the almost universal equation of menstrual blood with pollution, the high value accorded in some early medieval societies to women of childbearing age, or the detailed messages encoded in (covered or uncovered) body or facial hair.[4] Indeed, the semiotic or sign-bearing body is now so well established as a subject for study, and its symbolic value is being 'read' in so many ways, that medievalists are in some danger of erasing its physical presence almost entirely from their considerations.[5]

But bodies are inscribed with meanings almost from birth,

as Elisheva Baumgarten's comparative work on Jewish and Christian rituals of childbirth and early childhood underlines.[6] If we seek intersections between the bodily life cycle and the law, it is in fact to religious law that we most readily turn. As James Brundage has spent his career telling us, Christian can-onists, often influenced by Old Testament laws which were shared with the Jewish community (the Jews themselves con-tinuing to refine their laws into what would become the Babylonian Talmud of the second century CE), expended a great deal of effort creating a framework of acceptable behav-iours at different stages of life for males and females.[7] Many of these codes were enshrined in religious sermons, where the uncontrolled female body functioned as an allegory for a sinful life, and the horrors of childbirth were emphatically described to persuade young women to give up the worldly life altogether.[8] Yet at the same time, if sexual activity had to take place (a fact accepted by the canonists), then it had to be within strictly defined parameters, most of which focused on the status of the woman in the partnership. Christian and Jewish lawgivers viewed all non-procreative sexual activity as sinful, thus it fol-lowed that valid marital relations could occur only after puberty, and the woman's menstruation and pregnancy both functioned as prohibitive times. Marriage is identified by almost all of the literature as *the* definitive marker of the tran-sition between childhood and full adult status.

When we talk about the female 'life cycle', therefore, are we really dealing with the 'marital cycle'? Were we to explore the literature on women's life cycles from the past few years, we might be forgiven for thinking so. The bookshelves groan under the weight of studies devoted to widowhood,[9] incorpor-ate a fair few on motherhood,[10] even have one or two relating to marriage itself;[11] more recently there has been a scatter of books on single women.[12] Significantly, no such detailed studies have emerged on men, apart from odd chapters in histories of masculinity: as we shall see, this mirrors the pattern in the source materials.[13] Yet when we explored the idea of dividing women's lives using the marital cycle, an easy assumption – that the authors of chronicles, legal treatises, charters and

poetry actually used marriage as a key identifier – rapidly dissolved. A surprising number of extracts included here show
little or no interest in a woman's marital status: whilst it was
common for a married woman to be identified as 'wife of', the
business she was transacting might have demanded instead that
she identified herself as a member of her natal family, whether
married or not. Women's identity was thus a lot more fluid
than that of men, an issue which has long been recognized by
prosopographers seeking to catalogue individual lives in the
Middle Ages.

So where did the assumption that marriage was a key identifier come from? Has the marriage-related life cycle been
created out of studying legal sources, or do secular and ecclesiastical laws record other significant markers of the passing of
life? If religious law is concerned with the physical and morally
upright body, what does secular law address? At first sight, its
overwhelming concerns appear to be a) keeping the peace and/
or protecting the ruler's rights and prerogatives and b) the protection and transfer of property. In the latter area, a woman's
marital status certainly affected her access to, and ability to
manage, property. Generalizing broadly, all laws, early or late,
have some consideration of a woman's right – or not – to
inherit, and provision for a form of dowry, a gift from her own
family upon marriage. Once a daughter was married, the fact
she had received a dowry might preclude her having any further claim on her natal family's property. The same is again not
so obviously true of males, although marriage usually implied
setting up a new household and thus a need to gain access to a
portion of the patrimony.

One reason for the tighter control of women undoubtedly
stemmed from the fact that early medieval law codes, and later
laws based on the rediscovery of Roman law from the twelfth
century onwards, viewed women as perpetual minors whose
property and person required supervision from a male guardian. There is remarkable continuity between the need for such
a *mundoald* among early medieval law codes and the later
medieval practice of *mundium* or *couverture*.[14] Lombard law
held all women as legal minors throughout their lives, and the

English legal treatise 'Glanvill' stated that 'legally a woman is completely in the power of her husband'.[15] Women's marriage was noted because it brought with it a change of guardian, from father to husband, and a substantial transfer of property. Paradoxically, this legal disability only serves to increase the visibility of women in our sources, as the male guardians are at pains to identify their charges. We shall explore this further in Chapter 3 below.

But religious and secular law certainly did not exist in isolation from each other, and so we find the laws of early medieval rulers reflecting the gradual process of Christian conversion in Europe and taking on board some central elements of ecclesiastical law. Canon law, for example, prescribed the age of consent as fourteen for boys and twelve for girls, a scheme which recurs, explicitly or not, in several early medieval considerations of the issue.[16] Paradoxically, therefore, boys were deemed to be capable of maintaining a sexual, even marital, relationship long before they might hope to gain access to the property they needed to support any resultant family. (This was marginally less true for Jewish boys – bar mitzvahed and thus admitted into the adult male community at thirteen, they might marry rather younger than their Christian counterparts, but remain in the parental home after marriage.) But as Allen Frantzen has shown, the sexual activities of children were condemned by the Anglo-Saxon penitentials not on grounds of age – in fact they were given 'but little leeway' – but because they failed to fulfil the goal of procreation.[17]

Regulating sexual activity through the law was somewhat hit-and-miss: neither Roman law nor some of its successors committed themselves to defining an age in years at which girls would be capable of childbirth, despite setting out an age of consent. The central concern was in essence the age of menarche, but the laws, often composed and/or compiled by the literate and thus subject to heavy religious influence, carefully sideline any discussion of female biology by reducing this life event to an age-defined turning point. In doing so, however, they set an age that was rather wide of the mark when compared to other medieval views of the onset of periods. For the age of legal majority, twelve, was lower than that suggested by the medical community, which considered thirteen or fourteen the minimum age of sexual maturity. Core to the problem was the sinfulness of consummating a marriage when it was known that a girl could not yet have children. Marriage litigation in later medieval England reflects this concern, with use being made by both male and female litigants wishing to end marriages of the impediment of being below canonical age when their marriages were contracted, usually by their parents.[18] Marriage is therefore certainly central to the female life cycle in medieval Europe, even if there was a small minority of women who never married. We shall explore this further in each of the chapter introductions.

The second definition, the 'legal' life cycle, is one that takes its shaping and divisions from contemporary secular and religious law codes and legal documents such as property transfers. These of course varied between cultures, but both schemes of law paid a considerable amount of attention to women's lives, establishing prescriptive frameworks which were the focus of much early work on medieval women's history.[19] Many legal codes have been translated and used to illustrate the lives of women, to great effect, but legal documents of practice, although they have been examined in their thousands for numerous socio-economic studies of different regions, have received rather less attention for the light they shed on the female life cycle. Law, gender and life cycle together have only patchily been studied. Although recent studies of the life cycle, notably Deborah Youngs' work on the later Middle Ages, or Ivan Marcus' slightly older work on Jewish life cycles, incorporate evidence from legal prescriptions, these and other works have tended to find more inspiration for their studies in the colourful descriptions of family life in narrative sources (some of which are followed up in the present volume).[20]

Conversely, studies of the law, even those informed by recent currents in gender history, have only minimally addressed the issue of life cycle directly. It is possible that this neglect is due to a backlash against early work on women's lives, which took as its starting-point precisely those prescriptive sources that seemed to represent medieval views on women. This approach was criticized for its naivety – if women's lives as laid out in the prescriptive sources (including sermons and penitentials as well as articulated schemes of behaviour in the canons and secular legal systems) were simply an ideal which few, if any, could match in their day-to-day lives, then what was the value of such sources for the lives of 'real' women? This perfectly reasonable question, however, led to something of a rejection of a whole body of legal evidence by a generation of historians who turned instead to the approaches used by scholars of literary texts to tease out from narrative sources clues to day-to-day life. The Gender and Medieval Studies group, which emerged in the UK in the late 1980s, is still largely dominated by literature specialists rather than becoming the interdisciplinary group envisaged in its early years.

Why include legal materials, then? The answer lies in the literally thousands of charters, or documents of property transactions, which survive, especially in southern Europe. These reveal legal prescriptions in action, and demonstrate that the legal divisions of a woman's life, centred mainly on her marital status, had a profound effect on her ability to act on her own behalf. That is not to say that the letter of the law was followed every time – the adaptations visible in the documents say much about the notary's knowledge, but may also hint at the preferences of his client. We shall return to this issue. Suffice to say for the moment that the law focused particularly on issues of valid marriage and the legitimacy of children, as both impacted upon the smooth transfer of property between generations; legislators, therefore, were keen to ensure that women were controlled and passed from male (father) to male (husband) according to the correct protocols.

We might add to the two categories above a third one, the 'imagined' life cycle. This might well have been shaped by biology and law, but was deployed as a philosophical or literary tool to help medieval writers and thinkers explain the world around them. Most obviously, this category encompasses the 'ages of man' literature, studied by Elizabeth Sears twenty years ago and still influential in shaping our own considerations on life stages.[21] The various definitions of the ages of man, how-ever, had one thing in common: it is an inherently gendered scheme, and related quite explicitly to the male experience.[22]

We shall explore the different life stages as imagined in the sources further in the section introductions. However, there is one more issue worth noting here, and that is the problem of old age. As Shulamith Shahar asked several years ago, 'Who were old in the Middle Ages?'[23] Although work on medieval life expectancy is fragmentary at best, some broad comments can be made (and tested later on in the source material). First, there was an assumption that marriage would inevitably lead to child-bearing, and that medieval secular women were at an increased risk of early death because of their multiple pregnancies. Given that it is impossible to produce a statistically sound basis for this assumption, we might suggest that death in childbirth seems frequent because it is proportionately better-reported than other forms of death.[24] There were several reasons for this – death had occurred before the woman had lived out a full life; it had reper-cussions on the family and its property as the wife's blood relatives might reclaim what they saw as theirs; and it almost always led to the husband's remarriage and the appearance of a stepmother and stepsiblings, a potential source of tension.

Contrasted with this, the death of a woman in old age, hav-ing lived a full life, had far less impact on the written record. A 'full life', however, might only mean reaching menopause (a remarkably *invisible* life stage)[25] – women who lived much longer than this risked falling into a less enviable category, seen as 'hags' and 'crones', mistrusted, sometimes (as our poetry extracts reveal) ridiculed for their failing health and looks. And here is one of the most startling contrasts between secular and religious women – the latter, likely to live a longer life through their better diet, achieved only a greater respect if they survived into extreme old age, which was recorded and celebrated.[26] Old age, however, may not have been as gendered as other life stages. Pauline Stafford has suggested that certain functions, such as high office, had the potential to de-gender their female holders, and this model is useful when considering the life cycle.[27] For the elderly, their primary functions in life, whether as warriors (men), mothers (women) or agricultural workers (both), became more difficult to sustain in old age, as the body weakened and younger generations (including their own children) reached adulthood and began to fulfil those functions themselves. Old age may even have brought with it tensions relating to the release of property – we are familiar with stories of grown sons rebelling against their fathers, but the survival of an ageing dowager, with a legal right to the property she held, could be an equally tense situation.

The life cycle, then, offers a rich and challenging organizational scheme for our sources, and the different types of sources provide different definitions of the life cycle. The intersections between these are rich in potential for our understanding of how women's lives were understood and portrayed. Some extracts could have been used under several headings; some were sufficiently interesting to us that they were included despite ambiguities about which life stage they really represent. Some record exceptional women and circumstances, but most chart the mundane. The number of extracts in each section varies – this was not a conscious decision, but to some extent reflects the respective attention paid by medieval writers to each life stage, and tells us much about what aspects of secular women's lives were deemed worthy of attention. In the next section we shall consider the sources themselves.

THE SOURCES: HOW 'SECULAR' IS 'SECULAR'?

The sources collected in this volume are, for the most part, newly translated texts, and have been selected by the editors for their information about women, most of whose lives are unexceptional. Care must be taken not to assume that what is presented here represents 'typical' women from a given region at a given time, but it is important to acknowledge that few would have attracted attention from historians except, perhaps, as part of much larger samples used for statistical purposes. It is an indication of how historical fashions change that one Anglo-Saxon woman, who was described as 'a woman of no historic importance' by the translator of her will fifty years ago,[28] is now regularly used as an example in undergraduate medieval history courses. It is to be hoped that some of our texts will achieve similar prominence!

Insofar as we have been able, we have focused on women in secular life, that is, women who may well demonstrate piety in the sources in which they appear, but who did not enter the church as nuns nor achieve notoriety as saints (several saints' lives have been mined, however, for their rich descriptions). Secular life, for most, would have been centred around their families, whether natal or marital, work of all kinds (paid and unpaid) and the day-to-day business of food, shelter and clothing. For some this life was a struggle; others were sheltered from the struggle by their wealth and status. A significant number of the texts feature women in unusual circumstances – an unforeseen event or disaster thrusting her into the limelight in a way that neither she nor we might have expected. Whilst these experiences were hardly typical, they provoke questions about the wider context: we may only have one or two documents about the impact of the Arab sack of Barcelona at the end of the tenth century, for example, but they cause us to consider the wider human cost of medieval warfare, and the vulnerability of all caught up in it.

How women are presented depends to a certain extent on the type of source. We need to keep in mind the distinction between secular life and the means by which it was recorded, for it is a fact that almost all the materials translated here began life at the end of a medieval, usually male, cleric's pen. Literacy – and certainly the ability to write – was highly gendered. Substantial attention has been paid by scholars to the issue of female literacy and access to education, and source books of texts by women writers published – there are probably few undiscovered female authors still to find.[29] Women writers were the exception, and they usually lived their lives within an ecclesiastical context. Whereas they can be studied as a collective – for example, the literate nuns in Ottonian Germany – increasingly such women are studied on an individual basis with monographs devoted to them, like the recent study of Herrad of Hohenbourg's *Garden of Delights*.[30] They will not, however, appear much here.[31]

This does not mean, however, that women's voices are absent from the volume. It is a common motif of much work on medieval women to suggest that pretty much all we hear is filtered through a male, clerical screen. Some authors treat this fact with pessimism – using it to assert the oppressed and silenced nature of medieval women; others are more optimistic that the screen can occasionally be pulled back, read through, to reveal genuine medieval female voices. Recent work on anonymous early medieval sources has argued strongly that there is a pattern to women's concerns, particularly a greater emphasis on the family, and on female ancestors or protagonists, which can indicate female authorship of some of these texts.[32] That is not to say that all family-centred texts have to be authored by women, but often their own position within a dynasty could depend on their secure appropriation and shaping of its history. This process is most obvious within the field of female patronage, which has been studied as a means of accessing the opinions of elite women, but also of uncovering the strategies they used to combat often vulnerable positions.[33] It has also been argued by both editors of the present volume that memory and commemoration offer alternative routes into women's history.[34] That is to say, even the most unpromising texts can be made to offer up nuggets of information if the right questions are asked of them.

Two genres of narrative historical sources – historiography, writing about the past, and hagiography, writing about saints – need an extra word and special attention simply due to the fact that modern historians are so indebted to their descriptions of medieval life and thought.

Writing about the past in the form of annals (relatively short notes, year by year), chronicles (a roughly chronological account of the past: usually of one locality, region or principality) and histories (accounts of the past, often around a theme, such as crusading), is often set against the backdrop of a wider canvas, or the biographical genres of individual lives or collective biographies. These narrative texts are usually written for a specific purpose: whether apologetic (explaining a particular chain of events) or propagandistic (getting a message across), they are always partisan in that their authors express the viewpoint of their community and/or patron. Clearly, we have to understand where the author comes from and what reason he or she has to tell the story that unfolds. Since much medieval historiography is dynastic – and thus family-centred, modern historians increasingly pay attention to how all members of the family are represented. In particular, they attempt to identify the roles of men and women in this process, in the realization that the conventions of a particular genre might dictate that one should not identify explicitly a story based on the testimony of a woman, but that this does not mean that the story cannot have been generated by a woman. Identifying such concealment is not an easy task. For example, quite a number of medieval chronicles and histories are dedicated to noble women, suggesting that they might have been interested at one level or another in some of the contents of these texts. Few of the prologues are as detailed as William of Malmesbury's *History of the English Kings*, which explicitly records that Queen Edith/Matilda (d.1118) had had several conversations with the author. They talked about the origins of her family (the Wessex dynasty) and in particular the place of the famous author Aldhelm in that family. William also acknowledges the stimulus she gave him to write down his knowledge of kings past.[35]

Now the cynic might argue that the monk William was keen to flatter the queen, attributing intellectual curiosity to her which might not have existed. Both editors of the present volume would argue strongly that such cynicism is entirely misplaced. Because if the cynic had his way, what would one do with one of the most famous female historians of the Middle Ages, Anna Komnena, the Byzantine princess and younger contemporary of Queen Matilda, who, in the 1140s on the basis of scrupulously collected material (oral and written), wrote a history of her father? Of course hers is a partisan account, but at the same time it betrays an intellectual rigour and determination that is equal to any male account of the past we have.[36]

There are other reasons why, for our collection of texts, we have taken excerpts from medieval chronicles. As narratives of the past, these writings contain many decriptions of medieval life that are our only sources for the information they contain. Modern historians, influenced by postmodern interpretations of historical narrative as a construct and discourse, have on occasion dismissed the validity of using such descriptions as valid representations of past reality. Our point of view is that we cannot know to what extent a medieval author coloured, exaggerated or potentially misrepresented reality, but such ignorance can never be a reason for neglecting to read and ponder such sources. As long as we analyse the sources sensitively (by acknowledging the limits of our information) we can harvest them profitably. A case in point is the description of Ardres Castle's interior in the *Chronicle of the Counts of Guînes* by Lambert of Ardres. Georges Duby accepted the text entirely at face value and took it as a model for all castle life, while more recently Leonie Hicks has offered a more subtle interpretation based on extensive comparative material, not least from archaeological sources.[37] Clearly, careful interpretation of the description of the various chambers and who lived where is needed here. But the bottom line surely is that Lambert is highly unlikely to have painted a living environment of his patron's family in such fanciful terms as to make his description unacceptable for his contemporary audience.

Hagiography, that most generic of text forms, is similarly rich in incidental references to the daily lives of those who, for some reason or another, were touched by a saint and asked to recount their experience. Such testimonies were twofold, in that either they were aimed to elucidate biographical information about a saint and his or her behaviour, or, secondly and perhaps more importantly, they were about the posthumous power of the saint to procure miracles (and thus donations from those seeking help). This type of interview became ever more formalized as the twelfth century saw the rise of canonization inquests, where witnesses were summoned to attest to the veracity of miracles worked before or after death by local cult figures. Although such depositions underwent editing in their final redaction, their editors often left in the mundane details of the witnesses' daily routine, perhaps deliberately, to add credibility to the circumstances of the miracle witnessed. The value of the depositions for our purposes is that female witnesses were often treated differently – requiring the local priest's confirmation of their statements – but not omitted altogether. We are alert to Patrick Geary's warning that 'these texts are anything but a transparent window onto the everyday life of medieval people', but nor should the pictures contained in them be dismissed as without value because they occur within highly formulaic works.[38] To reiterate the distinction made above, fragments of secular lives can be preserved in the most ecclesiastical of sources.

Turning now to documentary sources, such as wills, agreements between parties, records of court cases and so on, these would at first sight appear to be less problematic than the narrative sources discussed above. However, whilst the distinction between narrative and documentary sources is a useful one, we must be careful not to exaggerate the reliability of charters' and wills' contents at the expense of the 'literary' quality of the narrative sources. Increasingly, historians and literary scholars are beginning to realize that in 'textual communities', a term aptly coined by Brian Stock, often the same people were responsible for the production of, say, charters and chronicles.[39] This is particularly, but not exclusively, true of the collections of charters preserved by monastic institutions, whose archivists were alive to the power of a text in the case of disputed rights or property. Such a realization then begins to explain why both types of sources were often revised to bring them up to date and to take account of changes in circumstances by interpolation (adding material within a text), omission (deleting material within a text), addition (adding extra details at the end of a text) or abbreviation (contracting a text). Very often too, as a result of copying a manuscript, various different versions of the same document or chronicle were in circulation, each of which carried some authenticity or validity for the community that kept them.[40]

Even if we have no reason to believe that a text has been

altered, the false distinction between narrative and documentary sources is hard to maintain when we examine the contents of such texts. Legal documents could tell a story (and fine-tune the contents) just as well as a chronicler or hagiographer could (and as we have noted, s/he could be one and the same). Transcriptions of witness statements could be arranged for maximum impact, regardless of the order in which they were taken; women's vulnerability might be played upon in order to circumvent some constraint on their actions. The stories told in documents, then, should all be treated with the same level of caution, and modern historians should be wary about being too categorical in deciding levels of truth in these texts. Nevertheless, recent work on women's wills has convincingly suggested that these have a much more 'autobiographical' nature than men's, and even if a will presented the testator as she wished to be remembered, that image is itself informative (see below, Chapter 5).

This leads on to a final point about transmission. The tiny minority of women who were literate and left written works to us have received a disproportionate level of attention from women's historians, and their works have been mined for information into the limitations of working as a female author (Judeo-Christian tradition having a strong aversion to women aspiring to preach and teach, for example). The work on medieval women outside this select circle has become ever more refined in its reading of male descriptions of female lives, yet work on finding female voices and ideas in this male-dominated written world is still surprisingly rare. Finding female voices in the sources is not difficult, but are these voices simply acts of clever ventriloquism by the male author of the work? In many cases they may be shaped by the expectations of the genre within which the author is working, but their inclusion should make us pause for thought. Similarly, female-authored legal documents may well adhere to the requirements set out by the law, and be drawn up by male notaries or scribes, but the wishes of their protagonists are suggestive, again, of a not wholly subsumed female voice. In the texts that follow, we have listened very hard for the female voices, often with unexpected results.

NOTES

1. And in the case of pioneers such as Eileen Power, rather earlier than that: see her ground-breaking book, *Medieval English Nunneries, c.1275–1535* (Cambridge, Cambridge University Press, 1922) and article, 'The position of women in the Middle Ages', in *The Legacy of the Middle Ages*, ed. C. G. Crump and E. F. Jacobs (Oxford: Clarendon Press, 1926), and subsequent work *Medieval Women*, ed. M. M. Postan (Cambridge: Cambridge University Press, 1975).

2. Among the authors who have mined these rich sources are Judith Bennett, who has published *Women in the Medieval English Countryside: Gender and Household in Brigstock before the Plague* (Oxford: Oxford University Press, 1987) and *Ale, Beer and Brewsters: Women's Work in a Changing World* (Oxford: Oxford University Press, 1996), and co-edited *Sisters and Workers in the Middle Ages* (Chicago: Chicago University Press, 1989); and Barbara Hanawalt, author of *The Ties that Bound: Peasant Families in Medieval England* (Oxford: Oxford University Press, 1986), *'Of Good and Ill Repute': Gender and Social Control in Medieval England* (Oxford: Oxford University Press, 1998) and *The Wealth of Wives: Women, Law and Economy in Late Medieval London* (Oxford: Oxford University Press, 2007).

3. See e.g. Joan Cadden, *The Meanings of Sex Difference in the Middle Ages* (Cambridge: Cambridge University Press, 1993).

4. See M. H. Green, 'Flowers, poisons and men: Menstruation in medieval western Europe' and Bettina Bildhauer, *'The Secrets of Women (c.*1300): A medieval perspective on menstruation', both in *Menstruation: A Cultural History*, ed. Andrew Shail and Gillian Howie (Basingstoke: Palgrave Macmillan, 2005). For a literary perspective, see also Peggy McCracken, *The Curse of Eve and the Wound of the Hero: Blood, Gender and Medieval Literature* (Philadelphia: University of Pennsylvania Press, 2003). The length, presence or absence of hair, bound or unbound, had a multiplicity of meanings, including signalling nobility, marital status or sexual orientation: see Robert Bartlett, 'Symbolic meanings of hair in the Middle Ages', *Transactions of the Royal Historical Society*, sixth series, 4 (1994), 43–60; Conrad Leyser, 'Long-haired kings and short-haired nuns: Writing on the body in Caesarius of Arles', *Studia Patristica*, 24 (1993), 143–50.

5. The exception is the pioneering volume edited by Sarah Kay and

Miri Rubin, *Framing Medieval Bodies* (Manchester: Manchester University Press, 1994), which skilfully combines both approaches.

6. Elisheva Baumgarten, *Mothers and Children: Jewish Family Life in Medieval Europe* (Princeton: Princeton University Press, 2004).

7. James Brundage, *Law, Sex and Christian Society in Medieval Europe* (Chicago: Chicago University Press, 1987) remains the best one-volume survey.

8. The archetypal medieval text is *Hali Meidenhad*: on texts of this type, see Jennifer Wynne Hellwarth, *The Reproductive Unconscious in Medieval and Early Modern England* (London: Routledge, 2002).

9. See Notes, Chapter 4, for bibliography on widows.

10. Apart from Baumgarten, already cited above, we have Clarissa W. Atkinson, *The Oldest Vocation: Christian Motherhood in the Middle Ages* (Ithaca: Cornell University Press, 1991); Mary Dockray Miller, *Motherhood and Mothering in Anglo-Saxon England* (New York: St Martins Press, 2000); and *Medieval Mothering*, ed. John Carmi Parsons and Bonnie Wheeler (New York: Garland, 1999).

11. Most recently, Philip Lyndon Reynolds, *Marriage in the Western Church: The Christianization of Marriage* (Leiden: Brill, 2001) and David D'Avray, *Medieval Marriage: Symbolism and Society* (Oxford: Oxford University Press, 2005).

12. *Singlewomen in the European Past, 1250–1800*, ed. Judith Bennett and Amy Froide (Philadelphia: University of Pennsylvania Press, 1999); *Young Medieval Women*, ed. Katherine Lewis, Noel James Menuge and Kim Phillips (Stroud: Alan Sutton, 1999); Kim M. Phillips, *Medieval Maidens: Young Women and Gender in England, 1270–1540* (Manchester: Manchester University Press, 2003).

13. See selected chapters in D. M. Hadley, ed., *Masculinity in Medieval Europe* (London: Longman, 1999); the exception is in work on the transition between boyhood and manhood, on which, compare the discussion in the introduction to Chapter 2, p. 44 and associated note 5) below.

14. There has been considerable work on this among legal historians as well as gender specialists. An extended discussion is Thomas Kuehn, *Law, Family and Women: Toward a Legal Anthropology of Renaissance Italy* (Chicago: Chicago University Press, 1991). See also Ellen Kittell, 'Guardianship over women in medieval Flanders: A reappraisal', *Journal of Social History*, 31 (1998); Theodore J. Rivers, 'Widows' rights in Anglo-Saxon law',

The American Journal of Legal History, 19 (1975), 208–15; *Consent and Coercion to Sex and Marriage in Ancient and Medieval Societies*, ed. Angeliki E. Laiou (Washington: Dumbarton Oaks, 1998); Ruth Mazo Karras, 'The history of marriage and the myth of *Friedelehe*', *Early Medieval Europe*, 14 (2006), 119–51.

15. Rothari law 204 in K. F. Drew, ed., *The Lombard Laws* (Philadelphia: University of Pennsylvania Press, 1973); *The Treatise on the Laws and Customs of the Realm of England Commonly Called Glanvill*, ed. G. D. G. Hall with an introduction by M. T. Clanchy (Oxford: Oxford University Press, 1993) (hereafter *Glanvill*), p. 60; Kuehn, *Law, Family and Women*, pp. 212–37.

16. Gratian, *Glossa ordinaria*, ad. X.4.2.3, in A. L. Richter and E. Friedberg, eds., *Corpus Iuris Canonici*, 2nd edn, 2 vols. (Leipzig: Tauschnitz, 1922).

17. Allen Frantzen, 'Where the boys are: Children and sex in the Anglo-Saxon penitentials', in Jeffrey Jerome Cohen and Bonnie Wheeler, eds., *Becoming Male in the Middle Ages* (New York: 2000), pp. 43–66.

18. R. H. Helmholz, *Marriage Litigation in Medieval England* (Cambridge: Cambridge University Press, 1974), pp. 60, 98–9 and cases on pp. 199–204; C. Donahue, *Law, Marriage and Society in the Later Middle Ages* (Cambridge: Cambridge University Press, 2007) for further discussion in chapters 3, 4 and 5 (pp. 63–218) and Frederick Pedersen, *Marriage Disputes in Medieval England* (London: Hambledon Continuum, 2000). See also the translation of a protracted case at York by P. J. P. Goldberg, *Women in England, 1275–1525* (Manchester: Manchester University Press, 1995), pp. 58–80.

19. The recent volume *Medieval Women and the Law*, ed. Noel James Menuge (Woodbridge: Boydell, 2000), however, challenged this approach by using alternative sources – and imaginatively paired chapters – to get at women's legal position. See also Hanawalt, *The Wealth of Wives*.

20. Deborah Youngs, *The Life Cycle in Western Europe, c.1300–1500* (Manchester: Manchester University Press, 2006); Ivan Marcus, *The Jewish Life Cycle: Rites of Passage from Biblical to Modern Times* (Washington: Washington University Press, 2004). It is to be hoped that the papers given at the 'Life Cycles and the Law' conference held at St Andrews in 2007 will eventually be published, adding to the field.

21. Youngs, *The Life Cycle*; Marcus, *Jewish Life Cycle*; Elizabeth Sears, *The Ages of Man: Interpretations of the Life Cycle* (Princeton: Princeton University Press, 1986); J. A. Burrow, *Ages of Man: Studies in Medieval Writing and Thought* (Oxford: Clarendon Press, 1986).

22. Kim Phillips, 'Maidenhood as the perfect age of women's life', in Lewis, Menuge and Phillips, eds., *Young Medieval Women*, pp. 1–24, at p. 3, notes that Mary Dove had already made this point: Mary Dove, *The Perfect Age of Man's Life* (Cambridge: Cambridge University Press, 1986).

23. Shulamith Shahar, 'Who were old in the Middle Ages?', *Social History of Medicine*, 6 (1993), 313–41.

24. Patricia Skinner, *Health and Medicine in Early Medieval Southern Italy* (Leiden: Brill, 1997), pp. 40–42.

25. Briefly treated by Darryl W. Amundsen and Carol Jean Diers, 'The age of menopause in medieval Europe', *Human Biology*, 45 (1973), 605–12.

26. Shulamith Shahar, *Growing Old in the Middle Ages: 'Winter Clothes Us in Shadow and Pain'* (London: Routledge, 1997).

27. Pauline Stafford, 'Emma: The powers of the queen in the eleventh century', reprinted in *ead., Gender, Family and the Legitimation of Power: England from the Ninth to the Twelfth Century* (Aldershot: Ashgate, 2006), Essay X.

28. *English Historical Documents*, Vol. 1: *c.*500–1042, ed. D. Whitelock, 1st edn (Oxford: Oxford University Press, 1953), no. 116, p. 524; 2nd edn (London: Eyre Methuen, 1979), no. 116, pp. 567–9, referring to the will of Wulfwaru.

29. The catalogue of books about women writers in the Middle Ages is now vast: one of the earliest and best was Peter Dronke, *Women Writers of the Middle Ages: A Critical Study of Texts from Perpetua to Margaret Porete* (Cambridge: Cambridge University Press, 1994). Others include translated collections such as *The Writings of Medieval Women*, ed. Marcelle Thiebaux (New York: Garland, 1997) and Carolyne Larrington, *Women and Writing in Medieval Europe* (London: Routledge, 1995). See also *The Cambridge Companion to Medieval Women's Writing*, ed. Carolyn Dinshaw and David Wallace (Cambridge: Cambridge University Press, 2003). The term 'literacy', of course, encompasses the ability to read, or write, or both, and it is commonly accepted that more people could read than write. Recent studies include: Rebecca Krug, *Reading Families: Women's Literate Practice in Late Medieval England* (Ithaca: Cornell University Press: 2002); *The*

Voice of Silence: Women, Literacy and Gender in the Low Countries and Rhineland, ed. T. de Hemptinne and M. Gongora Diaz (Leiden: Brepols, 2004) and *Voices in Dialogue: Reading Women in the Middle Ages*, ed. Linda Olson and Kathryn Kerby-Fulton (Notre Dame: University of Notre Dame Press, 2005).

30. K. Bodarwé, *Sanctimoniales litteratae. Schriftlichkeit und Bildung in den ottonischen Frauenkommunitäten Gandersheim, Essen und Quedlinburg* (Münster: Aschendorff, 2004); F. J. Griffiths, *The Garden of Delights: Reform and Renaissance for Women in the Twelfth Century* (Philadelphia: University of Pennsylvania Press, 2007).

31. See source collections that focus on ecclesiastical women, *Medieval Writings on Female Spirituality*, ed. Elizabeth Spearing (London and New York: Penguin, 2002); *Guidance for Women in Twelfth-Century Convents*, trans. V. Morton, with an interpretative essay by J. Wogan-Browne (Cambridge: D. S. Brewer, 2003).

32. Janet L. Nelson, 'Gender and genre in women historians of the early Middle Ages', in *L'historiographie médievale en Europe*, ed. J.-P. Genet (Paris: Éditions du CNRS, 1991), pp. 149–63, reprinted in *ead., The Frankish World, 750–900* (London: Hambledon, 1996), pp. 193–7; Elisabeth van Houts, 'Women and the writing of history in the early Middle Ages: The case of Abbess Matilda and Aethelweard,' *Early Medieval Europe*, 1 (1992), 53–68.

33. Pauline Stafford, *Queen Emma and Queen Edith: Queenship and Women's Power in Eleventh-century England* (Oxford: Blackwell, 1997) is a prime example of the effectiveness of such study. See also Patricia Skinner, '"Halt! Be men!": Sikelgaita of Salerno, gender and the Norman conquest of southern Italy', *Gender and History*, 12 (2000), 622–41, and June Hall McCash, *The Cultural Patronage of Medieval Women* (Athens: University of Georgia Press, 1995).

34. E. van Houts, *Memory and Gender in Medieval Europe 900–1200* (Basingstoke: Macmillan, 1999); Patricia Skinner, 'Memory and gender in medieval Italy', in *Men, Women and the Past in Medieval Europe*, ed. E. van Houts (London: Longman, 2000), pp. 36–52; *ead.*, 'Gender, memory and Jewish identity: Reading a family history from medieval Southern Italy', *Early Medieval Europe*, 13 (2005), 277–96.

35. *William of Malmesbury: Gesta regum Anglorum. The History of the English Kings*, 2 vols., Vol. 1, ed. R. A. B. Mynors,

R. M. Thomson and M. Winterbottom, (Oxford: Clarendon, 1998), pp. 8–9.

36. Anna Komnena, *The Alexiad*, trans. E. R. A. Sewter (London: Penguin, 2004).

37. G. Duby, *Women of the Twelfth Century*, 3 vols., Vol. 2: *Remembering the Dead*, trans. J. Birrell (Cambridge, 1998), pp. 106–9; L. Hicks, 'Women and the use of space in Normandy, c.1050–1300' (PhD thesis, University of Cambridge, 2002), pp. 25, 48–61 and her 'Magnificent entrances and undignified exits: Chronicling the symbolism of castle space in Normandy', *Journal of Medieval History*, 35 (2009), 52–69.

38. Patrick Geary, *Living with the Dead in the Middle Ages* (Ithaca: Cornell University Press, 1994), p. 12.

39. Brian Stock, *Implications of Literacy: Written Language and Modern Interpretation in the Eleventh and Twelfth Centuries* (Princeton: Princeton University Press, 1983).

40. See on this issue *Narrative and History in the Early Medieval West*, ed. Elizabeth M. Tyler and Ross Balzaretti (Turnhout: Brepols, 2006), in particular the contributions by Balzaretti, 'Spoken narratives in ninth-century Milanese records', Sarah Foot, 'Reading Anglo-Saxon charters: memory, record or story?' and Judith Jesch, 'Poets and history in the late Viking Age'.

A Note on the Texts

Translation of medieval sources is never a neutral act. Indeed, the current editors of *Gender and History* equate translation with hegemony, risking the imposition of meanings and structures not intended by the original author.[1] Along with substituting one word for another comes the act of interpretation, of choosing between alternative meanings, of reordering the sentence to render it into readable English. We have, on occasion, used the introductory sections for each translation to highlight any technical vocabulary. There are also some words in our translated texts which are highly obscure. In these cases we have left the words in the original language and set them in italics. Whereas in almost all cases we have tried to supply a possible meaning (in the form of an editorial interpolation following the words in question), in a few cases some words have had to remain untranslated. We have not aimed at consistency in the translation of terms or identification of sources across the various texts we have translated, since not only have we used existing translations in some cases, but also synchronizing them with the new translations we have made from sources from different European regions across a time span of many hundred years would have been a near-impossible (and in the end, undesirable) task. This is the main reason why on the whole we have left monetary values as they are expressed in the original language.

Above all, the purpose of this collection has been to make accessible, to those without the necessary linguistic background, a selection of texts that offer routes into investigating the lives of medieval secular women from a number of different angles. We have in all examples given the reference to the original sources, most of which exist in reliable editions; where these editions contain facing-page translations we – unless otherwise indicated – translated the text afresh. Through our translations we encourage the reader to explore those sources further. We are indebted to colleagues who have offered suggestions for texts, provided transcriptions and translations, or given permission for their work to be reproduced in this volume: they are recorded in the appropriate places. We hope that the newly translated excerpts included in this collection will stimulate students and general readers alike.

NOTE

1. Karen Adler, Ross Balzaretti and Michele Mitchell, 'Practising gender history', *Gender and History*, 20 (2008), 1–7, at 4.

A Note on Dates and Currencies

Many of the extracts translated, particularly those with a legal function (e.g. recording a property transaction such as a sale or a will), are dated and mention monetary amounts. Although we have rendered all dates into conventional modern-day form according to the Common Era (this term is preferred to Anno Domini, given that not all documents are written by Christians), the reader will encounter several systems at work, often more than one in the same document. The Roman Empire had used a fifteen-year cycle, and each year within this cycle was called an 'indiction' (and a further complication of the Roman calendar is that it did not start in January). The indiction system continued to be used in the Middle Ages by its heir, the Byzantine Empire, in the east, and by the writing office of the papacy in Rome and Avignon. Another system used was to denote a date by the year of the local or national ruler (a practice still used in English Chancery documents – for example, 2010 is the fifty-eighth year of Elizabeth II's reign), useful for charting the shifting political boundaries of medieval Europe. Jewish documents, on the other hand, did not recognize the Christian dating system, and used the number of years since the creation of the world (specifically the creation of Adam) as its starting-point (Anno Mundi – AM), a system also in use by the Byzantines, but with a different starting-point date for creation! (The Byzantines dated the creation to 5508 BC (in Common-Era terms – therefore, for example, their year 6644 – minus 5508 – becomes AD 1136.) The Muslim calendar, on the other hand, dated from the flight of Muhammad from Mecca to Medina (the Hegira), starting in approximately 622 CE

(thus, for example, 2010 CE – minus 622 – becomes 1388 AH).
Only from the eleventh century does the Common-Era year
(expressed as 'the year of our Lord') more frequently replace
these alternative systems in Christian documents.

Both Jewish and Gentile documents often specify the month,
and this, too, might vary from our use of numbered days. Jewish documents used the Hebrew months and Jewish festivals as
dating markers. The Christian month might be divided in
Roman terms, with terms such as the Kalends (the first of the
month) featuring in our sources and indicate the number of
days before that date (hence the second Kalends of April would
be 29 March). A final word of caution: although all the dating
systems in medieval Europe were based on ancient rules, they
were fluid in their interpretation and should not be entirely
relied upon. Sometimes a dating clause which is wrong, for
example, when a CE date does not correspond with the year
indicated by the indiction cited, can be a sign that the document itself is suspect, but scribes often made mistakes,
particularly when producing copies of older (and perhaps hard-
to-read) texts.

Moving on to the issue of currency, we meet an even more het-
erogenous picture across the regions of Europe and across time.
The key issue here is that medieval Europe was much more economically and politically fragmented than modern Europe, and
that the right to mint coins was a sign of rulership. Hence many
different currencies circulated round the Continent. Common
in many of the documents translated here is the term 'pound',
but this relates to a weight of coins (usually silver, occasionally
gold) rather than a currency itself. In England, silver shillings
and pence were used to make up pounds, and the pound sterling, introduced by King Henry II in 1158, expressed the
percentage of silver content in the pennies that made it up. And
pounds varied in weight across borders, so we see them quali-
fied for clarity (i.e. 'Genoese pounds').

The *solidus* is mentioned frequently in southern European
contracts: this was a gold coin emanating from the Byzantine
Empire, whose gold content fluctuated wildly and which was

often used more as an accounting tool rather than meaning actual coins in circulation. Smaller gold coins, named *tari*, were also used. Originally an Arabic coin, they were later minted by some of the towns in southern Italy, and an exchange rate of four *tari* to the *solidus* was the norm. Byzantine *tremisses* were worth one-third of a *solidus*. Another gold Byzantine coin was the *hyperperon*. In northern Europe, gold coinage was a rarity, and silver *denarii* (originally a Roman-Empire currency unit) were more commonly used, spreading into southern Europe relatively quickly, as a more flexible form of currency. In summary, the availability of coinage determined what was used when, and mixed currency use was common. The Italian towns, in particular, saw a thriving exchange trade, since almost all were the centres of individual states from the twelfth century onwards, and thus set their own weights and values for incoming merchants, a practice which was mirrored in southern France. The mark was also used as an amount in accounts, and was the equivalent of two-thirds of a pound. Fluidity is again the watchword, and mistakes were made in calculations, as the observant reader will note!

CHAPTER 1

BIRTH AND INFANCY

Introduction

Births were not regularly or systematically recorded until the fourteenth century, in Italy, and later elsewhere, reflecting the reality that many infants did not survive their first year. Nevertheless, medieval authors often commented on births, especially when writing biographies of prominent leaders. A good or bad birth might set the pattern for how the subject was portrayed – Peter of Eboli describes the birth of Tancred, failed challenger for the kingdom of Sicily at the end of the twelfth century, as that of an *abortivus* ('abortion/foetus') and graphically underlines the pretender's physical shortcomings in his illustrations. Earlier that same century, Abbot Guibert of Nogent remarks on the fact that he too survived, despite being born as 'almost an abortion'.[1] The miraculous nature of his survival only serves to reinforce the quasi-hagiographic account he gives of his mother. Indeed, Guibert's autobiographical text is clearly modelled on the saints' lives to which he was so regularly exposed. These often foreshadow their subjects' later greatness through in-*utero* portents experienced by their pregnant mothers.

Neither of these examples might be called typical, but they do indicate that the birth process excited interest and comment, and also reflect the growing emphasis, during the central and later Middle Ages, on birth as an indicator of social status. It is in the latter half of the eleventh century that we begin to see concerted efforts to compose family histories in order to record and deploy extended lineage as part of a claim to power, an example being the history of the counts of Anjou attributed to Count Fulk IV.[2] These, for the most part, privileged the male line, unless a greater claim to wealth or power could be made through a female ancestor. The emphasis on birth was in marked contrast to the earlier period, in which low birth could sometimes be overcome by great achievements and/or (in the case of women) a strategic marriage. The oft-quoted portrayal of slave-born Merovingian and Carolingian queens is the most obvious example.[3]

How then do our sources treat birth? Records tend to high-light the exceptional, as in most medieval sources. In the years prior to the first millennium, anxious aristocratic mothers-to-be might even fear giving birth to the Antichrist (text 1). We have already touched upon the comments that the survival of an unusually small foetus provoked, but birth abnormalities of any kind, such as physical deformities, or multiple births, were often thought of as indicators of the mother's moral shortcomings, and were reported because they were so unusual.[4] No blame seems to have been attached to the infant, however: indeed, it has been argued from archaeological evidence in England that children with birth defects often survived, and that special measures might even be taken to ensure their care.[5] Norse culture may not have been so forgiving: several Norwe-gian law codes of the twelfth and thirteenth centuries used physical criteria to judge whether a newborn should be recog-nized as a human, and as part of the community.[6]

Strikingly, there is little reference in the sources to the pos-sible risks of childbirth to the mother, despite the 'perils of pregnancy' forming a stock theme in much writing about medi-eval women. What do we know about women's experience of childbirth? Our evidence is fragmentary, partly because of the enclosed nature of the birthing room, and partly because only a minority of births, and those mainly in elite households, had a significance worthy of record.[7] Birth was, after all, an oft-repeated experience for medieval married (and some unmarried) women, and its very regularity and normality meant that it attracted little notice except, as already mentioned, when it heralded the arrival of a long-awaited heir, or went wrong in some way. The thirteenth-century encyclopaedist Bartholomew the Englishman, among others, notes that younger women with narrower bodies might well have difficulty in labour, but comments that the more difficult the birth, the more love the mother would have for her child![8] Nevertheless, it is clear from medical treatises and commentaries by sometimes hostile male witnesses, that supernatural aid was sought at this difficult moment, either from the saints or through charms and rituals which had little to do with Christianity (text 2).

Could the focus on the risks of pregnancy in fact derive from modern assumptions, influenced by the medicalization of childbirth in modern times, rather than medieval evidence? Certainly it has been argued recently that birth was increasingly removed from the control of women and their midwives to that of male doctors from the later Middle Ages onwards: for such a move to be successful and convincing, the risks had to be emphasized, and the practical care of female midwives, whose empirical knowledge was based largely on experience rather than education, discredited.[9] Birthing accounts emphasize the risk (albeit for specific reasons – see text 3). The formal account of Isabel de la Cavallería's labour perhaps epitomizes male interest in birth, for all that she was attended by midwives (text 4). It is no coincidence that the later Middle Ages also saw the revival of intervention in the form of caesarean sections.[10]

Most of the evidence we have for this shift is contained in medical and scientific treatises, which paid considerable attention to conception and birth. Although the inclusion of contraceptive methods tacitly acknowledged that there might be a demand for this type of remedy,[11] medical theorists were far more concerned with promoting, rather than suppressing, fertility. Fertility was, after all, a crucial and decisive factor in the fate of many marriages in the Middle Ages. Whilst secular and ecclesiastical law frowned upon divorce on the grounds of childlessness, there is no doubt that it was a major factor in many high-profile medieval divorce cases, and that it was the wife, rather than her husband, who was assumed to have had the problem in conceiving (text 5). For example, it is thought that the infertility of his first wife was the reason for the high-profile divorce of David, a wealthy Oxford Jew, from his first wife Muriel, in the early 1240s.[12] Male infertility, as distinct from impotence, was hardly recognized.

Pregnancy and motherhood not only provided a woman with some defence against being divorced, but also gave the wife greater material security when she was widowed. We also see legislators making provision for the support of children (text 6). As mother to children, she had cemented her place within her husband's family and would more often than not take control of her children's assets until they were of age, thus maintaining herself and her family. Fathers would make provision for their children even whilst the latter were still in the womb (text 7). Childless, a woman's ability to support herself after her husband's death, and her in-laws' wish to assist her, might be severely curtailed. This could lead to quite desperate measures to secure a child or simulate a pregnancy, as the extracts below illustrate. Although faked pregnancies and the substitution of babies went on to provide a rich seam for the imaginations of medieval jongleurs,[13] such instances must have been rare and the risk of discovery high (see texts 8–11 and cf. text 4).

Although the arrival of children was broadly welcomed, ambivalence surrounded the newly parturient woman. This is nowhere more clearly indicated than by the practice of 'churching', in which the new mother was temporarily excluded from her religious community for a lying-in period of some thirty to forty days immediately after the birth. She only re-entered it when coming to church for the first time afterwards, often on the day of her child's public baptism.[14]

It is very easy to slip into a discussion of birth seen from the mother's point of view, but what, if anything, do we know about attitudes towards female babies? The addition of a new member to the medieval community, especially that of a daughter, was greeted with mixed feelings, as the sources translated in this section reveal (texts 12 and 13). In Judeo-Christian culture, sons were inevitably favoured, despite the oft-quoted strictures of St Paul that 'there is no male and female . . . for you are all one in Christ Jesus'. Jewish culture, too, differentiated between male and female children, for only the former might grow up to become leaders of the community and religious teachers (although see below, Chapter 5, for evidence that this was not always strictly adhered to). The arrival of a son might also be crucial to the survival of a family line, and celebrated because of that fact. It is difficult to find any similar celebrations of a daughter's birth, although her arrival might at least prove a wife's ability to conceive. It is noteworthy that the Jewish husband's equivocal welcoming of a new daughter, reproduced below, is followed by his expectation that more children will follow, and the implication is that there is still time to have a son.[15]

Care was taken to ensure that the newborn was welcomed into the religious community as quickly as possible – we know this indirectly from rules surrounding the midwives' responsibilities. They, or even the parents, in the event of a baby emerging sickly or close to death, were charged with performing a brief and *ad hoc* baptism (text 14) – but its fate thereafter was entirely dependent on its social status and the commitment of its parents to its care. Baptism signalled the entry of a child into the community: in the case of the elite, it might have much greater significance (text 15). Children of the elite might be sent out to wet-nurses, either because the mother could not feed the child herself, or in the belief that suppressing lactation would enable the mother to become pregnant again more rapidly, but there was at least some ambivalence about this practice (text 16). Wet-nurses could be richly rewarded for their work, but were also hedged round with restrictions, deriving mainly from the ancients, as to their behaviour and diet. One of the most disturbing aspects of the wet-nursing industry was the requirement that the nurse put her client's needs first, even ahead of those of her own children.[16] We are unlikely ever to be able to reconstruct the experiences of the nurse's family, but should bear in mind that the material rewards of taking in a nursling – and for some women this income was vital to their family's survival – might have been counterbalanced by the emotional and physical effects of its arrival (text 17). For some women, becoming a child's nurse meant a physical relocation to the child's home. Although this could mean an improvement in her circumstances, there was always the risk of falling foul of the child's family should it meet with any mishaps. It is striking that, in hagiographic texts, saints not only make up for the inability of doctors in miracles of healing, but also for the shortcomings of incompetent or lazy nurses (texts 18 and 19).

Notwithstanding the strictures of medieval religions which embraced the newborn, feared for their souls at least and valued their existence, how gendered was the care of the very young? Although it is highly unlikely that medieval culture embraced the ancients' practice of exposing unwanted children to the elements – the lack of young girls in early medieval records does not justify the assumption that many were the victims of infanticide[17] – death could ensue from a change of nurse or, at the other end of the social spectrum, from disease and lack of nutrition in large peasant or poor urban households. Accidental deaths while playing, despite parental care, occurred in and around the house and even in bed.[18] Penitential texts criticize the practice of mothers taking their children into bed, and accidentally smothering them by overlaying, treating this together with deliberate homicide and other 'more serious' sins (text 20). Nevertheless, deliberate abandonment did take place, as is evidenced by the rise of foundling hospitals, such as Innocent III's foundation of Santo Spirito in Rome,[19] in the central and later Middle Ages. Abandonment was clearly a desperate act for the mother, with any number of possible causes – illegitimacy, poverty, a disability in the child, or a combination of these. As we see in the case of Castruccio Castracani below, fostering and bringing up such foundlings was praised as an act of Christian charity (text 21).

There are many questions remaining about the gendered experiences of newborns and infants in the Middle Ages: although clerical writers spent much time considering the nature of the child, only passing references relate to practical measures for bringing it up.[20] It would be interesting to investigate what proportion of babies farmed out to nurses were female, and whether there was an imbalance between the sexes. Work might be done on the family diaries, or *ricordanze*, of medieval Italy, which functioned both as records of additions to the family and account books. These have been mined for the experiences of women, but less attention has been paid to the birth records there. Similarly, the records of charitable institutions – most obviously again in Italy, whose culture of written records preceded much of Europe – would repay study from a gendered point of view to see whether more abandoned babies were female than male.[21] In times of hardship, were female children valued less than male? Were baby boys expected to grow into more useful members of the household – as workers, protectors or even as clerics – than their sisters? Or was the baby girl's future – as a carer to her father, if not to her own brood – as imagined by Walter of Châtillon, typical of attitudes to female offspring, and equally valued? Further work has still to be done.

1. *Fear of Giving Birth to the Antichrist, France, Mid-tenth Century*

This letter is from Adso of Montier-sur-Der to Queen Gerberga (d. c.969), wife of King Louis IV (936–54) of France, previously widow of Duke Gislebert II of Lotharingia (929–39), and was probably written in the years 949–54. Adso explicitly refers to her request to him for information about the Antichrist. The Antichrist was the Devil incarnate, who, it was widely believed, would rule for the final three and a half years of the world's existence before being defeated by God and the Last Judgement. The text in its various versions was very popular, with queens, in particular, perhaps afraid that one of their offspring might turn out to be the Antichrist.

Newly translated from: Adso Dervensis, *De ortu et tempore Antichristi necnon et tractatus qui ab eo dependunt*, ed. D. Verhelst, Corpus Christianorum Corpus Mediaevalis, 45 (Turnhout: Brepols, 1976), pp. 20–23, 28–9.

Letter from Monk Adso to Gerberga on the origin and time of the Antichrist

Brother Adso, the lowest of all her servants, wishes glory and eternal peace to her royal highness, in powerful dignity the most excellent lady, Queen Gerberga, beloved of God and loved by all his saints, mother of monks and leader of holy virgins.

Because I have acquired the favour of your mercy, lady mother, I have always been faithful to you in everything as is appropriate in a servant. Therefore, although my prayers do not deserve anything from God, I am asking the mercy of our God for you and your husband, the lord king, as well as for the wellbeing of your children. May He be willing to preserve the imperial dignity for you in this life and hereafter allow you to reign happily with Him in heaven. If the Lord gives you good fortune and grants you and your children a longer life, we know without doubt and believe that God's church must be exalted and our religious order must be multiplied more and more. As your faithful servant I wish this and strongly desire that if I were able to gain the whole realm for you, I would do so most readily. But since I am unable to do so, I will pray the Lord for the salvation of you and your children that His grace may always precede you in your work and that His glory may follow you with piety and mercy, in order that aiming at the divine commandments, you may fulfil the good, which you desire, so that the crown of the heavenly kingdom may be given to you.

You have a devout urge to listen to the scriptures and often talk about our Redeemer, you even wish to learn about the wickedness and persecution of the Antichrist and about his power and origin; since you have deigned to command me, your servant, I wish to write something for you about and to render insofar as is known about the Antichrist, although you do not need to hear this from me because you have with you Lord Rorico, the most sensible and wise pastor, who as most famous mirror of all wisdom and eloquence is absolutely essential in our time.

Wishing to be informed about the Antichrist, you must know firstly why he is so named. This is because he will be the opposite of Christ in all things and will do things contrary to Christ. Christ came humbly, he will come proudly. Christ came to raise the humble, he in contrast will reject the humble, encourage sinners, exalt the wicked, he will always exalt vice against virtue; he will teach to drive out the law of the gospel, recall the adoration of the demons in the world, will seek his own glory [John 7: 18] and will call himself almighty God. The Antichrist has many servants of his wickedness, many of whom have already lived, like Antiochus, Nero and Domitian. Now in our own time we know of many antichrists, for anyone, layman, canon, or even monk, who lives contrary to justice and attacks the rule of the order and blasphemes what is good [Rom. 14: 16] is an antichrist, a satanic servant.

Let us now, however, consider the origin of the Antichrist. What I am saying I have not thought out or invented myself, but by my careful reading found it written down in books. As our authorities say, the Antichrist will be born from the Jewish people, that is from the people of Dan, as the prophet says: 'Let Dan be a snake in the wayside, an adder on the path' [Gen. 49: 17]. He will sit in the wayside like a serpent and will be on the path so that he can attack those who walk in the paths of justice [Ps. 22: 3] and kill them with the poison of his evil. He will be born from the union of a father and mother, like other men, not, as some say, from a virgin alone. He will be conceived entirely in sin [Ps. 50: 7], will be generated in sin, and will be born in sin [John 9: 34]. At the very start of his conception the Devil will also enter his mother's womb and the Devil's power will foster and protect him in his mother's womb and will always be with him. Just as the Holy Spirit came into the mother of our Lord Jesus Christ and overshadowed her with His power and filled her with divinity so that she conceived of the Holy Spirit and what was born of her was divine and holy [Luke 1: 35], so too the Devil will descend into the mother of the Antichrist, will fill her entirely, completely absorb her, totally overpower her, completely possess her inside and out, so that with satanic support she will conceive through a man and what will be born from her will be thoroughly evil, totally lost. That is why man is called the 'son of perdition' [2 Thess. 2: 3], for he will destroy the human people as far as he is able to and will then be destroyed himself on the last day . . .

Since we have dealt with his beginning, let us now deal with his end. The Antichrist, son of the Devil, and the worst artisan of evil, as has been said, will plague the world with great persecution and torment all God's people with various tortures for three and a half years. After he has killed Elijah and Enoch and crowned with martyrdom the others who remained in faith, at last God's judgement will come upon him, as St Paul writes, saying: 'the Lord Jesus will kill him by the power of his own virtue', or whether the archangel Michael will kill him, he will be killed through the virtue of our Lord Jesus Christ and not through the virtue of any angel or archangel. The teachers say that Antichrist will be killed seated on his throne in his tent on the Mount of Olives in the place opposite to where the Lord ascended to heaven. You must know that after the Antichrist has been killed the Day of Judgement will not follow immediately, nor will the Lord come to judge at once [Isa. 3: 14], but as we learn from the Book of Daniel, the Lord will allow the elect forty days to do penance because they were seduced by the Antichrist. There is no one who knows how much time there may be after they shall have completed this penance until the Lord comes to judgement. But it remains in the providence of God, who will judge the world in that hour, in which before the world he ordained it was to be judged.

Thus, lady queen, I, your true servant, having faithfully fulfilled what you commanded, am now prepared to obey other commands which you may deem worthy to issue.

2. A Charm to be Spoken During the Birth of a Baby, England, Eleventh Century

Translated by T. Hunt from *Breviarium Bartholomei, De difficultate partus*, pars 6, dist 3; an eleventh-century Latin text edited from London BL MS Harley 3 fol. 128ra, in T. Hunt, *Popular Medicine in Thirteenth-century England* (Cambridge: D. S. Brewer, 1990), no. 38, p. 90.

We thank Dr Hunt warmly for allowing us to use his translation.

If these things are not sufficient, then if a priest or clergyman is present, let him read the writing on the parchment slip three times over the woman who is labouring to give birth. Thereafter let the woman put the parchment slip on her navel and gently bind it on her. And immediately, if God wishes, she will give birth without danger to herself or her child if she does this in good faith and devotion: 'In the name of the Father and the Son and the Holy Spirit, Amen. Mary begat Christ, Anna begat Mary, Elizabeth begat John the Baptist, Mary begat our Lord Jesus Christ without sin and pain. In His name, and by the merit of Holy Mary, his mother and virgin, and of St John the Baptist, we beseech that you, child, whether a boy or a girl, may leave your mother's womb without you or she dying; in the name of the Father and the Son and the Holy Spirit. Amen.'

3. Pregnant Woman's Delivery of a Stillborn Baby, Normandy, Mid-eleventh Century

The *Miracles of St Vulfran* were written by the monks' sacristan at Saint-Wandrille (Normandy) in the mid-eleventh century, before 1066. The miracle described seems like a stillbirth which occurred after a prolonged attempt to give birth, which lasted from St Sebastian's Feast on 20 January until one week after Easter (a moveable feast occurring between 22 March and 25 April). For a discussion of the text, see E. van Houts, 'Historiography and Hagiography at Saint-Wandrille: The *Inventio et miracula sancti Vulfranni*', *Anglo-Norman Studies*, 12 (1990), 233–51, at 236–8.

Newly translated from: *Miracula sancti Vulfranni*, par. 2, ed. AASS March iii, pp. 150–51.

Moreover, one ought not to pass over in silence what the divine virtue considered worthy to happen through the same saint [St Vulfran]: something that rarely or never had been seen by any mortal. There was a pregnant woman in the village of *Frigeia*, whose baby was due on the festival of St Sebastian. Contrary to Nature's way, she began to worry and, in imminent danger, was tormented by torture of her contractions as is common because she could not give birth. Lying on her bed she realized that she had nothing to expect except a deserved death. Such was her discomfort, weakness and difficulty that her labour lasted from the festival of St Sebastian until the octave of Easter. Then, having received more sensible advice that would pay off, she began to appeal to the mercy of the Lord and His mother to see if they felt her worthy of their compassion. She also frequently invoked the name of St Vulfran, whose vigils, which had been commonly celebrated until then, she had attended, and whose handmaiden she had become. She prayed for his usual piety that by his intercession she might appeal to the Almighty God's clemency that He deliver her from her present danger or that He might mercifully put an end to her life. Thus while she devoutly continued to pray, time and again repeating the name of the saint, asking faithfully that he would bring assistance, suddenly God's mercy revealed itself when her swollen stomach from her breast to her navel miraculously split lengthwise in half as if a field was newly ploughed. In agony on account of so much suffering, which had begun to distress her, her shouting prompted almost all her neighbours to come in. After they had entered and bewailed her as if already dead, they were not least surprised to notice her situation. Having taken counsel, they opened her stomach and found the baby's bones with its decaying flesh and removed it all from the half-dead woman. Later the woman returned to the holy patron because he had liberated her from an uncomfortable delivery and had completely cured her. Without delay and after many prayers, the splitting of her stomach had healed in such a way as if she had suffered of none of it, except that the token of the cut remained as proof of God's mercy and His servant's merit.

Thus, as we have said, liberated and restored to perfect health, she returned to Saint-Wandrille, where she told the events which we have narrated here as they had happened to her, while showing to all the scars on her stomach, deservedly bringing thanks to God and St Vulfran. Thereafter happy and filled with praise she returned home. These and many more things the glorious St Vulfran performed near God and His people.

4. Public Record of the Labour of Isabel de la Cavallería, Zaragoza, 10 January 1490

Translated by Professor Monserrat Cabre from the edition by María del Carmen García Herrero, 'Administrar el parto y recibir la criatura. Aportación al estudio de la obstetricia medieval', in *Homenaje al Profesor Emérito Antonio Ubieto Arteta* (Zaragoza: Universidad de Zaragoza, 1989), pp. 290–92.

We thank Professor Montserrat Cabre for allowing us to use her translation.

In the name of God. Amen. To be stated before everyone

that in the year of the nativity of our Lord Jesus Christ MCCCCLXXXX, the day counted as the tenth of the month of January, between the tenth and the eleventh hour before noon, in a room whose windows receive the light of the street, in the upper rooms of the houses of the magnificent lord Martín Gil de Palomar y de Gurrea, lord of the town of Argavieso, located in the parish of San Juan de Puent in the city of Zaragoza, facing the houses of Sir Sancho de Ayala, bookseller, as well as those which were owned by Sir Martín de Pertusa and also the public street called Guchillería; being there, the magnificent Isabel de la Cavallería, daughter of the magnificent and eminent lord Sir Alfonso de la Cavallería, and who had been the wife of the magnificent Pedro de Francia, deceased, who had been the lord of the town of Bureta, walking around the aforesaid room where the windows were open and some blessed candles lit, accompanied by two women who were holding her by her armpits, complaining about suffering from the pain of her pregnancy, going into and wanting to go into labour.

I, Domingo de Cuerla, Notary, together with the witnesses written and named below, were constituted there personally, having been called with much insistence by the aforesaid Isabel to attend her labour so that we could personally see and eyewitness the baby who would be delivered by the aforementioned daughter Isabel. And she said that she required me so that I, Notary, might write a public record and draw up a formal statement of the administration of her labour as well as of the baby who was about to be born.

And after, having said the above, in the aforesaid room and before Isabel, were personally constituted: Catalina de Cutanda, whose popular alias was de Salinas, widow, who had been the wife of Gabriel de Salinas, deceased, and Aina de Medina, wife of Gonzalvo Tizón, wallmaker, midwives, or popularly called *madrinas*, for the administering of labour, also especially called in to administer the labour of the aforesaid Isabel. To the request of Isabel, I, the aforesaid Domingo de la Cuerla, Notary, and in front of all the witnesses named below, touched with my hands their bodies and between their legs, with their skirts and clothes up to their shirts so that I could see and examine if the midwives were bringing any baby fraudulently, or if Isabel had any under her skirt. And I, the aforementioned notary and the witnesses, saw that neither Isabel nor the midwives had anything on but their personal clothes and dresses.

To the request of the aforesaid Isabel de la Cavallería, both midwives on their knees and touching with their hands an image of our Lord, Jesus Christ, and the four gospels, solemnly swore, kissing and adoring the aforesaid image and gospels, to administer well and without any fraud or trick the labour of the aforesaid Isabel. And having done this, a bed which was in the room was uncovered and I, the aforesaid notary and the witnesses, saw that there was nothing in it except the necessary and appropriate linen for its dressing. And having done this, and the aforesaid Isabel de la Cavallería continuously complaining about her suffering and going to go into labour, I, the aforesaid notary and the witnesses named below, were present there, watching Isabel de la Cavallería and the midwives and the other persons who were there, with the deliberate intent to ensure that they did not and could not do any trick in bringing any baby and changing one for another. And the aforesaid Isabel de la Cavallería, complaining about the pains of her labour, lying down on her back in the arms and legs of the aforesaid Lord Martín de Palomar y de Gurrea, Lord of Argavieso, who was sitting in a chair holding her with strength, the aforesaid Isabel having some relics on her belly and many blessed candles lit around, and the midwives were there, Aina, on her knees in front of the aforesaid Isabel, and the aforementioned Catalina Salinas was between the legs of the aforesaid Isabel de la Cavallería, sitting on a stool with a cloth laid out in her knees to administer the labour and to receive the baby who was about to be born, and there was a clean brass pot between the legs of the aforesaid Isabel, as we could see, where I, the notary and the witnesses saw and heard fall in the blood and the water which were coming out from the body of the aforesaid Isabel de la Cavallería while in labour pains. And thus, after very many big pains that the aforesaid Isabel de la Cavallería was suffering I, the notary and the witnesses named below and some other persons who were there and wanted to eyewitness the labour of the aforesaid Isabel de la Cavallería, saw how she gave birth and a baby came out of her body, completely wet and with his eyes closed. Catalina de Cutanda, alias Salinas, Midwife, received the baby in her hands and in the aforesaid cloth that she was holding. And having the baby in her hands, as has been said, I, the notary and the witnesses seeing it, saw that the umbilical cord was hanging from the placenta within the body of the aforesaid Isabel de la Cavallería and was affixed to the navel of the aforesaid newborn baby, and that the aforesaid midwife Salinas, administering the aforesaid labour, was working to receive and take it out, as she did and took out the placenta where the aforesaid baby had been nourished in the body of the aforesaid Isabel de la Cavallería, and I, the aforesaid notary and the witnesses, saw that placenta fall into the aforesaid pot with a lot of blood which was there. And thus, having done all of the above, the aforementioned Catalina de Cutanda, alias Salinas, Midwife, uncovered the aforesaid newborn baby that she had wrapped in the cloth where she had received it, and I, the notary and the witnesses mentioned below, and the other people who were there and wanted to see it, publicly eyewitnessed and saw that the newborn baby was a man, since he had all the male organs that men have, that is, his member and its companions, alias popularly called willy and balls.

And thus, having seen and examined the aforesaid baby and being a man as has been said, the aforementioned Catalina, midwife, before me, the notary and the witnesses mentioned below, cut the umbilical cord of the aforesaid child and wrapped him with the cloth that she had.

And having done all of the above, the aforementioned Isabel being sleepy and almost out of herself because of the hard labour, the aforesaid Martín de Gurrea, Lord of Argavieso, asked me, the aforesaid public notary, in his own name and as proxy of Isabel de la Cavallería, who had given birth, to write it down in a public record as many times as were necessary in order to maintain the right of Isabel de la Cavallería and to preserve her interest in the future.

That was done in the aforesaid city of Zaragoza, the aforesaid day, month and year, in the houses and place mentioned above.

All present witnesses of all this were: Master Pedro de Juana, Shoemaker, and Ferrando Dominguez, Notary, inhabitants of the city of Zaragoza.

5. William of Conches on Human Reproduction, Normandy, Mid-twelfth Century

William of Conches (*c.*1090–*c.*1154) wrote his encyclopaedic work on philosophy and Nature in the period *c.*1144–51 (probably in 1148/9), during which his patron, Count Geoffrey of Anjou (d. 1151) was also Duke of Normandy. William dedicated the work to him and meant it also for the education of his sons, among whom was Henry, later King Henry II (1154–89). The book is written as a dialogue between the duke and an anonymous philosopher, who presumably is William himself.

Newly translated from: *Guillelmi de Conchis dragmaticon philosophiae*, ed. I. Ronca, Corpus Christianorum Continuatio Mediaevalis, 152 (Turnhout: Brepols, 1997), Book 6, pars altera, c. 8, pp. 205–11.

On Coitus

1. Duke: Sperm results from the act of coitus. What kind of complexion is suitable to the performance of this act?

Philosopher: If you knew of all necessary things for this act, you would not doubt the type of complexion. Three things are necessary: semen that is ejaculated, heat which sets a man on fire and liquefies the semen (for we know that coldness freezes humours), and emotion which stiffens the penis and ejaculates the semen. Thus when the material is collected together in the male parts and dissolved and prepared, it is the emotion that expels the semen from the penis.

2. But because the penis is sensitive, the nerves generate a deep response; when the semen runs out, titillation causes the lasciviousness of lust. If therefore any one of these three [semen, heat and emotion] is lacking, the act of the coitus fails. A hot and dry combination opposes one quality of this act [wetness]; a cold and wet one opposes another [warmth]; a cold and dry

one opposes both. But a combination of hot and wet is suitable for the act on account of both qualities. So hot and wet men are suited to this act.

3. Duke: Since a woman is naturally cold and wet, why is it that she is more lustful than a man?

Philosopher: It is more difficult to light a fire with wet wood; however, once it is set alight, it burns longer and more vigorously. The lustful heat in a woman, who is by Nature more wet, once alight, burns more vigorously and longer. Again, the womb, which receives the semen, is cold; the semen of a man is hot and wet; the womb therefore is pleased to receive it. Do we not see snakes, seeking heat, entering the mouths of those who sleep? Therefore a woman's delight in coitus is twofold: namely, in the ejaculation of her own semen and in the reception of that of another; the man's [delight] on the other hand is single, namely only in the ejaculation.

[. . .]

8. On the inside the womb is hairy in order that it retains the semen better. It has seven cells with human figures imprinted on them in the manner of a seal; as a result a woman can prepare for seven and not more [children] in one birth. As a result of frequent love-making, a prostitute's womb is covered in slime, with the hairs, which are meant to retain the semen, covered up: hence in the manner of oiled marble it instantly rejects what it receives.

9. Duke: This reminds me of what you have just said to me that without semen women can never conceive; but this is not plausible. We have met women who were raped, who have suffered violence despite their wailing, and still have conceived. It seems that they never experienced delight in the act. But without delight they cannot produce sperm.

10. Philosopher: Although the act of rape displeases at the start, in the end as a result of carnal weakness, it pleases. There are two wills in humans: a reasonable and a natural will, which we always experience in conflict: what pleases the flesh often displeases reason. Therefore in rape it is not the will of reason, but the will of the flesh. And what doubt is there that the sperm of the mother is in those she has conceived, when you see

similar sons born from mothers and taking on their [mothers']
weaknesses?

11. Duke: We often see legitimately married women who
sleep only with their husbands with great delight, yet they
never conceive. I would like to understand the reasons for this.

Philosopher: The reason can lie as much with the woman
herself or with the man. It sometimes happens that the womb
is too fatty and as a result the mouth of the womb on the inside
is obstructed and that therefore the semen cannot reach the
place of conception. Sometimes it is constrained by too much
dryness, and sometimes the interior of the womb is lined with
slimy secretions. Sometimes the womb lacks retentive power
and its power to reject prevails. Or sometimes the bindings that
ought to be tight are too weak.

12. Sometimes even when nothing is wrong with the womb
a woman still does not conceive. Because of the quality of the
sperm from either partner or both: if the sperm is too hot, it
dries out and is destructive; if it is cold, it congeals; if it is too
moist, it dissipates; if it is too dry, it becomes hard and not easy
to be assimilated.

6. The Welsh Law of Women on Provision for Mother and Baby, Early Thirteenth Century

This is a collection of legal texts which was compiled in the early thirteenth century, but goes back to earlier times. The text is known in
Welsh and Latin. The present translation is based on the latter, which
has survived in a manuscript in Aberystwyth.

Newly translated from: NLW MS Peniarth 28, edited in *The Latin
Texts of the Welsh Laws*, ed. H. D. Emanuel (Cardiff: Wales Univer-
sity Press, 1967) and in *The Welsh Law of Women*, ed. D. Jenkins and
M. F. Owen (Cardiff: University of Wales Press, 1980), pp. 147–59.

On the Law of Girls and Women

If a man accepts a woman as his wife and gives her a marriage
gift and then makes her pregnant, and if she is dismissed before

she gives birth, the period from when she was dismissed will be owed to her for the bringing up [of the child]. She shall bring up the child, willingly or not, for one year and a half. He shall give her for the bringing up a fat sheep with fleece and lamb; and also an iron pan or four pence; and a unit of grain for making pottage or *rynnyon* for the baby; and three loads of wood; then two ells of white cloth for swaddling the child, or four pence; then two ells of striped cloth or twelve pence; then a fat cow with calf; then three loads, namely one of grain, one of barley and one of oats. All this shall be given to the mother if she wants them.

If any pregnant woman shall be made to miscarry between the fourth day and the full month, the person through whose fault this happened shall give her a fourth of the [child's] price, according to its status; and this shall be called *gwayth kyndelwaut*, because it is not yet formed. If it happens in the second, third or fourth month, a third part of its price according to its status shall be given. If someone does it in the fifth month or after the foetus has quickened, half its price shall be given.

7. A Bequest of Moveables to a Pregnant Wife, Genoa, 5 March 1156

Scriba's cartulary – a collection of charters copied in sequence on to a continuous roll – is a list of business transactions carried out in the city of Genoa and recorded by Scriba for the parties concerned. Values are expressed in Genoese pounds, which are pounds of silver, and *solidi*, which are gold coins. Similar records to this one exist in a number of Italian and southern French cities and will be used throughout this source book. Although the editors do not comment, it appears that the testator in this case might have made his will in the Holy Land, to be then inscribed back home in Genoa, to judge from the internal references in the will.

Newly translated from: *Il Cartolare di Giovanni Scriba*, Vol. 1, ed. M. Chiaudano and M. Moresco (Turin: S. Lattes & Co., 1935), document 47, pp. 23–5.

*

Witnesses: Arnaldus Tolose, Martin Pezol, Lombardus of S. Egidii, Bonus John Balbus, Bertram Ermengardus, Manfredus de Cari, Paul of Mt Pesulani

I, Raimondus Pictenadus, will for my soul forty *solidi* for the intercession, monument, masses and distribution to the poor according to the judgement of Peter, my brother, and Poncius de Bitteri; the rest of the things [are] in their power, and which they should sell within a year and a half, and with the price pay to the Hospital of Jerusalem twenty *solidi* and to the Fraternity of the Temple fifty *solidi*. I institute as my heir according to Falcidian law he or she with whom my wife is pregnant and let he or she be content with it. I institute Guilelma, my wife, as the heir of all my other goods, except for the part which I have in the slaves Martin and John, whom I leave to my brother Peter, asking him to pay to my wife, or her true representative, ten Genoese pounds' worth of pepper or money within a year and a half. Everything which is written in this papyrus from * downwards my wife can claim whenever she wishes, and I order that it be paid to her. I wish my body to be buried in the Church of the Holy Sepulchre. If this my will is lacking in any solemnity in law, I wish it to obtain such by force of codicils or another last will. Done in the lodging of this same witness, 1156, the fifth day from the beginning of March, in the third indiction.

[An inventory of goods follows:]

2 *sospeales*, a small chest, 7 tables of *aneto*, 2 wineskins, a *mastra*, 2 eating benches and 2 eating tables, and 4 benches to sit in a shop, a cushion store, a *seiar*, a brazier, shutters, 2 hemp stalls on which they work cloths, a cloak of rabbit fur lined with scarlet, a wolfskin cloak, * three and a half Genoese pounds. A mortar of bronze, 2 pestles, 2 fire pans, an iron tripod on which to place dishes, an iron grate, a bronze bowl, 4 ash trays, a bronze candlestick, 2 bronze chandeliers, a painted dish from Almaria and a dish of bronze, 2 bronze basins, 2 cauldrons and 2 *pairolos*, a bronze icing pail, 2 gold rings and a silver spoon (broken), 2 covered pans, a bronze lamp, a bronze *dozol* with hanger, a painted bed, 2 feather quilts, 2 cushions, one of hide and one called wool carpet and gilded, a

leather couch, 2 covers, 2 sheets and a canopy, an *orinale* and an axe, and a balance with 5 bronze weights, and a mark of bronze, and a clay cup, and a horn water cup, and a bronze ladle, and an iron spoon, a glass plate, a saucer with a cup of glass, a saucer with a cup of wood, a box, a side of bacon, a trinket box [lit: a box where all minute things are put], 2 fur capes, 2 *baracamos iauni*, a furry spotted skin, an old silk cover. All these things which are written here are the portion of my wife, worth ten Genoese pounds and four *solidi*, and a kitchen and a salt pan.

8. Faked Pregnancies and Substituted Children: Galbert of Bruges on Walter of Vladsloo, Flanders, Early Twelfth Century

In 1127–8 Galbert of Bruges, a notary, wrote an account of the murder and betrayal of Count Charles the Good (1119–27), who had been killed on 2 March 1127 while praying in church. The following section relates to Walter of Vladsloo, Lord of Eine, near Oudenaarde. As butler to the count and a so-called 'peer', he belonged to the highest Flemish aristocracy and was one of the traitors. Bertulf was the count's chancellor (*c*.1091–1127), and the head of the Erchembalds, a family of unfree birth whose members had climbed up the social ladder by becoming wealthy citizens of Bruges. Their low social origins, however, also added to the family's stigma as they were widely held responsible for the murder of Count Charles.

Newly translated from: *Galbertus Brugensis, De multro, traditione et occisione gloriosi Karoli comitis Flandriarum*, ed. J. Rider, Corpus Christianorum Continuatio Mediaevalis, 131 (Turnhout: Brepols, 1994), par. 89, p. 139.

By God's harsh and horrible judgement, it happened that Walter of Vladsloo, one of the country's peers, fell from his speeding horse while he was on a military expedition and, a broken man, died after having been ill for a few days. It was certainly true that he had been an accomplice in the betrayal of his lord [Count

Charles the Good], the father of the whole country of Flanders. In order to be most intimately involved with the traitors he had even married off to one of Bertulf's nieces a certain adopted boy, who was in fact the son of a shoemaker whom his wife had pretended was his own. Walter had really believed that he was the father of the boy whom the mother falsely had pretended to have given birth to as his wife. But the child she had given birth to had died immediately at birth. Therefore she had substituted the shoemaker's son, who had been born around the same time, and in secret she had sent her own dead child to the wife of the shoemaker, to whom she gave cash in order that she would pretend to have given birth to the dead child and not disclose to her husband what she had done. When the stolen and adopted son had grown up, and while everyone believed that he was Walter's son, the provost [Bertulf] came and gave in marriage his niece, the daughter of his brother's son, to that false son, so that bound together strongly as a result of the marriage – under all circumstances – they would become bolder, stronger and more powerful. However, after Walter's death, his wife let it be known publicly that the boy had been adopted as a son and was not the real son, whom [she said] Walter had entrusted to a certain burgher with a promise of three hundred pounds. And so God's plan foiled that of the provost, who, deceived by God's plan, through that marriage had wanted to exalt his family proudly and arrogantly by linking it to the shoemaker's son. It was true that no one dared to raise a hand against Walter, although an accomplice to treason, on account of the fact that he was a peer of the country and second only to the count. But God, to whom his punishment was left, removed him by a lingering death from the view of the faithful.

9. A Substituted Child, Normandy, Eleventh Century

A charter from the Monastery of Jumièges, written between 1080 and 1084, documents the extraordinary case of a substituted child, which took place in the late 1060s in a complicated property dispute. The ordeal of hot iron, which the mother of the substituted child undergoes, was a medieval form of judgement. The accused was required to pick a hot iron from a fire. A burned hand was interpreted as divine judgement of the accused person's guilt, whereas no visible injury signified the person's innocence. The document, which still survives as an original, is written in the first person by Rainald, a royal chaplain, who ultimately passed some of the property he was given back to the monastery.

Newly translated from: *Regesta regum Anglo-Normannorum: The Acta of William the Conqueror*, ed. D. Bates (Oxford: Clarendon Press, 1998), no. 162, pp. 530–33.

In the days of Richard, Count of the Normans, and of his son Robert, and of William, son of Robert, there was a chaplain of theirs, named Ernald of Bayeux, a man rich in lands and houses both inside and outside the city [of Bayeux], which he had bought with his own gold and silver. When he died, during the reign of William, Duke of the Normans, Stephen, nephew of the aforementioned Ernald, entered the inheritance of his uncle's estate, according to the laws of succession, by grant of William, Duke of the Normans. This Stephen had a little son by a certain widow, called Oringa, the sister of a Norman called Ambarius of Bayeux. When the child died, without Stephen's knowledge, the ingenious woman rented a boy from a woman who lived in the village of Martragny, paying her ten shillings a year, and the woman was called Ulberga. Stephen believed the child his and lawfully made him heir of his allodial property [land free of obligations to a lord], that is, of the houses he had at the gate of the trees inside the city, and of 12 acres of land at the golden spring outside the city and of some fields from which he derived income. Then after first the wife of Stephen and later Stephen himself passed away, the said woman [Ulberga] from Martragny, not receiving the rent she was accustomed to receiving for her son, demanded the return of the child, but could not have him back from the relatives of Stephen's wife.

Word of her claim reached Duke William, who by now had become King [of England], and his wife, Matilda, in the village of Bonneville. The king arranged to have a hearing to determine whether the woman should receive back her child. King William,

Archbishop John, Roger de Beaumont and a number of others adjudicated that the woman claiming the boy should receive back her son by means of the ordeal of hot iron if God should preserve her unharmed. King William and his wife, Matilda, sent me, Rainald, his clerk, to Bayeux to witness the ordeal, and at the king's behest, William the Archdeacon, now Abbot of Fécamp, Gotselin the Archdeacon, Robert of Lille, with his wife, Albereda, Evremar of Bayeux and quite a few other good men of the city went with me. When the ordeal was carried out in the small monastery of Saint-Vigor, the woman reclaiming her son was unharmed by the judgement of God as I and the other named people observed. And when the king learned this from me and the other aforesaid men, he laid claim to Stephen's possession and gave it to the queen, and the queen gave me, with the approval of the king, the houses and 12 acres I mentioned before, and the fields, and all of Stephen's allodial property. The other things of Stephen, which belonged to the Church of St John, the king had already given to the clerk, Thomas, later Archbishop [of York]. [. . .] To Geoffrey, the clerk surnamed 'Masculus', I gave one field from the allodial possession in return for which he will serve me, and another one to Evremar in return for eleven shillings per year; for which, the same Evremar is to look out for my interest at pleadings, if necessary, and whenever during the year I come to Bayeux he is to provide me, at his own expense, with wine and beer and good bread for the first night, according to custom, and to feed my horses, and for this I have the witness of my lady, the queen. And, if necessary, he would advance to me up to a hundred shillings at Bayeux. And a third field I gave to Vitalis the clerk, that he should serve me. [. . .] All these things which I have described can be verified by Vitalis the clerk, who was with me throughout.

10. *A Substituted Child, England, Twelfth Century*

This case of a substituted child is known from the *Life of St Hugh of Avallon*, Bishop of Lincoln (1186–1200), but also from documents from the king's court at Michaelmas [29 September] in 1194, which allow us to identify the people concerned. William of Hartshill took his brother Thomas of Saleby and his wife Agnes to court as they had, so he claimed, defrauded him from his inheritance by asserting that Grace was their daughter. In fact, as the story relates, she was a substituted child. For Grace's marriages, see Chapter 2, text 36.

Newly translated from: *Magna vita sancti Hugonis: The Life of St Hugh of Lincoln*, 2 vols., Vol. 2, ed. D. L. Douie and D. H. Farmer (Oxford: Oxford University Press, 1985), Book 4, c. 5, pp. 20–21.

In the area of Lincoln lived a man [Thomas of Saleby], already of advanced years, who had a barren wife [Agnes]. He also had a brother [William of Hartshill], a hard-working and prudent knight, who by hereditary right was considered to be his successor should he die without issue. His wife hated the brother, for fear that as her husband's widow she would be put under his authority, and for this reason she never showed him any affection. Inspired by the crime of a snake's wickedness and with the aim to preclude him from gaining an inheritance, because she did not have a child of her own she substituted for it another child. It is reported that, swollen by internal fraud, she tied a pillow round her waist and pretended that her swollen womb was caused by pregnancy, whereas she was really breeding a shocking crime. The knight to whose prejudice the deceitful trick was put into place, realizing that he was being duped, but not being sufficient either to prove or to stop the ingenious crime, brought it to the attention of his friends. He investigated their advice thoroughly, but found little that was suitable.

Meanwhile, the woman went to her bed and, faking labour, gave herself over to groans. She then brought out into the open a baby girl [Grace], whom she had recently procured from a young woman in a nearby village; and as if she had really given birth to her, brought her up with all care and devotion. She called the true mother to her and delegated to her the task of looking after her own child. All this happened not far from Lincoln, when the Easter festival of the resurrection of the Lord was about to begin.

11. Pope Gregory XI Issues a Pardon over a False Pregnancy, Villeneuve-lès-Avignon, 27 July 1372

The Apostolic See is another term for the papacy, which stood at the head of the church, and was often referred to as 'Mother'. Any cases brought before local bishops or clerics could be referred upwards to the Pope for advice and judgement. In this instance, the Bishop of Sabina, one of the parties in the dispute, is represented by an advocate, termed his procurator. The practice of issuing papal dispensations was well entrenched by the fourteenth century; in this example, the involvement of the Jewish woman – the reason why this text is included in Simonsohn's edition (see below) – is of rather less interest than the obvious desperation of the central figure of the tale, Beatrix. The dating of the document follows Roman style, identifying the day as six before Kalends (the first of August) in the second year of the pope's reign.

Newly translated from: Shlomo Simonsohn, *The Apostolic See and the Jews: Documents 492–1404* (Toronto: Pontifical Institute of Medieval Studies, 1988), document 429.

Memo for the future: The Apostolic See, a pious mother, always opens and extends her door of mercy to her erring children if they return to her with a humble spirit after their excesses, and she knows that having weighed the quality of person, place or time, the sin can be put right beneficially in God's name. Indeed on this matter there came recently to our hearing a tale worthy of belief. Once a certain Isoard Cabassole, a soldier of Cavaillon, died intestate, and a dispute arose between our venerable Brother Philip, the Bishop of Sabina, the brother of the above Isoard, who claimed that as the nearest relative to Isoard his moveable and landed property should come to him by right of succession; and Beatrix, beloved daughter in Christ, the widow of the same Isoard, who claimed that after his death she remained pregnant and so the material in question should come by law to her unborn child, the one to be born from her. The dispute came in this way to the communal court of our venerable brother, the Bishop of Cavaillon, when Beatrix, perceiving that she was not pregnant, and thus her [right to] take possession of the goods expiring [lit.: 'running out of breath'] and this case depending on it, she had procured, through these beloved children in Christ: Augerius Augerii, a cleric and son of the same Beatrix; Ludovic of Rovreto, cleric of Cavaillon; Rixenda de Areis, citizen of Aquensem; Joanna, wife of Peter Gauterius, layman of Cavaillon; Alasacia Alphanta de Saumanna, a woman; and Gemma, a Jewess of the same diocese, a certain near-abortive [possibly premature] and another baptized child buried in the cemetery of St Michael Cavaillon, which children were exhumed and taken out of the cemetery and brought to her, so that it might be supposed that one of them was an abortive child expelled from her own body, and she accepted one of them afterwards and lied that she had miscarried it.

Which matters, spreading by public fame, came to the notice of Raymond de Luco, cleric of Carpentras and our Brother Francis, Bishop of Cavaillon, Vicar-general, and also at the instance of Michael Iausserandi de Carumbo, layman, of the diocese of Carpentras, the procurator of the Bishop of Sabina, who ordered Beatrix, a first, second, third and last time, that as certain agreed periods were elapsed, she should appear personally before him in order to respond to questioning on the matter; but Beatrix contumaciously refused to appear in this way. Next Stephen, Abbot of the Monastery of St Victor in Marseilles of the Order of St Benedict, then rector in the county of Venaissin, belonging to us and to the immediate Roman Catholic church, where those named above lived, sent this mother to be heard by Hugh de Luca de Draguinhano, expert in law, and the case to be brought to an end. The said Hugh, having advanced some matters in the case, ordered Beatrix to be summoned and ordered that she should appear before him to purge the previous contumacy within a certain time, at the application of the above communal court, and respond to questioning, and to do and receive other things which justice demanded on pain of a penalty of three hundred marks of silver. And because the said Beatrix contumaciously refused either in this period or after the expected time to appear, the aforementioned Hugh, mitigating and moderating the amount of three hundred marks, condemned Beatrix to pay to the communal court five hundred pounds of crowns, and did no more in the case, which we wished to have presented for pronouncement. We, therefore, having certain cases placed before us, and in consideration of the above Bishop of Sabina, who humbly prayed to us that we should treat mercifully these people culpable of the sin, in this way agreed to the request of the bishop and the supplicants, and remitted and excused any corporal, criminal or civil penalty which Beatrix, Augerius, Ludovic, Rixenda, Joanna, Alasacia and Gemma had incurred or might incur as a result of their wrongdoing together or singly; and as far as the five hundred pounds owed to us and the Roman Catholic church by Beatrix, by apostolic authority we remitted this and broke off all proceedings and annulled them, restraining the rector of the above county and the judges of the court, who are busy at the current time, from pursuing any criminal case or debt for us from them, and any such case pursued in contravention of this order will be null and void.

Done at Villanova, Diocese of Avignon, sixth Kalends of August, second year.

12. Reaction to the Birth of a Daughter: Walter of Châtillon, France, Twelfth Century

Walter of Châtillon (c.1130–d. 1176 or later) was a theologian and poet who wrote both satirical poetry and more serious treatises. The poem translated here may have been written in his student days at the University of Paris.

Newly translated from: *Die Lieder Walters von Chatillon in der Handschrift 351 von St Omer*, ed. K. Strecker (Berlin: Wiedmannsche Buchhandlung, 1925), poem 20, p. 33.

The mildness of spring returns, painting the meadows with flowers.

The surface of the ground smiles at our moods, hungering
    for nourishment, and is a resting-place for love.
Two nearly opposite forces mixed their effects, the
    seed plot blossomed and Nature gave a return:
From discord, concord; the planting produced fruit.
Then others rejoiced, whom Cupid had favoured, but
    like an old wound the birth affected me badly;
Mine is the life of the lonely and wretched, completely
    destroyed by a broken love.
I, the unfortunate, deserve her; she should have been
    called Day,
Destined by Nature to be my daughter, a day which
    so very suddenly dawned as my relative.
Grow then, little girl, the future support of your father in
    his querulous old age, when his eyes will dim;
As the diligent servant of my mind you will do more
    than a son.

13. A Jewish Husband in Dispute with his Wife, Cairo, Tenth to Twelfth Centuries

This is one of many thousands of texts found in the *genizah*, or Jewish
document store, of Fustat (the old name for Cairo). Their preservation
was due to the Jewish practice of keeping any document which might
include the name of God. Shelomo Goitein's six-volume masterpiece
makes extensive use of these texts, which, nevertheless, still have not
been fully edited.

    Reproduced from: S. D. Goitein, *A Mediterranean Society: The
Jewish Communities of the World as Portrayed in the Cairo Genizah*,
Vol. 3: *The Family* (Berkeley: University of California Press, 1978),
p. 228.

O, noble woman, give up your bad feelings and seek reconcili-
ation. I am happy with my child. What? Because the first one is
a girl I should hate her? God forbid! What I say is this: God has
made my lot pleasant. It is an auspicious sign for me and for you.

14. Conciliar Advice on Lay Baptism,
Trier (?), 1277

This text is often cited as evidence that midwives were allowed to baptize. In fact it is clear that it was making provision for *anyone* to baptize newborns, provided they followed the correct form of words. The date of the ecclesiastical council at which this ruling was made is uncertain, but is believed to be 1227 or 1277. The value of the text is increased by its acknowledgement that it was preferable to allow baptism in any language – hence the reference to French and German vernacular versions – than to wait for a priest (with the correct Latin) to arrive.

Newly translated from: J. D. Mansi, *Sacrorum consilium nova et amplissima collectio*, 31 vols., Vol. 24 (Venice, 1759–98), cols. 191–206, on the Council of Trier 'ut creditur 1277'.

On Baptism and its Types

Baptism should be celebrated in the communal font in this form: 'N, I baptize you in the name of the Father and of the Son and of the Holy Spirit.' And the laity, women too, should be taught by their priests how to baptize in this way, so that at the critical moment of necessity they know, and can clearly pronounce, with the greatest clarity, exactly all the aforementioned words in the baptism, in which rests all the force of the sacrament. And the Gallic priests should teach the lay people in Romance how they should baptize their small children in times of necessity. Both father and mother when they try should baptize: 'Je te baptoi en nomme do patre et do fis et do sainte esprit.' The Germans, however, should say: 'Jeh deussen dicj N in me name des vaderez in de des sonnes in de des heiligen geistos.'

15. A Royal Baptism, England, Late
Eleventh Century

Queen Matilda (d. 1083) stood as godmother to Edith/Matilda (later Queen Matilda (d. 1118), who was wife of King Henry I of England

(1100–35), and herself the mother of Empress Matilda (d. 1167)). The story was told in a letter of Gilbert Foliot to Brian Fitzcount, one of the supporters of Empress Matilda for the crown of England in 1143/4. The prophetic element in the story is credited to eyewitnesses.

Newly translated from: *The Letters and Charters of Gilbert Foliot*, ed. A. Morey and C. N. L. Brooke (Cambridge: Cambridge University Press, 1967), letter 26, pp. 60–66, at 66.

We have heard some holy reports about the mother [Edith/Matilda] of the Empress [Matilda], according to which, from her earliest days in the cradle, she was destined to the royal dignity as revealed by a sign of God. For when Queen Matilda, the wife of King William, lifted her [Edith/Matilda] from the sacred font, the little girl stretched out her hand, clutched the veil on the queen's head and folded it over her own. Some people who ponder things very deeply, one of whom is still alive, explained it as a sign that revealed a very clear indication of the royal dignity to which she was later elevated.

16. A Noblewoman Breastfeeding her own Children: Ida of Bouillon, Late Eleventh Century

Ida of Bouillon (d. 1113) married Count Eustace II of Boulogne (d. *c*.1088) in *c*.1057. Her biography was probably composed at the order of her daughter-in-law, Mary of Scotland (d. 1115), or her granddaughter, Queen Matilda of England (d. 1153), and written by a monk of the monastery at Waast. As a result, the biography has a particularly religious flavour. According to St Paul, a married couple owed each other sexual contact, but only for the purpose of procreation. As virginal behaviour (i.e. sexual abstention) was deemed to be the norm, one could therefore argue that a married woman was a virgin if she only had sex with her husband for the purpose of having children. As a young woman, Ida is said to have had a vision prophesying the greatness of her three sons: Count Eustace III (d. *c*.1125), Godfrey of Bouillon (d. 1100) and Baldwin of Antioch/Jerusalem (d. 1118). Baldwin was the first crusader to be elected King of Jerusalem, in 1100.

Newly translated from: *Beatae Idae vita auctore monacho Wastensi coaevo*, ed. J. P. Migne, Patrologia Latina, Vol. 155, cols. 437–47, at 438–9.

After a fitting and honourable welcome [at Boulogne], Ida was married to Eustace, Count of Boulogne, according to the rite of the Catholic Church. When the wedding had been solemnly celebrated, Ida loved faithfully God's mysterious things, under worthy guidance, while she did not closely scrutinize matters pertaining to the world. Naturally keeping chaste in marriage, according to the apostle's precepts, she nevertheless gave what she owed to her husband, and, as if she did not have a husband, bore him three sons, as was indicated above, in the presence of God's clemency and as revealed through the prophecy of the above- mentioned vision.

The eldest son was Eustace, a powerful man in secular affairs and an outstanding layman in religion. Imitating his father's nobility, which is well known, he held his inheritance with great strength. The second son was Godfrey, named after his [maternal] grandfather, whose lands he held and who with God's will triumphed over the Turks and under new grace was predestined to become the first king of Jerusalem. Although born later, but therefore no less powerful in deeds or authority, the third son was Baldwin, of good memory, Lord and Proconsul of Antioch and its surroundings, who, later, after the death of his brother Godfrey was given the royal honour so that he could fill the vacant throne [of Jerusalem].

It is clear that the venerable Ida was the mother of these remarkable sons, because while they were still in their cradle she did not allow them to be fed with milk other than from her own breasts out of fear that they be contaminated with bad habits.

17. King Roger of Sicily Rewards the Wet-nurse of his Son, Henry, Southern Italy, 1136

Apart from its slightly unusual content, this document resembles many others recording property transactions in the region. It probably owes its existence to the fact that King Roger's first wife, Elvira of

Castile, had died in 1135. The wet-nurse in this case was therefore arguably propelled into prominence as a surrogate mother for the infant Henry. Sadly, the child died young, and Roger remarried: his second wife also bore a son named Henry.

Newly translated from: *Syllabus Graecarum membranarum*, ed. F. Trinchera (Naples: Joseph Cattaneo, 1865), 117 (1136), pp. 155–7.

Roger in Christ God, pious and powerful king. Just as the builder, building a house, does not only use large square stones, but also small ones, for his house, so a good king who rewards his subjects for their good deeds and through this builds his own house should not only give large rewards, but also smaller thanks. On account of this, Adelina, the wife of Adam, nourished my legitimate son Henry, giving a small gift. And so our power gave to her and her successors a property called Rachala Exames in our territory of Boiki, with its rights: five pairs of oxen and five peasants, whose names are Moyses, son of Solimen; Nemes, his brother; their brothers, Ises and Mouleasen; and Mouhammout, son of Abderrachmet Bouliptis.

Which, under this seal and document, we gave to the said Adelina and her husband to have, with their heirs; in the month of April, fourth indiction, year 6644.

Roger in Christ God, pious and powerful king and aid to Christians.

18. Nurse and Infant, Normandy, Mid-eleventh Century

For details about this work, see the introduction to text 3 above.

Newly translated from: *Miracula sancti Vulfranni*, par. 14, ed. AASS, March iii, pp. 154–5.

The other [son] was younger and was hardly more than two years old when, to the greater glory of God, he experienced grave danger, close to that from which no mortal returns. For on the third day after his mother had returned from the shrine of the saint, as we have told above, the nurse held the small boy at her breast and in a childlike manner soothed the crying child with her usual caresses. But when she noticed that he began to cry louder she took off the sharp pin which fastened at her neck the dress she was wearing, so that instantly the little boy stopped crying. But by having taken it off, she did not realize the danger, for he put it in his mouth, as is the habit of children of that age, and it got stuck between his tongue and his palate against the narrow opening of his throat. The discomfort greatly distressed him, for he could neither swallow nor spit it out, and he began to cry again loudly. When the father returned from the nearby wood and saw his beloved little boy crying he asked for the reason. When he understood what had happened he was seriously shaken and quickly picked up the boy. Having opened the little boy's mouth, he moved softly the tops of his fingers so that he might dislodge the sharp object; he used all his ingenuity and wisdom, but contrary to what he tried to achieve his attempt was in vain. For as a result of the soft touch the sharp pin got dislodged and dropped into the large back of the child's throat and in its fall disappeared inside the child's body. When the mother, who had entered after the father, saw this she wailed loudly and, as if insane, lifted the child in her arms to take him to the shrine of the holy confessor, praying to St Vulfran: 'Free my son and return him to me at once in good health.' The father, however, fearing that something worse might happen during the journey, held her back so that she stayed at home despite how ill the child was. Both offered thanks to the saint and asked devotedly that he would consider it worthy to act as the saviour for them and their child's health. What then? Within an hour the little boy had quietened down as if nothing had happened to him, for he cried no longer, nor was he in distress; in fact, as he had done before he ate and drank, played and slept. On the third day, after the food he had taken had been digested, the whole copper object, undamaged by the interior passage and without any hurt to his bowels, fell in the privy. Is it not miraculous how through all the twists of the boy's intestines, as if through fine small round tubes, the copper sharp object, now going up high, now going down low, could travel without getting stuck anywhere or causing wounds, and so at last through Nature's lower parts find a way out all in one piece?

19. Nurse and Infant, Normandy,
Early Twelfth Century

This story belongs to a collection of miracles of St Nicholas written by a monk of Bec (Normandy) in the early twelfth century.

Newly translated from: *Miracula sancti Nicolai conscripta a monacho Beccensi*, Vol. 2, ed. A. Poncelet, *Catalogus codicum hagiographicorum Latinorum Bibliotheca Nationali Parisiensis*, ed. Hagiographi Bollandiana (Brussels, 1890), c. 20, p. 416.

It is said by those who know, on account of their reading and listening, that one day, when the most holy man was still a baby, after she had forgotten to prepare his cradle his nurse took him out of the bath. By chance, a lame and blind man was present. Having remembered what she had neglectfully forgotten to do, through God's will and direction, she put the small boy on the knee of the sick man, who was sitting nearby, while she prepared the cradle. Having accomplished this task, she took the child and laid him in his cradle, fastening the strings, as is the habit of nurses. The lame man, who until that moment had dragged himself over the floor and who had never had the strength to walk, suddenly stood up completely recovered, regained his sight, began to walk and run as if he had never suffered any affliction, while praising God for having bestowed this gift on him through such a small child.

20. Penitential Texts on Child Deaths,
Spain, Ninth to Eleventh Centuries

Penitentials were books of punishments which priests referred to when handing out penances to their sinning parishioners after confession. The three Spanish books of penitentials, *Vigilanum* (V), *Cordubense* (C) and *Silense* (S), date from the late-ninth, early-eleventh and mid-eleventh centuries respectively. They are described by their editors as being somewhat more rigorous in their punishments than contemporary northern European examples.

Newly translated from: *Paenitentialia Hispaniae*, ed. Ludger Körntgen and Francis Bezler, Corpus Christianorum, Series Latina, 156A (Turnhout: Brepols, 1998), pp. 7, 8, 24 and 66.

V: X, 50: If a woman kills a child in the womb by a potion or other means, let her do penance for 15 years. Similarly for children already born.

V: X, 51: But if a poor woman rushes to do this, let her do penance for 7 years.

C: IX, 147: If a woman conceives and kills her child through a potion or other means, let her do 21 years' penance.

S: VI, 83: If a woman should kill her child whether in the womb or newborn with a potion or other art, let her do 15 years' penance.

S: VI, 84: But if she is a poor woman, 10 years.

V: X, 54: If a woman or another crushes her infant, it should be judged homicide.

[Silense has the same statement almost verbatim: S: VI, 82.]

V: X, 55: If anyone causes an abortion, let them do 3 years' penance.

V: X, 57: If a woman should kill her child in the womb before it quickens [lit.: 'before it has a soul'], let her do 3 years' penance.

V: X, 58: If it is after quickening, then it should be judged as murder.

S: VI, 85: And if it is before the child quickens, 3 years.

S: VI, 86: But if after quickening, it is judged murder.

21. Care of an Abandoned Baby, Italy, Late Thirteenth Century

This story, although written in the early sixteenth century, concerns Castruccio Castracani, Duke of Lucca (1281–1328). The theme of humble beginnings triumphing had resonance in the Italy of Machiavelli's time, but the story of the child's abandonment is timeless.

Newly translated from: Niccolò Machiavelli, *Tutte Le Opere*, ed. Mario Martelli (Florence: Sansoni, 1971).

Master Antonio had a vineyard behind the house in which he lived. This was not difficult to enter from many directions since it had only gardens at its boundaries. It happened that one morning, shortly after sunrise, Madonna Dianora (for that was what Master Antonio's sister was called) went out into the vineyard, collecting certain herbs to make her condiments as is the custom with women, when she heard a rustle under one of the vines in the grass, and, turning her eyes that way, heard something like crying. Making her way towards the noise, she discovered the hands and face of a baby who, wrapped up in the leaves, appeared to be calling for help. So she, partly marvelling, partly astonished, but full of compassion and wonder, picked him up and carried him to the house, washed him and wrapped him in white linens as is the custom, and when Master Antonio returned to the house she presented the baby to him. He, hearing the tale and seeing the infant, was filled with no less wonder and piety than the woman had been, and, discussing among themselves what action they should take, they decided to raise him, since he was a priest and she did not have children. They took on a wet-nurse into the house, and nourished him as if he had been their son, and having baptized him, named him after Castruccio, their father.

CHAPTER 2

GIRLS AND YOUNG WOMEN

Introduction

Work on the experience of medieval children has tended to view them as a de-gendered group, on account of their pre-pubescence. But a child's future was decided from the moment of its birth. Gender was of course only one factor, and class might be argued to be far more decisive in the decisions made about a child's upbringing, health, education and economic well-being. But the possibilities for a child's future, particularly in times of economic hardship, were far more limited for girls, who might at best hope to remain with their parents or be placed in service, than they were for boys, who had the additional opportunity of being given as oblates by their parents to the Church.[1]

In this section we have combined the experiences of young girls and young single women. We originally planned to separate these two groups, influenced to a certain extent by the medieval idea of the life cycle, which distinguished between the child (*puer/puella*) and the youth/young man or woman (*adolescens, iuvenis*). However, our investigation of the available source material soon revealed that little girls are a singularly elusive group to find. As with babies, only those who attracted attention for their unusual gifts or qualities (such as young saints), or because their lives took an unexpected turn, appear in the literature (texts 22 to 25). Otherwise, they were, to our male authors, an unremarkable community, and it is easy to believe that passivity, silence and obedient service (texts 26 and 27) were indeed what was required of a good daughter, just as the advice manuals prescribed.[2] The main exception to their being confined was due to the fact that young girls, particularly those from poorer families, might enter other households as servants, willingly or not, and we have evidence of the contractual arrangements made when they did so (text 28). There is also considerable evidence for female slavery in medieval Europe, the persistence of which has been attributed to their position as domestics and their use as sexual partners (texts 29 to 32).[3]

Only as they approached menarche did girls elicit more attention,[4] but here a clear gender division becomes apparent in their progress through the life cycle. The life stages known as 'adolescence' and 'youth', whilst not dependent on puberty, variable in their boundaries and lasting rather longer than modern-day conceptions of the term, were recognizable to medieval authors as stages that *men* went through to achieve social and legal maturity, not women. Georges Duby's depiction of medieval youth culture has been influential in shaping our perception of this as a distinct moment in the medieval male life cycle, and Ruth Mazo Karras has developed the idea of medieval youth as a transitional stage in a number of male life experiences played out at court, at work or, later on, at university.[5] And, most recently, in the context of the children's crusades, William MacLehose has explored contemporary medieval disagreement about boundaries between fragile and mature childhood on the one hand and young and old youth on the other.[6]

Youth as a stage in female lives, however, is rather less easy to define or tease out. A recent volume of essays on young medieval women found the idea of female youth only in creative fictions of womanhood, in literary and hagiographic texts, rather than enshrined in legal sources.[7] That is, ideas about female youth belong precisely to the category of imagined life stages – possible to imagine, but harder to find in practice. Female youth is evasive, not because of gender-blindness among historians, but because the potential for a visibly different life stage between childhood and marriage was much more limited for women than for men. As Deborah Youngs acutely observes, 'Whilst their youth was acknowledged, the perceived moral dangers of single women meant that the earlier they attained adulthood – mainly through marriage – the better.'[8] Young single women, therefore, were something of an endangered species in the Middle Ages.

This anxiety to ensure a young girl's progression into marriage (discussed further in Chapter 3, below) is reflected in betrothal arrangements early in her life (texts 33 and 34), even to the extent of sending her away to live with her future husband's family in case of imminent danger (text 35). In the case of heiresses, shockingly early marriages, worthy even of note by contemporaries, might be sanctioned by the girl's family (text 36). Puberty was a dangerous time for girls, and the possibility of illicit sexual relations or even assault was not confined to the pages of hagiography (texts 37 and 38). Fear for women's honour is most clearly expressed in some of the letters of guidance written by clergymen to young women who were sent reluctantly to nunneries after their fiancés were killed. Although we do not have the women's view, these male 'agony-aunt' letters contain an interesting take on these young women's lives. What they have in common is the picture of the horror of married life (which the woman would have led if her betrothed had not lost his life), including dramatic descriptions of death in childbirth, noisy children and impatient husbands. They also, unsurprisingly, exalt the notion of the marriage to Christ as a superior life to its secular counterpart. Reading these letters against the grain allows us, above all, to reconstruct the apparent haste with which the girls were sent away from home, and also the shock the girls experienced at the abandonment of the prospect of a married life.[9]

Marriage also demanded economic resources in the form of a dowry, and the concern to secure this is widely visible in charters, where the main economic barrier to marriage – the lack thereof – formed the basis of litigation (text 39) or was addressed as a charitable act (texts 40 and 41). There was, however, an inherent tension between ensuring young girls were married off, and not marrying them off before they were capable of procreation.

For more explicit information on how medieval authors understood the latter issue, we have to turn to medical treatises.

These, like prescriptive sources, gave weight to healthy, pro-
ductive marriages, and thus have considerable material on sex
and female fertility. Again, though, they must be treated with
caution if we are seeking to understand the realities of women's
lives in the Middle Ages. This is because much of the medical
knowledge on display was directly or indirectly drawn from
ancient sources, and medical works belonged to a tradition of
intellectual study. Indeed, a distinction is often drawn in the
history of medicine between such theoretical works and handbooks of medical practice, which are rarer and usually later in
date. Medical books inform us of numerous contraceptive
methods, for instance, but we cannot assume that this indicates
widespread use.

Nevertheless, we do have some evidence of practical medicine in action. Some of it is recorded not in medical handbooks
at all, but in saints' lives, where the patient ultimately receives
a cure through faith, after the cures prescribed by doctors fail.[10]
The attention paid to problems in conception includes specific
reference to whether the girl was menstruating, and in some
cases specific ages were reported. The twelfth-century treatise
which would later circulate in Europe under the title *Trotula*
discusses menstruation thus:

> This purgation occurs in women around the thirteenth year, or a
> little earlier or a little later, depending on the degree to which
> they have an excess or dearth of heat or cold.[11]

The medical literature, therefore, would suggest that the legal
age of twelve for girls cited in some medieval law codes was
rather too young for a valid marriage, and we might in this case
think that it was more accurate than the religious literature.
Medical historians such as Darryl Amundsen and Carol Jean
Diers have suggested that thirteen or fourteen might be seen as
a realistic age for menarche in medieval women, a figure with
which Joan Cadden agrees, but which Clarissa Atkinson has
criticized for still being 'improbably early'. Numerous medical
texts, clearly alive to the unlikelihood of girls being ready for
marriage at twelve, in fact advise against beginning a childbearing

career the moment one was physically able, citing the dangers to the health of both mother and child.[12] Such admonitions were backed up by hagiographical texts (text 42).

The onset of sexual maturity, then, can be taken as a marker of the end of girlhood for the majority of women, but it was accompanied with a deep-seated horror of menstruation among our writers, which had its roots in pre-Christian ideas of pollution. Hence the drive towards procreative marriage, for it was well understood that menstruation stopped during pregnancy (text 43).

We must not forget the small minority whose lives did not progress to the next stage, marriage. Single, never-married women have formed the focus of recent attention by Judith Bennett, who terms their existence 'lesbian-like' without implying that this meant having sexual relations with other women.[13] Most of these entered all-female communities of nuns: very few were able to live independent, secular lives. Some daughters of high birth might find themselves confined to a nunnery – whether or not they had taken vows – in order to preserve their chastity. As mentioned above, economic hardship might prevent marriage if a girl could not bring a dowry with her, and for some young women the struggle to survive without male support forced them into prostitution, which Christian writers strove to understand and remedy (text 44). The fallen woman and the idealized virgin are both visible in literary texts, which satirize the consequences of illicit sexual relations (text 45) and celebrate perpetual virginity (text 46). Ultimately, however, all three types stood outside the boundaries of acceptable behaviour. Had Ermengarde of Brittany persisted in her chastity without becoming cloistered, she might have attracted suspicion and censure (although compare texts 47 to 49). The single, never-married woman might truly be said to 'challenge the boundaries' of the gender roles assigned to her far more than those who took the veil and ended up under male domination just as surely as if they had found a husband. Predictably enough, therefore, her existence as anything other than marginal has been largely written out of the record.

22. A Jewish Girl's Charitable Act, Cairo, Mid-eleventh Century

For details of the source from which this text is taken, see above, Chapter 1, text 13.

Reproduced from: S. D. Goitein, *A Mediterranean Society: The Jewish Communities of the World as Portrayed in the Cairo Genizah*, Vol. 3: *The Family* (Berkeley: University of California Press, 1975), p. 235.

Joseph ben Musa Taherti writes to Nahray ben Nissim:

A little girl gets new clothes on New Year's Eve – a father in Al-Mahdiyya sends her old clothes to Fustat to be sold and the proceeds to be used for the maintenance of orphans in Jerusalem. She has the right to sell them and buy herself something, but has been taught charity.

23. Little Girls' Pastimes: Liutberga, Germany, Ninth Century

Liutberga (see below, texts 26 and 49) lived in the ninth century, in northern Germany. She became a servant of Countess Gisla (daughter of Count Hessi in Saxony), and looked first after Gisla, then became the housekeeper to Gisla's son Berhard and also acted as nurse to his two sets of children. After a spell as a recluse, she retired to Wendhausen, where she died between 860 and 865. See S. F. Wemple, *Women in Frankish Society. Marriage and Cloister* 500–900 (Philadelphia: University of Pennsylvania Press, 1981), pp. 99–100, 173–4. This excerpt offers a glimpse of what she remembered of her childhood.

Newly translated from: *Das Leben der Liutbirga. Eine Quellen zur Geschichte der Sachsen in karolingischer Seit*, ed. O. Menzel, Deutsches Mittelalter, Kritische Studientexte des Reichsinstituts für ältere deutsche Geschichtskunde, MGH, 3 (Leipzig: Verlag Karl W. Hiersemann, 1937), c. 28, p. 32.

*

On another occasion in a similar fashion the Devil with great insults confronted her at her anchorage and began to mock her sanctity; he recalled how as a small girl she had once played a trick on a girlfriend of the same age. While being both engaged on some joint piece of work she had broken a needle. When her friend left, she secretly took the friend's needle and put her own broken one in its place. And [the Devil] congratulated her on her deception as if she had done a great deed: 'Hey, where was your sanctity and your precious behaviour then, when you felt not ashamed to act as a thief?' Liutberga still remembered what she had done as a little girl when she first learned the art of needlework and until she had committed her sin – which she had never confessed – to oblivion.

24. *Little Girls' Pastimes: Joan of Arc, France, Early Fifteenth Century*

Joan of Arc was born in Domrémy (northern France) in 1412. After her involvement in the fight against the English, she was captured by them and put on trial for heresy at Rouen (then occupied by the English). This is an excerpt from the proceedings of the third day, Saturday 24 February 1431, pertaining to her years as a young girl at her home village. The last paragraph of this extract refers to the fact that Joan usually wore a male outfit, suitable for fighting; only at the end of her trial did she reluctantly agree to wear a dress.

Newly translated from: *Procès de condamnation de Jeanne d'Arc*, 3 vols., Vol. 1, ed. P. Tisset, Y. Lanhers (Paris: Klincksieck, 1960, 1971), pp. 65–7.

Asked if she did not take the animals to the fields, she said that she had answered this elsewhere, and that after she had grown up, and had reached the age of understanding, she did not generally look after animals, but certainly helped to take them to the meadows and for fear of the soldiers, to a castle called 'Isle'; but she did not recall whether or not she tended them when she was young.

Item: She was questioned about a certain tree growing near her village. To which she answered that, fairly near Domrémy, there was a certain tree called the Tree of Ladies, but others called it the Tree of Fairies, 'des Faees' in French; and nearby was a fountain. And she has heard it said that when sick with fever some people drank of this fountain and sought its water to restore their health. And she had seen it herself; but she did not know whether they were cured this way or not. Item: She said she heard that the sick, when they could rise, went to the tree and walked around it. And it was a big tree, a beech, from which they get the may flowers, 'le beau may' in French; and it is said to belong to milord Pierre de Bourlemont, knight. Item: She said that sometimes she would run around with the other young girls, making garlands for Our Lady of Domrémy there. And often she had heard old people say (who did not belong to her family) that there were fairies there. She heard a certain Joan, the wife of Mayor Aubery of Domrémy, godmother to the Joan who was speaking, say that she had seen fairies; but she herself did not know whether it was true or not. Item: She said that she herself never saw fairies at the tree that she knew; but [asked] if she saw them elsewhere, she did not know if she had seen them or not. Item: She said that she had seen young girls putting garlands on the branches of the tree, and she herself sometimes hung them there with them [the other girls]; sometimes they took them away, and sometimes they left them there. Item: She said that since she knew that she had to come to France, she had taken little part in games or frivolous behaviour, the least possible; and she did not know whether she had danced near the tree since she had grown to the age of understanding. Although she certainly danced there occasionally with the children, but then she more often sang than danced.

Item: She said that there was a wood, called the oak wood, 'le Bois-chesnu', in French, which can be seen from her father's door and is not more than half a league away. Item: She did not know, nor had she ever heard, that fairies lived there; but she did hear her brother say that in the country around it was said she, Joan, received her message from the Tree of Ladies; but she said she had not done this, and she denied it to her brother.

Item: She also said that when she came to the king, some people asked her if there was in her region a wood called the oak wood; for there were prophecies which said that from this wood a young girl would come who would do wonderful things; but Joan said that she put no faith in that.

Asked if she wanted to have a woman's dress, she answered: 'Give me one. I will take it and go away: otherwise I will not have it; and I am content with this, since it pleases God that I wear it.'

25. Little Girls at School: Froissart's L'Espinette amoureuse, 1365–72

Jean Froissart (c.1337–c.1405) was a chronicler and poet who frequented the English court and received patronage from several European rulers on his travels. He is best known for his account of the early years of the Hundred Years War. This text, however, shows a different side to his work.

Newly translated from: Jean Froissart, L'Espinette amoureuse, ed. Anthime Fourrier (Paris: Klincksieck, repr. 2002), p. 50. The text is reproduced and discussed in Jens N. Faaborg, Les enfants dans la littérature française du moyen âge (Copenhagen: Museum Tusculanum, 1997), pp. 214–15.

> When I was no more than twelve . . .
> They sent me to school,
> Where they school the unlearned,
> There were little girls there
> Who were my pastime playthings
> And I, who was a virgin then,
> Would give them pins
> Or an apple or a pear
> And it seemed to me, if you were to ask,
> That I gained great prowess through their grace;
> And also truly it came out,
> I will say without a doubt.

And then I shared among them,
'When the time will come among us
Whom will I be able to love?'
One should not blame me for this
If my nature leads me to this
Because in many places one passes up
That much joy and honour can come
From love as well as arms.

26. A Young Girl at Work: Liutberga, Germany, Ninth Century

For information about Liutberga, see above, text 23.

Newly translated from: *Das Leben der Liutbirga. Eine Quellen zur Geschichte der Sachsen in karolingischer Seit*, ed. O. Menzel, Deutsches Mittelalter, Kritische Studientexte des Reichsinstituts für ältere deutsche Geschichtskunde, MGH, 3 (Leipzig: Verlag Karl W. Hiersemann, 1937), c. 3-6, pp. 11–14.

When the said matron [Gisla] went on a business journey because she had to visit her estates in many regions, she came to a certain place when it was time to look for somewhere to stay the night. The nunnery there had a nearby guesthouse and its buildings provided comfortably for her needs. Amongst the serving-girls one stood out, for this one young girl seemed superior to her contemporaries in beauty and intelligence. With the attitude of a perfect servant in every respect she gave orders to all others with speed and skill. Silently observing her appearance and seeing her in action the matron began to make enquiries as to who she was, where her family lived and what her social status was. She replied sensibly and in an orderly way, explaining that she had come from a place called 'Solazburg' and that her parents were of respectable status; she explained her present circumstances and that she would have made a vow [to be a nun] were it not for her young age. Gisla at once made up her mind and with great persuasion she began to exhort the girl to accompany her and to commit herself to her trust, swearing by God that the girl would be able to live with her forever, as if she were one of her daughters.

Putting faith in these promises, Liutbirga joined Gisla on her journey, and I believe, with the consent of divine providence, and mutual agreement, the wish of both women was fulfilled. For, as she later asserted, she had vowed to go on pilgrimage, and God, to whom she had dedicated herself in spirit, had given her this opportunity. And so the said Liutbirga travelled with the said matron Gisla to her estates and the girl joined her in the exercise of charity more and more, and day by day in a short time she was loved by all, not only by those with whom she came into contact, but also by those who came to know her. The girl stayed on in the home of her lady; a talented girl, she increased the flowers of her virtue year upon year. She was wise in counsel, true to her word, dedicated to her work, generous in alms, constant in her efforts and outstanding in piety; she excelled in her efforts on behalf of others, caring for the sick and solving disputes. Embracing all who were afflicted by misery, she loved everyone and everyone loved her. Possessing these gifts and similar talents, she increased them daily and, step by step, she climbed the road to the summit of perfection, pleasing God as well as mankind.

The said young woman Liutbirga was, as we have already said, clever and of strong moral character; without blemish, especially, she persevered in the praise of God, devoutly offering in her heart the sacrifice of her spirit to the Lord in psalms, hymns and sacred songs, according to the apostle. And so as to briefly set out the manner of her effort, everything she deemed good and pleasing to God she embraced with total affection of her heart. Yet she avoided evil and worldly vice as if they were a steep precipice. Incessantly she studied the sacred scriptures and by daily meditation made a little progress every time until she reached a profound understanding; and if the weakness of her sex had not prevented her, she would have become even more learned.

*

She was exceptionally capable in the various arts of women's work, to the extent that the people with whom she dealt and those living further afield called her the 'daedala' [lit: 'the very skilled']. She remained faithful to the very needy and, whenever necessary, she was so merciful that she was known as the 'mother of the poor'. And it so happened that her happy fame spread, so that many of the aristocracy, nobles and matrons, got to hear of her and flocked to her in a huge effort to offer her friendship and love; it was wonderful how she was first known and then loved, and how she gained many more friends in the place of her pilgrimage than she had had in her homeland.

27. A Peasant Girl at Work: Alpais of Cudot, France, Mid-twelfth Century

The *Life* of Alpais of Cudot (*c.*1150–*c.*1211) throws light on the early life of a young woman of peasant stock in northern France in the second half of the twelfth century. Alpais was born in Cudot, near the Cistercian monastery of Écharlis (diocese of Sens), where the monk, Peter, wrote her *Life* in *c.*1180.

Newly translated from: *Leben und Visionen der Alpais von Cudot (1150–1211)*, ed. E. Stein, Scriptoralia, 77 (Tübingen: G. Narr, 1995), c. 1-2, pp. 120–23.

The most celebrated virgin was born of poor parents in the small village of Cudot near Écharlis, the site of our monastery, and her first name was Alpais. The etymology of the girl's name reflects her life very well, for Alpais can mean 'high peace' or 'high hope' or even 'increasing hope' or perhaps even 'elevated foot'. [. . .] Her father Bernard provided food by the labour of his own hands and 'in the sweat of his brow he ate his own bread' [Gen. 3: 19]. With the help of two oxen he tilled his own plot of land. In this agricultural labour, his twelve-year-old daughter, his eldest child, helped him. In front of her father, prodding the plough oxen with a stick, she forced them to furrow the land. With manure and cow dung placed on her shoulders, she accompanied her father to fertilize the field and garden. But because her young upper arms could not support the very heavy load, he tied the rope of the basket to her forearms. Carrying this load on her shoulders, with her arms and shoulders bearing the weight, she shared her father's work as much as she could. Rejecting leisure, which is the mind's enemy, day and night she exhausted her tender small body as a result of the heavy labour. Because her brothers were younger [than her], they looked after their father's cows and herds in the fields. On Sundays and festivals, when other girls went to dances and idle pleasures and vainly occupied themselves, Alpais herded the oxen and cattle to the pastures so that she drove them away from the vegetables, the produce of the neighbours; no one was ever disturbed by her, nor was anybody ever in the least distressed by what she lightly did or said to anyone. In fact, at home she sat in silence, devoting herself exclusively to God, whom alone she strove to please; the young girl invoked His virgin mother with intense prayers, while shedding copious tears. With the body of a young girl, but with the mind of an old woman, by passing her youth in ways [far] from those of childhood – in fact, old for her age – she ignored any forbidden longing. Instead within her heart's chamber, having shed tears over her pillow, daily she offered herself again and again as a living, holy and immaculate host to her spouse [i.e. Christ], pleasing God; for the love of whom she had embraced keeping her virginity with such a desire that she had never given a playful kiss to anyone nor with a dishonest word or act offended anyone's chaste eyes.

When the young girl could not any longer bear such tasks because all the muscles within her had broken and torn as a result of the continuous hard labour, she drew from within her heart deep breaths which changed the colour of her beautiful face, and her exterior showed already the clear signs of her internal pain. What more? In the grip of continuous weakening, for almost a whole year she lay on a hard and rough bed made up of dirty straw without feathers or bedlinen. She lost

all appetite for food and drink. Emaciated by the long fasting
and having lain in bed on her back for so long that her breast
and shoulders, her loins and all her inner organs right up to her
intestines were destroyed and rotten, she inspired such horror
in those who came to see her and brought forth such stench
that even her mother – for her father was already dead – and
her brothers, sharing in her suffering, despite their brotherly
love refused to go near her on account of the intolerable stench
of her wounds. Her mother, however, who suffered more seriously from her daughter's illness because she loved her with
even stronger maternal affection, every day wished for her
daughter to die in order that at least her suffering might stop
with her death. And because she was poor and had nothing
that she could give her, she threw a piece of barley bread to
Alpais, as if to a dog from afar, because of the intolerable
stench. Alpais could neither catch the bread with her hand, nor
could she bring it to her mouth, because her hands were already
withered, and, on account of the completely rotten flesh, loos-
ened and disjointed from the arms and, with feet already dead,
her family denied her the one duty which they owed her. She
became such a burden and nuisance for her brothers that they
begged their mother to stop feeding her, so that, forced by hunger, she would die. And so it happened that, as much from lack
of food as from her continuous habit of daily fasting, her throat
became so dry and arid that, deterred by the pain which was
constantly pressing her, she had given over to oblivion all appetite for food: so that whenever she was given food, she was
horrified, as if prepared for torture. A drink of water took such
labour that the sound of water trickling down her dry throat
could be heard by bystanders as if water was flowing down
from one rock to another. She had become unused to taking
food as a result of the fasting and the lack of food and the con-
tinuing deterioration of her weakness, fasting first for two or
three days, and then for weeks. Consequently, she was reduced
to such weakness that in no way could she bring her hand,
lame with rottenness, to her mouth, or lift her foot, already
withered, nor even without assistance turn from one side to the
other in order that by changing position she might refresh her

tired body. And because the intolerable stench which exuded from the ulcerated limbs prevented anybody from coming close to her, deprived of human consolation she prayed to God and His holy mother that they have compassion for her with loud sighs.

28. A Contract Placing a Girl in Service, Amalfi, 1090

This text is discussed alongside other similar placements of children in Patricia Skinner, '"The light of my eyes": Medieval motherhood in the Mediterranean', *Women's History Review*, 6 (1997), 391–410. Although the transaction appears to have arisen from a debt, we should note that the girl would ultimately benefit from her period in effective servitude, and she is specifically recorded agreeing to her mother's actions (whether willingly or not). The items in the contract referred to as *cumpitum*, *coctum* and *capitallunclu* are very obscure and difficult to translate, but their probable meaning is 'a quilt, a pan and a pillow'. The relative value of *tari* in relation to *solidi* is that one *solidus* was worth four *tari*.

Newly translated from: *Codice Diplomatico Amalfitano*, ed. R. Filangieri di Candida (Naples: Tipografico Silvio Morano, 1917), document 85, pp. 136–7.

In the name of our Lord and saviour, Jesus Christ. On the first day of June in the thirteenth indiction, at Amalfi.

I, Asterada, widow of the late Visantius of the city of Salerno, on this day willingly hand over and assign to you, Master Ursus, son of Master Sergius Meiadirtu and to Rogata, your wife, my daughter named Sica. For this reason, from this day forward and for all the days of your life she should serve and obey you, and whatever service and order you should order her to do by day and night my daughter should do and complete for you with faithfulness and speed and without any fraud or ill-will.

And you must feed her and clothe her and give her shoes, for the right reasons and to the best of your ability, and you must do good by her, so that you will have from her mercy and a good reputation.

And if she should flee from you and come to me or to my property, wherever I may be staying, I shall bring her back and return her to you any way I can without your scolding or ill-will. If she flees from you to any other place, you or your agents will have the power to apprehend her with this charter and to restrain her and return her to your service; but you should discipline her mercifully according to the fault she has committed, and we shall defend your right to her from all men.

And for this you gave to me four *tari*, but for this I returned them to you on account of my daughter's debt. At your deaths you must give to her a benediction of eight gold *tari* and a bed, *cumpitum*, and *coctum*, and *capitallunclu*, and a cauldron, and a frying pan and the clothes that she has at that time. And after both your deaths and with that benediction she shall remain fully and permanently free.

And if either party in this charter should go against it, let them pay to the party who remains firm a penalty of twenty Byzantine *solidi*, and let this charter remain firm.

And everything above pleases me, Sica, fully.

+ Gregory, son of Leo, is a witness.

+ Leo, son of Manso de Leo Galloppi, is a witness.

+ Lupinus, son of Sergius de Lupino de Mauro the Count, is a witness.

+ I, John the scribe, son of Sergius, wrote it.

+ John, son of Master Musco de John de Pantaleo, is a witness to the veracity of this charter and saw and read the copy.

+ Maurus, son of Master Sergius Count Mauronis, is a witness that he saw and read the charter, of which this is a copy.

+ Pantaleo, son of Master Muski de Master Constantine, is a witness to the veracity of this charter and saw and read the copy.

+ I, Constantine the scribe, son of the above Master John the scribe, copied this charter with my own hands just as I saw and read it and did not leave out or add anything. Done in the month of June, in the third indiction, in the year of our Lord, 1090.

29. Slave Girls Among the Rus', Tenth Century

This is a famous description of the funeral of a viking Rus' leader, buried together with his slave girl, by Ibn Fadlan. He was a diplomat/travel writer from Baghdad (perhaps the member of an embassy), sent out in 921–2 on a journey into Russia (possibly the Bulgarian territories on the Upper Volga), to report back on its inhabitants and customs. It is generally agreed that Ibn Fadlan met the Rus' people, who were descended from Scandinavian settlers in northern Russia. What is less clear is the extent to which the customs described are Scandinavian or Slavic, or a mixture of both. Regardless of the specific ethnicity of the funeral reported here, the account is vivid and, for our sensibilities, profoundly shocking.

We thank Professor Montgomery for allowing us to reproduce excerpts from his translation in his article, 'Ibn Fadlan and the Rusiyah', *Journal of Arabic and Islamic Studies*, Vol. 3 (2000) pp. 1–25.

I saw the Rusiyah when they had arrived on their trading expedition and had disembarked at the River Atil. I have never seen more perfect physiques than theirs – they are like palm trees, are fair and reddish, and do not wear the tunic or the caftan. The men wear cloaks, with which they cover one half of their body, leaving one of their arms uncovered. [. . .]

They are the filthiest of all Allah's creatures: they do not clean themselves after excreting or urinating or wash themselves when in a state of ritual impurity after coitus and do not even wash their hands after food. Indeed they are like asses which roam in the fields.

They arrive from their territory and moor their boats by the Atil, building large wooden houses on its banks. They gather in the house in groups of eleven-and-twenty, sometimes more, sometimes less. Each of them has a couch on which he sits. They are accompanied by beautiful slave girls for trading. One man will have intercourse with his slave girl while his companion looks on. Sometimes a group of them come together to do this, each in front of the other. Sometimes, indeed, the merchant will come in to buy a slave girl from one of them, and he will chance upon [the man] having intercourse with her, but the Rus' will not leave her alone until he has satisfied his urge. They cannot, of course, avoid washing their faces and their heads each day, which they do with the filthiest and most polluted water imaginable. I shall explain. Every day, a slave girl arrives in the morning with a large basin containing water, which she hands to her owner. He washes his hands and his face and his hair in the water, then dips his comb in the water and brushes his hair, blows his nose and spits in the basin. There is no filthy impurity which he will not do in this water. When he no longer requires it, the slave girl takes the basin to the man beside him, and he goes through the same routine as his comrade. She continues to carry it from one man to the next until she has gone round everyone in the house, with each of them blowing his nose and spitting, washing his face and hair in the basin. [. . .]

I was told that when their chieftains die, the least they do is to cremate them. I was very keen to verify this, when I learned of the death of one of their great men. They placed him in his grave and built a roof over him for ten days, until they had finished making and sewing his funeral garments.

In the case of a poor man, they build a small boat for him, place him inside and burn it. In the case of a rich man, they gather together his possessions and divide them into three: one-third for his family, one-third to use for his funeral garments, and one-third with which they procure the alcohol which they drink on the day when his slave girl kills herself and is cremated together with her master. (They are addicted to the alcohol which they drink night and day. Sometimes one of them dies with the cup still in his hand.)

When their chieftain dies, his family ask his slave girls and slave boys: 'Who among you will die with him?' and some of them reply, 'I shall.' Having said this, it becomes incumbent upon that person and it is impossible ever to turn back. Should that person try to, it is not permitted. It is usually slave girls who make this offer.

When that man whom I mentioned earlier died, they said to

his slave girls, 'Who will die with him?' and one of them said, 'I shall.' So they placed two slave girls in charge of her, to take care of her and to accompany her wherever she went, even to the point of occasionally washing her feet with their own hands. They set about attending to the dead man, preparing his clothes for him and setting right all he needed. Every day the slave girl would drink the alcohol and would sing merrily and cheerfully.

On the day when he and the slave girl were to be burned I arrived at the river where his ship was. To my surprise I discovered that it had been beached and that four planks of birch and other types of wood had been placed against it. Around them there had also been placed what resembled huge mounds of wood. Then the ship was hauled up and placed on top of this wood. They advanced, going to and fro around the boat, uttering words which I did not understand, while he was still in his grave and had not been exhumed.

Then they produced a couch and placed it on the ship, covering it with quilts and cushions made of Byzantine silk brocade. Then a crone arrived whom they called the 'Angel of Death', and she spread on the couch the coverings which we have mentioned. She is responsible for having his garments sewn up and putting him in order and it is she who kills the slave girls. I myself saw her: a gloomy, corpulent woman, neither young nor old . . .

Meanwhile, the slave girl who wished to be killed was coming and going, entering one pavilion after another. The owner of the pavilion would have intercourse with her and say to her, 'Tell your master that I have done this purely from love for you.'

At the time of evening prayer on the Friday they brought the slave girl to a thing which they had constructed like a door frame. She placed her feet on the hands of the men and appeared above that door frame. She said some words, and they brought her down. Then they lifted her up a second time, and she did what she had done the first time. They brought her down and then lifted her up a third time, and she did what she had done on the first two occasions. They next handed her a hen. She cut off its head and threw it away. They took the hen and threw it on board the ship.

I quizzed the interpreter about her actions and he said, 'The first time they lifted her, she said, "Behold, I see my father and my mother." The second time she said, "Behold, I see all of my dead kindred, seated." The third time she said, "Behold, I see my master, seated in Paradise. Paradise is beautiful and verdant. He is accompanied by his men and his retainers. He summons me, so bring me to him."' So they brought her to the ship, and she removed two bracelets which she was wearing, handing them to the woman called the Angel of Death, the one who was to kill her. She also removed two anklets which she was wearing, handing them to the two slave girls who had waited upon her: they were the daughters of the crone known as the Angel of Death. Then they lifted her on to the ship, but did not bring her into the pavilion. The men came with their shields and sticks and handed her a cup of alcohol, over which she sang and then drank. The interpreter said to me, 'Thereby she bids her female companions farewell.' She was handed another cup, which she took and chanted over for a long time, while the crone urged her to drink it and to enter the pavilion in which her master lay. I saw that she was befuddled and wanted to enter the pavilion, but she had put her head between the pavilion and the ship. The crone grabbed hold of her head and dragged her into the pavilion, entering it at the same time. The men began to bang their shields with the sticks so that her screams could not be heard and so terrify the other slave girls, who would not then seek to die with their masters.

Six men entered the pavilion and all had intercourse with the slave girl. They laid her down beside her master and two of them took hold of her feet, two of them her hands. The crone called the Angel of Death placed a rope around her neck in such a way that the ends crossed one another and handed it to two of the men to pull on it. She advanced with a broad-bladed dagger and began to thrust it in and out between her ribs, now here, now there, while the two men throttled her with the rope until she died.

30. Manumission of a Female Slave, Genoa, 12 May 1159

For an explanation of the source of this document, see above, Chapter 1, text 7.

We might note here that the freed slave was able to pay for her freedom with a significant sum of money, the source of which is not stated.

Newly translated from: *Il Cartolare di Giovanni Scriba*, Vol. 1, ed. M. Chiaudano and M. Moresco (Turin: S. Lattes & Co., 1935), document 537, pp. 288–9.

Algarda is freed.

Witnesses: Ansaldus Mallon, Bisaça, Oliver Nivetella, Bonus Vassallus Nivetella, W. Treia, Lanfrancus de Reco and Girardus de Lavania.

I, Malovrer, through the love of God and for the thirty-five-*solidi*-worth of Genoese *denarii* which I received from you, Algarda, my slave, daughter of the late Anselm, declare you to be free and absolve you from any bond of service, and permit you to go anywhere you wish, and do what you wish just as a freewoman [does], exempt from any condition of servitude. I also promise to you, on penalty of ten Genoese pounds of best gold, that neither I nor my heirs will weaken this liberty, and that we shall defend it for you from all men. [A further penalty clause follows.]

31. Sales of Female Slaves, Crete, 1301

The involvement of the Italian maritime republics in the slave trade was undoubtedly boosted by the establishment of colonies in the eastern Mediterranean. In this case we see the activities of merchants in Venetian-ruled Crete. The entries here were short notes made by an official notary or scribe on a roll or in his notebook, preparatory to writing up the transactions in full for the clients, hence some still were

'To be completed and dated', and where the notary was unsure of the name of the slave being sold he simply left a gap, indicated here as —. Entry 262 refers to the need to make two full documents instead of one, possibly because the buyer might have been representing a society rather than his own interests. Similarly, the scribe did not write out the full legal text of each transaction, but instead abbreviated it as 'etc.'. And because entries follow each other he was able to cross-refer to people he had already referred to. The last entry, in particular, raises doubts about the theory that baptism as a Christian could precipitate emancipation.

Newly translated from: *Benvenuto de Brixano, Notaio in Candia,* 1301–1302, ed. Raimondo Morozzo della Rocca, Fonti per la Storia di Venezia, sez. 3: Archivi Notarili (Venice: Alfieri Editore, 1950), *passim.*

Entry 10: 9 April 1301

I, Emanuel Vergici, inhabitant of Candia [Heraklion, Crete], make clear that I and my heirs give, sell and hand over to you, Elie Le Ferandine de Marseia, and your heirs, my slave whom I bought from the Turks, named Maria, from now and henceforward, etc. The price was twenty-five *perpera*. And I give you security.

Witnesses: Comes and Mencius.

To be completed and dated.

Entry 11: 9 April 1301

I, the above Emanuel, declare that I and my heirs sell to you, Johanneto Leucari, my slave named —, whom I bought from the Turks, to you, Zaneto Leucari, with all trust etc. The price was eighteen *perpera*, which you gave me. And I give you security.

Witnesses: Comes and Mencius.

To be completed and dated.

Entry 46: 19 April 1301

I, Emanuel Vergici, inhabitant of Candia, make clear that I and my heirs give and sell to you —, widow of Bande, my slave whom I bought from the Turks, named Herini, from now and henceforward etc. The price was twenty-seven *perpera*, which you gave me. And I give you security.

Witnesses: Nicolaus de Amigo and Comes.
To be completed and dated.

Entry 63: 27 April 1301

I, Floria, widow of John Prodecale, inhabitant of Candia, make clear that I and my heirs give, sell and hand over to you, Nicolo Prizolo, Notary, my slave named Maria, whom I bought when she came from Turkey. From now and henceforward, etc. The price was twenty *perpera*, which you gave me. And I give you security.

Witnesses: Michael Contarino and Paduanus.
To be completed and dated.

Entry 119: 15 May 1301

I, Emanuel Vergici, inhabitant of Candia, and my heirs, make clear that I and my heirs give and sell to you, Emanuel, son of the priest Nichipori, inhabitant of the said Candia and to your heirs, my slave whom I brought with me from Turkey, named Herini, from now and henceforward etc. The price was eighteen *perpera*, which you gave me. And I give you security.

Witnesses: Comes and N. Prizolo.
To be completed and dated.

Entry 120: 15 May 1301

I, Emanuel Vergici, inhabitant of Candia, and my heirs, make clear that I give, sell and hand over to you, John, son of the said priest Nichipori Ialina, and to your heirs, my slave whom I bought from the Turks, named Cally, from now and henceforward etc. The price was eighteen *perpera*, which you gave me. And I give you security.

Witnesses: Comes and N. Prizolo.
To be completed and dated.

Entry 172: 6 June 1301

I, Nicholas Reer, Catalan, inhabitant of Candia, and my heirs, make clear that I give, sell and hand over to you, Antonio Taliacute, inhabitant of Candia, and your heirs, my slave named Maria, whom I bought from the Turks in Turkey. The price was six *hyperpera*, which you have already paid me, and I give you security in perpetuity. If anyone, etc. Witnesses: Marcus Pascaligo and Comes.

To be completed and dated.

Entry 186: 17 June 1301

I, Magonus de La Sala, inhabitant of Constantinople, and my heirs, give, sell and hand over to you, Victor Paulo, inhabitant of Candia and your heirs, my [female] slave named Dullac of the Tartar race. From now and in the future in full virtue and power etc. The price was twenty-five *perpera*, which you have already paid. And I give you peace and security. If anyone, etc.

Witnesses: Emanuel, Notary, and Comes, Vicedominus, all of the Treasury.

To be completed and dated.

Entry 256: 1 August 1301

I, Roger Rogerio, inhabitant of Candia, and my heirs, give, sell and hand over to you, Beruze Cornario, my slave named Maria, whom I bought from the Turks, from now and henceforward etc. The price was seventeen *perpera*, which you paid me. And I give you security. If anyone, etc.

Witnesses: Marinus Barbadico, Marcus and N. Prizolo.

To be completed and dated.

Entry 258: 3 August 1301

I, Martin de Monigo, Genoese, and my heirs, give, sell and hand over to you, Philip Capelo, inhabitant of Candia, and your heirs, my slave named Bulgarum, of the Bulgar race, from now and henceforward, with all virtue and power etc. The price was ten *perpera*, which you paid me. And I give you security.

Witnesses: Vincentius, John Ravasii, Andreas of Vicenza and Vicedominus Jacob de Mezo.

To be completed and dated.

Entry 260: 3 August 1301

I, the above Martin, and my heirs, give, sell and hand over to you, Boniudeo, a doctor of physic, inhabitant of Candia, and your heirs, my slave named Balaba, of the — race, with full virtue and power etc. The price was sixteen *perpera*, which you have already given me, and if, etc.

Witnesses: Vincentius, John Ravasii, Andreas of Vicenza and Vicedominus Jacob de Mezo.

To be completed and dated.

Entry 261: 3 August 1301

I, Vasalinus —, of Genoa, and my heirs, give, sell and hand over to you, John de Molino, and your heirs, my slave named –, of the Tartar race, from now and henceforward, in full virtue and power etc. The price was twenty-two *perpera*, which you have already given me. And I give you security.

Witnesses: Pispolo, Vincentius, P. Fradelo, Rubeus Paradiso and Vicedominus Jacob de Mezo.

To be completed and dated.

Entry 262: 5 August 1301

I, Vasalinus Belegerio, inhabitant of Genoa, with my heirs, give, sell and hand over to you, Francisco Forciti, of the society of Perugians, inhabitant of Florence, and your heirs, my slave named Bersaba and her son named Beigoba, and a daughter named Cuise, of the race of the Cumans, from now and henceforward etc. The price was fifty *perpera*, which you gave me. And I give you security. If anyone, etc.

Witnesses: Pispolo, Vincentius, P. Fradelo, Rubeus Paradiso and Vicedominus Jacob de Mezo.

To be completed and dated. Two charters must be made.

Entry 263: 5 August 1301

I, the above Vasalinus, with my heirs, give, sell and hand over to you, Jacob Fuscari, of the district of St Paul, my slave named Berta, of the race of the Turks, from now and henceforward, etc. The price was twenty-two *perpera*, which you gave me. And I give you security. If anyone, etc.

Witnesses: Pispolo, Vincentius, P. Fradelo, Rubeus Paradiso and Vicedominus Jacob de Mezo.

To be completed and dated.

Entry 264: 5 August 1301

I, the above Vasalinus, with my heirs, give, sell and hand over to you, Angelo and N. Caravelo, my slave named — of the race of —, with her daughter named —, from now and henceforward etc. The price was twenty *perpera*, which you gave me. And I give you security. If anyone, etc.

Witnesses: Pispolo, Vincentius, P. Fradelo, Rubeus Paradiso and Vicedominus Jacob de Mezo.

To be completed and dated.

Entry 265: 5 August 1301

I, the Vasalinus Belegerio above, with my heirs, give, sell and hand over to you, Marino de Molino, inhabitant of Candia, my slave named — of the race of —, from now and henceforward, in full virtue and power etc. The price was twenty *perpera*, which you gave me. And I give you security. If anyone, etc.

Witnesses: Pispolo, Vincentius, P. Fradelo, Rubeus Paradiso and Vicedominus Jacob de Mezo.

To be completed and dated.

Entry 266: 5 August 1301

I, the above Vasalinus Belegerio, with my heirs, give, sell and hand over to you, Marco Taliapetra, my slave named Vida, of the race of the Cumans, from now and henceforward in full virtue and power etc. The price was twenty *perpera*, which you gave me. And I give you security. If anyone, etc.

Witnesses: Pispolo, Vincentius, P. Fradelo, Rubeus Paradiso and Vicedominus Jacob de Mezo.

To be completed and dated.

Entry 268: 5 August 1301

I, the above Vasalinus, with my heirs, give, sell and hand over to you, Nicolas Pascaligo, inhabitant of Candia, my slave named — of the race of —, from now and henceforward, etc. The price was twenty-one *perpera*, which you gave me. And I give you security. If anyone, etc.

Witnesses: Luchas de Lucha, Stephanelus, Notary, and the above.

Entry 269: 5 August 1301

I, the above Vasalinus, of Genoa, with my heirs, give, sell and hand over to you, Setelcol, widow of Master Leo, inhabitant of Candia, and your heirs, my slave named –, of the race of –, from now and henceforward, etc. The price was twenty-two *perpera*, which you gave me. And I give you security. If anyone, etc.

Witnesses: Comes, Iacobus de Grado, Stephen Bono, Vido Balistarius and the above vicedominus.

To be completed and dated.

Entry 270: 5 August 1301

I, the above Vasalinus, with my heirs, give, sell and hand over to you, Vido Balistario, inhabitant of Candia, and your heirs, my slave named —, of the race of —, with her son named —, from now and henceforward etc. The price was twenty-two *perpera*, which you gave me. And I give you security. If anyone, etc.

Witnesses: Iacobus de Grado, John Ravesii and the above vicedominus.

To be completed and dated.

Entry 271: 5 August 1301

I, the above Vasalinus, with my heirs, give, sell and hand over to you, Jacob de Mezo, of the Venetians of the district of St Paul, and your heirs, my slave named Batana, of the Tartar race, whose baptismal name is Simona, from now and henceforward, etc. The price was eighteen *perpera*, which you gave me. And I give you security. If anyone, etc.

Witnesses: Iacobus de Grado, Vido Balistarius, Michealinus Balistarius and the above vicedominus.

To be completed and dated.

32. A Fugitive Slave, Crete, 1315

Complementing the texts in 31, here we see another side to the life of a female slave.

Newly translated from: *Duca di Candia: Bandi*, ed. Paola Ratti

Vidulich, Fonti per la Storia di Venezia, sez. 1: Archivi Pubblici (Venice: Il Comitato Editore, 1965), p. 31.

6 March 1315

A public announcement was made by John de Xeno that if anyone has, or is keeping, or knows the whereabouts of Crusi, the slave of Lady Benevenuta, widow of Master Pascal, they must present her or show her to her lord within eight days, or pay a fine set by him.

33. Anglo-Saxon Customs on Engagement, Eleventh Century

The *Wifmannes beweddung* is a very rare description, in Old English, of arrangements for a girl's betrothal; it probably dates to the episcopacy of Wulfstan II of York (1002–23). See P. Wormald, *The Making of English Law: King Alfred to the Twelfth Century* (Oxford: Blackwell, 1999), pp. 385–6.

Newly translated from: *Die Gesetze der Angelsachsen*, 3 vols., Vol. 1, ed. F. Liebermann (Halle: M. Niemeyer, 1903–16), pp. 442–4.

How a Man Shall Betroth a Woman, and How He Should Make Such Arrangement.

1. If a man wishes to betroth a young woman or a widow, and if she and her kinsmen agree, it is right that, in the first instance, the fiancé promises and binds himself to her advocates, in good faith, according to God's law and the legitimate custom of the people, that he wishes her as his bride to maintain her according to God's law as one should maintain a wife; and his friends must provide surety.

2. Next, it has to be established who will pay for her upbringing. The fiancé must give his word, and his friends must provide surety.

3. Then, the fiancé must let it be known what he gives her in return for her acceptance of his offer, and what he will give her in case she survives him.

4. If the agreement is then made, it is right that she is entitled to one half of what he has, and to all, if they have a child together, provided she does not enter into another marriage.

5. He must confirm all that he has promised with an oath of good faith, and his friends must provide surety.

6. If they agree on all aspects, the kinsmen shall then give their kinswoman to the fiancé as his wife and give her in legitimate wedlock to him who has demanded her; and he who is in charge of the betrothal must receive the surety.

7. If, however, one wishes her to leave the region for that of another thegn, it is necessary that her friends receive a formal promise that she will not suffer any harm, and that if she commits an offence, the friends shall be allowed to assist her in case she may not have the wherewithal to pay a fine herself.

8. At the wedding, there shall be by a priest authorized to say Mass, who should arrange their union with God's blessing for all prosperity.

9. It is also good to enquire carefully that they are not too closely related by blood, out of fear that one would need to split up those who previously had been united by mistake.

34. An Anglo-Jewish Betrothal Contract, 1271

This betrothal contract, made four years before the prospective wedding, is a good example of how marriages could be arranged with very little intervention from the protagonists. We should note, however, that the engaged couple still had the choice whether to go through with the marriage, otherwise the careful stipulations as to what would happen should the wedding not go ahead would be redundant.

The document cites English currency, measured in pounds, shillings and pence; a mark was used as an accounting unit and was worth thirteen shillings and four pence. The date refers to how many years into the sixth millennium it was since the creation of Adam, hence the phrase 'of the six thousand'.

*

Newly translated from: Michael Adler, *Jews of Medieval England*
(London: JHSE, 1939), pp. 43–5.

On Friday, the third day of Shevat, in the year thirty-one of the
six thousand [5031], we, the undersigned, having received a
blessing from a minyan of ten persons [the minimum number of
Jewish males able to form a valid court], constituted ourselves
as a Beth Din [court of justice] to arrange matters between
R. Benjamin, the son of Joseph Jechiel, and Belassez, the daughter
of Rabbi Berechya [Benedict]. The said Belassez has betrothed
her daughter Judith, the daughter of R. Hayim, to Aaron, the
son of R. Benjamin, upon the following conditions:

The said Belassez promised to the said Aaron as a dowry
twenty marks sterling and the twenty-four books [of the Bible]
properly provided with punctuation, and the Masora [critical
notes], and both written upon calfskin: on every page there are six
columns, and the Targum [translation] of the Pentateuch [the first
five books of the Old Testament] and of the Haftaroth [selections
for reading in synagogue] are all therein written separately. From
today, Belassez has handed to the said R. Benjamin the said book
to keep it for the use of the young couple. She has further handed
to him the said twenty marks that they may be lent out at interest
to non-Jews until the young Aaron, his son, has grown up.

And when the time arrives for the wedding to take place,
when Aaron takes in marriage the said Judith, the daughter of
R. Hayim, it will behove his father, the said R. Benjamin to give
to his son Aaron and to the said Judith, his wife, twenty marks
sterling, and more (if the sum has grown from the original
twenty marks by way of interest). It will further be the duty of
the said R. Benjamin to provide both bride and bridegroom
with clothing suitable for their station, both for weekdays and
for the Sabbath, by the marriage ceremony, and to pay for the
wedding feast out of the interest which has accrued from the
original twenty marks. The said R. Benjamin may not make
any further claim upon the said Belassez either in respect of the
dowry or the cost of the wedding ceremony.

With good fortune, the wedding shall take place in the
month of Adar in the year 5035, if nothing untoward has hap-

pened to either of them, such as occurs to people. But if, God forbid, anything has accidentally befallen either of them, then the nuptials shall be solemnized, with good fortune, in another month after the disappearance of such an impediment.

Now and henceforth the said R. Benjamin pledges all his property, landed or moveable, therefrom to pay the above-mentioned twenty marks and to give them, together with the above-mentioned book, to Aaron, his son, and to Judith at the time of their marriage.

And if, God forbid, the marriage arrangements should not go well, so that the said Aaron does not wed the said Judith, it will behove the said R. Benjamin to return to the said Belassez the said book which she gave to him, or he may pay her six marks for the book, which will then become his property, and he shall also repay the said twenty marks which she delivered to him in view of the marriage. The said R. Benjamin shall take an oath as to the amount of money that has been earned from the time he received the twenty marks until the time he returned them, and will refund to the said Belassez half of the interest, reserving the other half for himself.

The said R. Benjamin has undertaken to observe all the above conditions under penalty of excommunication and has also sworn by holding a sacred emblem in his hand according the oath of the law to be faithful to them; so, likewise, has the said Belassez taken a similar oath on her part to observe the agreement.

They therefore at once each of them place a deposit of one hundred shillings sterling as a token of good faith in the hands of the Beth Din with the following undertaking: Should the said Aaron, the son of R. Benjamin, grow up and the time for his wedding arrive and he refuse to wed the said Judith, the daughter of R. Hayim, in accordance with the above stipulations, and to lead her under the *chupah*, and to make her a marriage settlement to the value of one hundred pounds as is the custom of the island, or if the said R. Benjamin refuses to abide by the above conditions, R. Benjamin shall lose the said deposit, which shall be paid to the said Belassez without any argument of any kind; and the said R. Benjamin shall pay her the money within seven days. On the other hand, if the said Judith, the daughter of R. Hayim, refuses to go under the *chupah* and be duly married to the said Aaron according to these conditions, then the said Belassez shall lose her deposit, which is to be paid to the said R. Benjamin within seven days.

And they have sworn and entered into a solemn oath of excommunication before us, and what we have commanded them to fulfil, we have written and attested, and all is of lasting validity.

Judah, son of Rabbi Meir
Abraham Hayim, Rabbi, son of Rabbi Joseph
Joseph, son of Rabbi Joshua

35. A Muslim Girl Sent Early to be Married, Sicily, Twelfth Century

The background to this text is the advance of the Normans into Sicily in the eleventh and twelfth centuries. The narrator is Ibn Jubayr (1145–1217), a Spanish Muslim and geographer, who made a journey from his homeland via Sicily and Egypt. Compare a similar tale recounted by the Christian author Geoffrey of Malaterra, *De rebus gestis Rogerii Calabriae et Siciliae comitis*, 2nd edn, ed. E. Pontieri, Rerum Italicarum Scriptores (Bologna: N. Zanichelli, 1927–8), p. 33, where a Muslim kills his sister rather than allow her to be captured and raped by the Normans.

Newly translated from: *Viaggio del Kinanu* by Ibn Jubayr, in M. Amari, *Biblioteca arabo-sicula*, Vol. 1 (Rome and Turin: Ermanno Loesher, 1880), p. 45.

There is another most singular example of the troubles of the Sicilian Muslims, of which we were the witnesses, and it is such that you will feel that it will break your heart, and you will be filled with compassion and pity. One of the first men of this city sent his son to a pilgrim, who was our companion, asking him to accept his little daughter, young, but of an age to marry, and to marry her himself if she was suitable for him, or, if not, to give her as the wife to whichever of his countrymen liked her. Thus, he asked him to take the girl with him, she voluntarily abandoning her father and brothers out of a wish to free herself from the troubles [of the country] and the desire to stay in a Muslim land. Her father and brothers were happy to agree to this and said they wanted to find a way to save themselves in a Muslim land as well once the embargo preventing them from leaving was lifted.

The pilgrim to whom this offer was made accepted it willingly. We cannot understand how a man could possibly have come to such harsh conditions that he would give such a dear commission so easily to someone else; to commit his own daughter to someone who would take her to a strange land; [how he could] bear the separation, resist the desire [to keep her] and the heartbreak of living without her. No less singular appeared to us [the virtue of] the girl, may God guard her and keep her in grace, who abandoned her family for the love of Islam ... Consulted by her father about the choice that he wanted to make, the girl replied to him, 'If you keep me here you will have to answer for me [before God].' She had lost her mother, but she still had two brothers and a sister.

36. The Case of Grace of Saleby, England, Twelfth Century

This extract continues the story begun above, Chapter 1, text 10. As for the wordplay on 'forester' at the end of the text, the author interestingly hints at the widespread hatred of royal foresters in England. After the Norman conquest of England in 1066, the king reserved large swathes of countryside for himself as hunting grounds, protected by his officers, the foresters, whose name derives from 'forest'. As a result local people were forbidden their age-old use of these lands for gathering firewood and hunting birds and animals. The word 'forest' derives from the Latin, *forestem silvam*, which literally means 'outside the wood', namely the area that had not been fenced off. And it is precisely this unfenced area that the Norman kings reserved for themselves. The author then jokingly explains that after their death foresters will not be allowed into heaven, but themselves will have 'to stay outside' [*stare foris*] heaven in the same way that ordinary people were kept outside the royal hunting grounds.

Newly translated from: *Magna vita sancti Hugonis: The Life of St Hugh of Lincoln*, 2 vols., Vol. 2, ed. D. L. Douie and D. H. Farmer (Oxford: Oxford University Press, 1985), Book 4, c. 5, pp. 23–7.

Therefore, according to the sentence of the wise man, 'No head is more cunning than that of the serpent' and 'no iniquity more iniquitous than that of a woman' [Eccles. 25: 22, 26]. Both these sayings can evidently be applied to this woman [Agnes, widow of Thomas of Saleby], whose fury and rage were so overwhelming and persistent that the final loss of her husband was not enough for her unless she executed her wicked plot against his brother as well. Despite her well-deserved excommunication, she persisted in her false tale by arguing that the inheritance belonged to her child [Grace]. While the lawful heir [William of Hartshill] was thus being excluded from his brother's inheritance, the king gave the infant and her inheritance as a gift to a certain young man who was the brother of Hugh of Neville, the chief forester in the kingdom. Despite the fact that she was barely four years old, he [Adam of Neville] decided that he ought to marry her solemnly in a wedding ceremony, so ensuring that he should not be deprived for any reason from the acquisition of this patrimony. When this was reported to the bishop, who had often issued edicts against under-age marriages, he immediately issued a special prohibition that no priest or faithful Christian should be present at this wedding. In considering this case he took into account both the eternal and temporal security of many people, for even before the truth of the matter had been fully assessed and discussed according to common law, he advised that such a marriage would be prejudicial to both parties concerned. Immediately thereafter, as the bishop had left on account of some business he had to do with the king in Normandy, the young man's associates and relatives came together in a remote village, and there in the presence of the church [congregation],

exploiting either the naivety or greed of the parish priest, they
married the peasant-girl toddler of servile status to a knight.
Such was their greed to grab someone else's rights that neither
her low birth nor the clear betrayal of her well-being could prevent this doomed wedding. As soon as the bishop came back
from overseas, he was told what had happened. The priest who
had celebrated the wedding was suspended and deprived of
both his office and benefice by the bishop; all others, who had
transgressed his orders and contumaciously refused to appear
before him, were publicly excommunicated.

Meanwhile, the false mother's maid, who had searched for
and found the child of the other mother, came, conscience-
stricken, first to the priest in charge of confession at the Church
of Lincoln – the Subdean Master William of Bramfeld, of pious
memory – and then, at his behest, to the bishop, to whom, in
floods of tears, she told all that had happened. Then the bishop,
in full knowledge of the facts, for a while kept secretly to himself what he had heard, but on the following day he ordered
that his sentence be publicly reissued every Sunday in all
churches throughout the area.

Some time later the miserable woman, instigator of this evil
act, realized what she had done and was horrified by the ruin
she had caused. In the event, together with the above-mentioned
maidservant, her confidante and accomplice, she sensibly
decided to go to the bishop, to whom she first tearfully in private
and then with trembling voice in the presence of many good
men – amongst whom was the author of this account – confessed
that she had betrayed her own husband and tricked his brother,
the former to his death and the latter out of his due inheritance.
All this was then carefully reported by the bishop to the Archbishop of Canterbury [Hubert Walter, 1193–1205], who at the
time was also chief justice of the whole kingdom [1193–8], and
to the brothers and friends of the above-mentioned despoiler of
someone else's lands, and also to almost all the nobles and barons of the English court.

Nonetheless, the husband of the girl – who was herself innocent of any wrongdoing – and his advisers held on to the
possessions which had been criminally obtained, arguing that

according to the laws of England a child was deemed legitimate whom a woman's husband during his life had accepted as legitimate. The application of this sentence thus prevented the legitimate heir from entering his inheritance. Meanwhile, however, more out of respect for the bishop than because the evidence of the case was almost universally known, no definite judicial sentence was given against Adam of Neville.

When again this most zealous defender of justice was about to cross to Normandy, on his departure he many times publicly proclaimed that if the knight took her as his wife as he intended, he should know that he had married a serf and that he would not enjoy her for very long. Once again, wicked men conspired and fixed a day for both parties to come to a definitive conclusion to the litigation at London that would exclude further postponement.

Adam of Neville – for this is the name of the girl's husband – accompanied by a crowd of relatives, hastened to London, where on the night before the day on which the judges had promised that they would adjudicate to him the lands outright which up till then had only been in his custody, he found lodgings not far from the city. While his cronies and advisers in the city discussed carefully the contents of the sentence to be given with the justices, he amused himself in a tavern and, a bit drunk, fell into bed, where he suddenly died in his sleep. And so, alone and without preparation, because he had not thought anything of this kind would happen to him, he was brought before the tribunal of a more just judge in order to receive retribution for his deeds. It is to be feared that there, with fitting shame, he would hear from the mouth of the very strict judge the judgement that his true acolyte [Bishop Hugh] had so often issued. Whenever the holy man [Bishop Hugh] would hear the name 'forester' (previously unknown and foreign), and the increasing complaints from the foresters' victims here and everywhere, he used to say, alluding to their barbarous name: 'These men are as justly and appropriately called "foresters", for they will stay outside God's kingdom.'

This man, being thus snatched away and expelled from the world by God, his widow, although still not ripe for marriage, was given with someone else's lands to the king's chamberlain

[Norman de Camera]. He died too, albeit after the saint's [Bishop Hugh's] departure from this world, and then the unlucky girl was handed over to a third husband [Brian de Insula], much more evil than the previous two, who because of the numerous crimes he had committed against many churches, had often been excommunicated. What his future holds for him is illustrated in no uncertain manner by his past behaviour, unless he accepts advice. The woman who orchestrated the whole affair ended a life somewhat protracted by bitterness and distress in a tragic death.

37. A Narrow Escape from Assault: Christina of Markyate, Huntingdon, Twelfth Century

Christina of Markyate was the daughter of a wealthy merchant (who is named as Autti in the extract below) who lived at Huntingdon, where as a young girl she experienced the unwanted attention of her maternal aunt's former lover, Ranulf Flambard, Bishop of Durham (1099–1128). The incident related here can be dated to the 1090s. Since Christina ultimately became a recluse and nun, the story, which no doubt is based on her own account, nevertheless is coloured by her intense religious vocation from a young age. See also Chapter 3, text 85.

Newly translated from: *Vie de Christine de Markyate*, 2 vols., Vol. 1, ed. and trans. P. L'Hermite-Leclercq and A.-M. Legras (Paris: CNRS, 2007), c. 5–6, p. 80.

Ranulf, Bishop of Durham – before he became bishop – was chief justice of the whole of England, second after the king, and had a relationship with Christina's maternal aunt, Alveva, by whom he had children. Afterwards he had given her as wife to one of the burghers of Huntingdon, and for her sake he honoured the rest of her family. He always stayed with her when he travelled from Northumbria to London, or on his way back. One day, when Ranulf was with Alveva, as was common, his friend Autti and his children came to visit him, and it so happened that the bishop couldn't take his eyes off the beautiful girl and instantly the instigator of lust, Satan, set his heart on fire so that he badly wanted her. From then on, he applied himself to seek how he might get hold of her and at last he had her unsuspectingly brought to him in his chamber, furnished with handsome tapestries, where he himself slept at night. Apart from the innocent girl, the only ones present were some members of the bishop's household, while her father and mother, together with the others who had come with her, kept to themselves in the hall, indulging in drinking. When night fell, the bishop secretly signalled to his men that they depart from the room, leaving their lord and Christina, that is the wolf and the lamb, together in the same room. What shame. The lewd bishop shamelessly grabbed the virgin by the sleeve of her tunic and with the mouth with which he was used to prepare the divine mystery he solicited her to commit a sinful deed. What could the miserable adolescent do, caught up in such narrow straits? Call her parents? They had gone to sleep. On no account did she wish to consent, but neither did she openly dare to resist. For if she openly resisted him there was no doubt that she would be overpowered.

Hear now how she cleverly took action. When she looked at the door she saw that although it was closed, it had not been locked, and she said: 'Let me go, so that I can lock the door. For even if we do not fear God, we must take care that no one can catch us doing this.' He asked her to swear that she would not deceive him and that she would indeed lock the door as she had said. And she swore to him. Then, as he let her go, she instantly ran out of the room and from the outside firmly locked the door and quickly ran home.

38. Alleged Rape of an Eleven-year-old Girl, London, 1320

This particular case is mentioned in a number of documents: 1) The record of the first appeal in the king's bench against Reymund of

Limoges (Easter 1320). 2) Reymund's suit against Joan's father, Eustace the saddler, for damages (autumn 1320). 3) The record of the second appeal, commenced before the coroners of London on 7 February 1321. 4) The report of the oral proceedings upon the second appeal in the London eyre on 26 February 1321.

An appeal was a criminal prosecution brought by the victim or (in the case of homicide) the victim's next of kin, and trial 'in the king's bench' meant trial in the crown court, which was notionally (but not often) held before the king himself, and heard those cases which concerned the king. A prosecution could alternatively be brought 'at the king's suit', i.e. via an indictment (the formal accusation of a crime), as is done today. Coroners were royal officials who investigated sudden or unexplained death; they also performed other functions on behalf of the Crown. An eyre means sessions, which were held by a special commission to try all cases. They were rare by this date (1320) and had not been held in London since the previous century. In London, the eyre was held at the Tower because it was a royal court.

The chronology of the case is as follows: Joan, daughter of Eustace the saddler of London, at the age of eleven, claimed to have been raped by Reymund of Limoges, a wine merchant of Bordeaux, on 9 or 19 March 1320. Her father, on her behalf, brought the appeal first to the king's bench and then before the justices in eyre in London. The date, place and circumstances are contested by the defendant. On 2 June 1320, Joan abandoned her appeal, Reymund was arraigned at the king's suit, and on 25 June 1320 he was acquitted by a jury in the king's bench. After the eyre of London commenced, Joan began a second appeal before the coroners of London, which was transferred to be brought before the justices in eyre at the Tower of London, where she made her formal accusation again on 26 February 1321. Because this last formal accusation varied from that given before the coroners, and because Reymund had already been acquitted, the judges decided that the case had failed and that Joan should be put in custody for her false claim, to await the king's grace (i.e. the king would determine the punishment). Reymund, meanwhile, had commenced a lawsuit against Joan's father and others for maliciously abetting the first case (see 2, below); Reymund's case was still pending in June 1321, but since no trace can be found of it thereafter, it was probably abandoned.

Newly translated from: Saddler v. Limoges, in *The Eyre of London 14: Edward II A.D. 1321*, Vol. 1, *Year Books of Edward II*, Vol. 26 (Part 1), ed. and trans. H. M. Cam (London: Selden Society, 1968), pp. 87–92. We thank Jonathan Rose for drawing our attention to the case, and John Baker for helping to make sense of the chronology and contents of the court proceedings and for help with the revised translation.

1) The Record of the First Appeal in the King's Bench against Reymund of Limoges (Easter 1320)

London: The sheriffs were commanded to arrest Reymund of Limoges, that they should have him here before the king on this day, namely a fortnight after Easter [13 April 1320], to answer to Joan, the daughter of Eustace the saddler, of London, concerning rape and breach of the king's peace, of which she accuses him. And the sheriffs returned the names of the pledges [witnesses who swore oaths as to the faithfulness of the accused] for prosecuting, Eustace the saddler and John le Boys; and also that they would have the said Reymund before the king on the required day. And now the said Joan comes, and likewise the said Reymund. And the said Joan accuses the said Reymund of rape and breach of the king's peace, saying that the said Reymund, on the night of Sunday next before the feast of Gregory the Pope in the thirteenth year of the reign of the king who now is [9 March 1320], at the hour of curfew, in the City of London, in Walbrook ward in the parish of St Mary of Woolchurch Haw, hard by the house of the said Eustace, by force and arms and against the will of the said Joan took her by her left hand and led her away to the room of the same Reymund in the parish of St Martin in the Vintry, and there flung her to the ground and lay with her against her will, feloniously as a felon against the king, and utterly robbed her of her virginity against the peace of the lord king and his crown and dignity. And having committed the said felony, he took to flight, and the said Joan pursued him, raising the hue and cry from ward to ward, to the next four wards, and as far as the court of the lord king, and so the said Reymund is arrested at the suit of the same Joan. And if the said Reymund will deny the said felony, the same Joan is ready to prove [it] against him [as the court shall award].

And the said Reymund comes and says that he is a clerk and that he cannot answer to this without his ordinaries [ecclesiastical persons who had jurisdiction within their own parish]. And that it may be known in what manner he should be delivered to the ordinary, inquiry into the truth of the matter is to be made by the country. Therefore let a jury thereof come before the lord king on the octave of Trinity [2 June 1320] wherever etc.

Afterwards on that day the said Reymund comes, led by the marshal. And likewise the said Joan. And likewise the jury. And the said Reymund, notwithstanding that he had said before that he was a clerk, says now that he is in no way guilty of the felony, and for good and ill puts himself upon the said jury [submitting himself to jury trial]. And when the said jurors come back with their verdict, the said Joan, being formally called, does not come to prosecute her said appeal. Therefore let those pledging to prosecute be merciful and let her be arrested. But she is forgiven because she is underage. And the said Reymund, as regards the suit of the said Joan, is discharged. And as to the lord king's suit, being asked how he wishes to clear himself, he denies all felony and rape and whatever is against the king's peace, and says that he is in no way guilty, and for good and ill puts himself on the country [allows himself to be tried by a jury]. Therefore let a jury thereon come before the king on the morrow of St John the Baptist [25 June 1320].

On which day the said Reymund comes, led by the marshal. And likewise the jury. Who say on their oath that the said Reymund is in no way guilty of the said rape and felony. Therefore he is discharged thereof. Asked what damages the said Reymund has sustained by the said occasion, they say that he has suffered damages to the value of forty pounds. Being questioned as to whether the said Joan is able to pay the said damages, they say no. Being questioned also as to who were the abettors of the said appeal, and by whose abetment the said appeal was framed, they say that Eustace the saddler, of

London, John the Botoner le Clop', John Longchamp, Thomas Shereman of Walbrook and John de Goiz, locksmith, were abettors of the said appeal. Therefore the sheriffs are commanded to distrain them by all their lands [temporarily seize their lands to enforce obedience to a court order] etc., and to produce them in person before the king on the octave of Michaelmas [6 October 1320] to answer both to the lord king and to the said Reymund.

2) Reymund's Suit Against Joan's Father, Eustace the Saddler, For Damages (Autumn 1320)

London: Reymund of Limoges proffers himself, on the fourth day, against Eustace the saddler; John Botoner le Clop', John Longchamp, Thomas Sherman of Walbrook and John de Goys, locksmith, in the plea that they falsely and maliciously abetted Joan, the daughter of Eustace the saddler, of London, in the king's court here, in appealing the said Reymund of rape and breach of the king's peace, causing the same Reymund to suffer damages of forty pounds, as was found by a certain jury, and whereof the said Reymund was cleared here in the king's court. [Martinmas] London: Eustace the saddler, John Botoner le Clop', Thomas Sherman of Walbrook and John de Goys, locksmith, were attached to answer to Reymund of Limoges in a plea: why they falsely and maliciously abetted Joan, the daughter of Eustace the saddler, of London, before the king in his court, in appealing the said Reymund of rape and breach of the king's peace. Whereof the same Reymund was discharged by the inquest of the country [jury trial] on which he put himself. Whereof the same Reymund complains that the said Eustace and the others on the Thursday following next the feast of the Purification of the Blessed Virgin Mary in the thirteenth year of the reign of the king who now is [7 February 1320 – note that the date of the alleged rape was either 9 or 19 March] in the parish of St Martin in the Vintry falsely and maliciously abetted Joan, the daughter of Eustace the saddler, in appealing the said Reymund, before the king in his court, of the rape of the said Joan and of breach of the king's peace. In consequence of which, the same Reymund was arrested on Palm Sunday of the said year [23 March 1320] and imprisoned until the morrow of St John's [25 June 1320]. Whereby he says he has suffered loss and damage to the value of one hundred pounds. And because of this he produces this lawsuit.

And the said Eustace and the others come by John Bernard, their attorney, and deny force and all abetment etc., and say that they are in no way guilty thereof, and of this they put themselves on the country [under jury trial]. And the said Reymund likewise. Therefore let a jury thereon come before the king a fortnight after St Hilary [27 January 1321].

3) The Record of the Second Appeal, Commenced Before the Coroners of London on 7 February 1321

Joan, the daughter of Eustace the saddler, came before the coroners of London on the Saturday following next after the feast of the Purification of St Mary, in the fourteenth year of the reign of the king who now is [7 February 1321] and made her appeal against Reymund of Limoges of rape and breach of the lord king's peace in these words: Joan, the daughter of Eustace the saddler, appeals Reymund of Limoges of the rape of her body, committed feloniously and against the peace: that is to say, on Sunday in mid-Lent in the thirteenth year of the reign of our lord the king who now is [9 March 1320], whom God preserve, namely, in Walbrook, in the parish of our Lady of Woolchurch Haw in London, two feet from the house of the said Eustace, the said Reymund came after the hour of curfew, feloniously as a felon; and he took the body of the said Joan, aged eleven years, and carried her off and took her into the house of the said Reymund, that is to say, to the house rented by Ellis Pers in the parish of St Martin in the Vintry in London, into his chamber, that is to say, into a solar in the upper storey, and kept the said Joan there all night, and there deflowered her, feloniously as a felon, against her will and against the king's peace, and so vilely and cruelly handled her limbs that her life was despaired of, and still is, and she has lost all hope of recovering her health. Wherefore the said Joan prays the aid of our lord the king, that law and right may be done to her for this felony committed in contempt of our lord the king and his crown and against the peace.

[The part of the text which follows records Joan's formal accusation made at the Tower of London.]

And she found pledges to prosecute her said appeal, namely Henry the Saddler, Porter, and William at the Wood, Saddler. Therefore the sheriffs were commanded to arraign the said Reymund to be before justices here. And the said Joan comes, and likewise the said Reymund, arrested by the sheriffs. And the said Joan accuses the said Reymund of the rape of her virginity, committed in the said place on the Wednesday next before Palm Sunday in the said year [19 March 1320] against the king's peace and his crown and dignity. And this she offers to prove as [the court shall award].

And the said Reymund denies all rape and felony etc. And he says that the said Joan in her appeal that she made before the coroners asserted that she had been raped on the night of the Sunday in mid-Lent in the thirteenth year of the reign of the king who now is [9 March 1320]. And now in her appeal which she makes before the justices, here she asserts that she was raped on the Wednesday aforesaid [19 March 1320], and she does not prosecute the appeal which she made before the coroners, which is, so to say, the original one. And he asks to take advantage of this variance, above all, because she could not twice be deprived of one and the same virginity. And the said Joan cannot deny this.

Therefore the said Reymund is cleared forever as regards the lawsuit of Joan herself. And the said Joan is to be put in prison for her said false appeal; but she is pardoned because she is underage.

And as to the king's suit, the said Reymund, being asked how he wishes to clear himself of the said rape and felony, says that he had elsewhere, before Henry le Scrope and his fellows, justices of the king's bench, been acquitted of the said rape and felony by the jury of the country under which he had put himself, for good and ill. And he puts forward [the copy of] the record of the acquittal of the said Reymund under the seal of the same Henry, together with the king's writ, directed to the same Henry, for sending that copy to the justices here, and also a writ of the lord the king to the justices here [commanding them] to admit that copy and to do further what they rightly should. And the said copy having been inspected, it was found that the same Reymund had been acquitted of rape and felony at the king's suit. Therefore he is cleared thereof.

4) The Report of the Oral Proceedings of the Second Appeal in the London Eyre on 26 February 1321

Joan, the daughter of Eustace the saddler, of London, who is here, appeals [Reymund] of L., who is here, of rape of her virginity and breach of our lord the king's peace, in that, whereas this Joan the daughter of Eustace the saddler, of London, who is here, was in the peace of God and in the peace of our lord the king on the Tuesday [sic] next before Palm Sunday in the thirteenth year of the king who now is, at sunset, in the City of London in the ward of Walbrook, and in the parish of our Lady of W. [St Mary of Woolchurch Haw], hard by the house of the aforesaid Eustace the saddler and at three foot from that house, in the high street of our lord the king, there came the aforesaid [Reymund] of L. With force and arms, namely, etc., feloniously as a felon against our lord the king who now is, by way of ambush and assault aforethought, took this same Joan by her hand, and against her consent and her will led her to the chamber of this same [Reymund] in the house rented by Ellis Pers, which is in the parish of St Martin in the Vintry, of London, which chamber extends south and north: one end of it abutting the high street of our lord the king which is called the Vintry, and the other end [being] three perches from the River Thames; which chamber lengthways adjoins the house of Sir Hugh Gisors towards the north and the house of James Beauflour towards the west. And in the middle of the room the same [Reymund], who is here, feloniously as a felon against our lord the king, in ambush and premeditated assault, against the peace of our lord the king who now is etc., and his crown and dignity, took this same Joan, the daughter [of Eustace], who is here, between his arms, and against her consent and will laid her on the ground with her belly upwards and her back on the ground, and with his right hand raised the clothes of the same Joan, the daughter of Eustace, up to her navel, she being clothed in a blue coat and a shift of light cloth, and feloniously as a felon against our lord the king who now is, with both hands separated the legs and thighs of this same Joan, and with his right hand took his male organ of – length, and put it in the vulva of this same Joan, and broke her watershed, and possessed her sexually so thoroughly that she was bleeding, against the peace of our lord the king, his crown and dignity. And so as soon as this same [Reymund] of L. had committed this felony and rape he straightaway took flight. And this same Joan who is here raised the hue and cry, and pursued him from ward to ward, as far as the next four surrounding wards, and from the ward to the beadles [parish officers], and from the beadles to the sheriffs, and from the sheriffs to the coroners, and from the coroners to the Tower of our lord the king, and from the Tower of London to the justices of the eyre, so that he was arraigned at her lawsuit.

And if [Reymund] of L., who is here, will deny this felony and rape, this same Joan, who is here, is ready to make [such] proof against him as this court shall award that she ought against a man, as a woman ravished of her virginity.

[Then follows a lengthy discussion on the merits of the case, as Reymund had been acquitted previously for the same crime.]

He [Reymund] was given a day on the morrow to hear his judgement. Then the parties came, and Passeley [the judge] rehearsed [the plea] as above. And he said that because the warrant for this appeal is the plaint, and it varies as above, the court awards that you take nothing by your appeal, and that Joan remain [in prison]; but because Joan is underage, the king's mercy is available to her. And because we find by this record that you were acquitted of this same deed at the king's suit, so that the king cannot have further suit against you, therefore [you are discharged] indefinitely.

39. Securing a Dowry by Litigation, Calabria, 1093

This and the following document provide snapshots of the Greek community in Calabria, by this time under Norman rule. Note here that Theodote's case is judged in her favour, and that she was able to act without male intervention.

Newly translated from: F. Trinchera, ed., *Syllabus Graecarum membranarum* (Naples: Joseph Cattaneo, 1865), 56, pp. 72–4.

Stilo [Calabria], 1093

In the month of January, in the year 6601, in the fifth indiction. When I, Count [Roger I, 1072–1101] came to Stilo, there came to me Simeon and Chamenias and their brothers, accusing Theodote, the daughter of Gannadeos, that the said Theodote had unjustly taken from them the property of Pillikiani. On this I, Count Roger, ordered the daughter of Gannadeos, Theodote, to come to my court. She came and was asked by me and my judges whether it was as her accusers stated, that she had taken from them the property of Pillikiano. The woman responded in my presence that neither through imperial power, nor through usurpation did they hold these properties. 'My father Gannadeos possessed and ruled these lands as master and judge and gave them to me as my dowry.'

After she said this I ordered Simeon to show us witnesses [to the effect that] after the death of Gannadeos Theodote had seized the said properties, so that the woman might be convinced. But the accusers could not show us this either by written document or by witnesses. These being absent, Theodote came with my judges before me, Count Roger —: they are the Bishop of Mesimerion, and Maleinos, and Erminnon and the rest of the judges of Stilo; and I asked them and they swore to me all that was known about the property called Pillikiano, saying, as if with one mouth, that it was true and evident that for years Gannadeos had held and ruled the properties and 'We have not heard that the accusers of his daughter were ever its lords.'

I, Count Roger, hearing this and learning the truth from my judges, restored the property to Theodote, the daughter of Gannadeos, and about this I ordered all under my rule, generals and viscounts, that wherever there are possessions of Gannadeos, except those of mine and my lords, these should belong to the daughter[s] of Gannadeos, Theodote and Alphara, wherever they may be in my territory of Calabria. And I also order that none of my officials should challenge you in this decision, made under my seal, else they will incur our anger; nor should anyone take from the said sisters' property or vines, either by day or night, but let the sisters hold them, and throw out the said Simeon and his brothers from the properties. This I confirmed and affixed my lead seal to, in the month and indiction stated.

Roger, Count of Calabria and Sicily

40. Securing a Dowry by Adoption, Southern Italy, 1170

Newly translated from: F. Trinchera, ed., *Syllabus Graecarum membranarum* (Naples: Joseph Cattaneo, 1865), 177, pp. 232–3.

Oletta [Auletta], September 1170

In the name of the Father and Son and Holy Spirit. Since God our Lord says: 'I will be a father to them and they will be my children', and calls us to be his adopted, so I, Bonus de Bonadia, take in adoption the daughter of my wife Maria, named Marotta, and I will have her in place of a daughter and she will be a shareholder in my property, moveable and immoveable, on these terms, that I will have all of it in my power as long as I live. If she takes a husband in my lifetime, then it will be incumbent upon me to act to her as a father acts towards his own daughters; and at the end of my life, if she wishes to act for my soul as I would like, then she should have everything just as if she were a true and legitimate daughter, acknowledging and serving no master, just as I have done. If indeed she does not want to make a gift for my soul as I would like, then I shall dispose of my goods by a will according to the customs of this place. Afterwards she will subject to the law, just as I am. And let her travel where she is permitted, as she has accepted the dominion and power from me. And if anyone should at any time rise up against this recognition, starting any action or dispute, may they pay the treasurer thirty-six *nomismata*, and, notwithstanding, she and her heirs should possess their inheritance firmly and without injury. The present document was written by the hand of Basil the notary, son of Komitis, in the year 6679, fourth indiction, in the month of September, in the presence of the judges of Oletta and honest witnesses.

Nikolaos the judge, son of Vitalis the judge, witness, wrote a cross with my own hand.

Witness: John de Optima, wrote a cross with my own hand.

Leo the judge, son of Komitis the judge and notary, son of Basil the notary, witness, with my own hand wrote a cross.

Witness: Satrianos, son of Niketas Proximi, witness.

Vitalis, son of Ursini, witness.

In the time of our most pious lord, Count Henry [Orrikos] and the *strategos* of Oletta.

Basil, the son of the priest Nikolaos de Kappello [wrote this].

41. Securing a Dowry through Charity, Trento, 1301

This will is interesting among the numerous women's wills preserved in the Trento archive because it epitomizes the idea that wealthy women participated in active charity, often targeted at other women. Osbeta's bequests to several 'natural daughters', of men whose relationship to her is unknown, surely points to a concern to provide a dowry of some sort for these disadvantaged women. Osbeta's world is in fact a very female one, from the beneficiaries of her will to her clients, and even her choice of burial place.

Newly translated from: 50 *testamenti medioevali nell'archivio capitolare di Trento (secoli XII–XV)*, ed. Luciano Maino, 3rd edn (Ferrara: Liberty House, 2001), 10, pp. 70–72.

In the year of our Lord, 1311. Ninth indiction. On Sunday 5 December. At Trento, in the house of Mistress Brigide, daughter of the late Gerard Chalochi. In the presence of [seven named male witnesses] and others asked and called to witness.

There, Mistress Osbeta, wife of the late Brugne de Avolano, lying ill in her bed, but sound of mind, considering the fragility of human nature and not wishing to die intestate, made her will about her moveable and immoveable goods and chattels, saying:

'First, I wish to be buried at the Church of St Vigilius, in the tomb of my mother. I also will and leave six and a half Veronese pounds to the canons, chaplains and clerics of the above-mentioned Church of St Vigilius, to say anniversary masses every year, specifically fifty Veronese *solidi* for my anniversary, forty Veronese *solidi* for my father Master Muse's anniversary, and forty small Veronese *solidi* for my mother Elisabet's, dividing the aforementioned money proportionately between the said canons, chaplains and clerics, through the payments of the people mentioned below.

[There follows a list of five tenants of houses belonging to Osbeta, paying her a total of one hundred and forty *solidi*, thus exceeding the sum she wishes spent on the masses.]

'Also, I will to the building works of the Church of St Mary twenty *solidi*. To the building works of the Church of St Peter I will twenty *solidi*. To the building works of the Church of St Mary Magdalene I will twenty *solidi*.

'I will to the poor of St Martin twenty Veronese *solidi*. I will to a certain hermit and a certain female hermit in Trento and around Trento five Veronese *solidi*. I will twenty Veronese pounds to buy a jug of oil to illuminate the altar of St Maxentius. And I will to the preaching brothers twenty Veronese *solidi*. And I will to the Franciscan friars twenty *solidi*. I will to the eremitic brothers twenty *solidi*. I will to the Franciscan sisters of St Michael ten Veronese *solidi*. And I will to the sisters of Sorbano ten Veronese *solidi*. And I will to the sisters of St Anne de Supramonte ten Veronese *solidi*.

'And I will for my soul to the Mistress Brigide aforementioned, daughter of the late Gerard Chalochi, thirty-four Veronese pounds of gold, which she owes me from a loan I made to her. And I will to Margaret, the natural daughter of the late Master Nicolas, my guest, five Veronese pounds. And I will to both the natural daughters of the late William de Marchadentis ten Veronese pounds. And I will to both the natural daughters of the late – Muse [possibly her father] ten Veronese pounds.

'And I state and acknowledge that Mistress Ordana is beholden to pay me two hundred Veronese pounds in a loan and no more. And Bartholomew the tailor [one of the witnesses] owes me thirty-four Veronese pounds of gold and no more.

'In all my goods, moveable and immoveable, and in all my affairs and business, I institute as my heir my brother, Master Jacob, Canon of St Vigilius. I wish this spoken will to have the force of a testament, and if it cannot, having overlooked some solemnity or for some other cause, I wish to add a codicil or other legal will which can give it that legal validity.'

Gislembert de Maieris, Notary of Lord Henry, Count of Lomello, heard and wrote down these things.

42. *Menstruation: St Trophimena Intervenes in a Case of Underage Marriage, Amalfi, Ninth Century*

This fascinating account of a dysfunctional marriage in ninth-century Amalfi is replete with allusions to the onset of periods, without ever referring directly to the young bride's malaise.

Newly translated from: *Historia inventionis ac translationis et miracula S. Trophimene*, cols. 35–7 in *Acta sanctorum, Iulii V* (Antwerp: Société des Bollandistes, 1709), originally in Patricia Skinner, *Health and Medicine in Early Medieval Southern Italy* (Leiden: Brill, 1997), pp. 148–51.

*

In the time of the most pious prefect [of Amalfi], Pulchari, a certain girl named Theodonanda was given in marriage to a man named Mauro. Having consummated the marriage, because she was not yet nubile she lay close to death for a long time; each day she expected the wretched end to her torture. At that time there was a powerful doctor, Hieronymus, providing good health with the best medicines at Salerno. When her parents brought her to him in order that he might find some medicinal remedy for her, he rejected her, saying, 'Her illness is incurable, I will not be able to help her.' They pleaded with him to show her some pity and after several prayers, overcome, he asked, 'How long has this discharge troubled her?' They replied, 'Four months. Because of this, brought to desperation by her harsh misery, we came so that, through the mercy of God, she might receive good health through you.'

At these pleas, the doctor, a servant of God, was overcome and began to consult immense volumes of books on his art, to see if by chance he could through reading recognize a cure for this illness: when he had read through all his diseases, and could find nowhere which illness she was suffering from, he said, 'Go away from here, brethren, because I cannot offer her any medical help; know this, however: either she will be cured through the mercy of God, or she will be punished through just judgement.' Hearing these words, they began to shed bitter tears, and, bidding farewell, they came to Reginna, so that, just as the doctor had said, they might mourn their dead. And, discussing their plight and coming to agreement, they got up to take her to the basilica of St Trophimena (it was not at all far from the same church's enclosure). The girl was brought to the tomb of St Trophimena. A nun named Agatha took her and laid her in a ladylike way in front of the altar, praying, and then waited with her parents for three days for her to come out. Such was the illness of her body that she waved her arms back and forth, [. . .] lying down on the ground, she called out, just as a bird of prey does as it hovers.

And when the girl was tired by these fatigues, her parents left her with the nun, and she slept a little in front of the altar, and, behold, the girl went out on tiptoe and headed for the river alone, for the hollow riverbed was not yet hastened [i.e. everything was dry, an allusion to her lack of menstruation]. And, behold, she saw the most beautiful girl of all, who gave her three blows on the back and said, 'Why have you dared to leave the church? Go back, and always fear me.' When the agitated girl went back and told the nun, she rejoiced ceaselessly that St Trophimena had appeared to her specially. Having experienced this blessing, the nun saw the pavement sweating large quantities of oil, full of perfume, and prayed intently to God, invoking the saint. She ordered the girl to undress and anointed her tiny body with the holy oil, and immediately she was cured from her illness.

43. Innocent III on the Horrors of Menstrual Blood, Italy, Before 1198

In this passage, Pope Innocent III reprises attitudes which can be traced back to ancient Greek and Jewish attitudes towards menstrual blood. On the former, see Lesley Dean-Jones, 'The cultural construct of the female body in classical Greek science', in Women's History and Ancient History, ed. Sarah B. Pomeroy (Durham: University of North Carolina Press, 1991), pp. 111–37.

Newly translated from: Lotharii cardinalis (Innocenti III): De miseria humane conditionis, Vol. 1, ed. Michele Maccarrone (Lucca: Thesauri Mundi, 1955), pp. 11–12.

What Type of Food the Foetus is Nourished With in the Womb
But listen to what type of food the foetus is nourished with in the womb: it is menstrual blood which comes forth, but ceases to come out of the woman after conception, so that the foetus might be nourished within the woman.

This blood is said to be so abominable and foul that contact with it causes seeds not to germinate and vineyards to dry up, grass to die, trees to drop their fruit, and if dogs eat it they become rabid. In the conception of a foetus, the strength of the

seed is restricted [by contact with the blood] so that lepers and
those with elephantiasis are born from such corruption.
Whence, according to the law of Moses, a woman who is menstruating is held to be unclean, and anyone who lies with her is
ordered to be put to death. On account of this uncleanness of
menstruation it is ruled that if a woman brings forth a male
child she should stop coming to the church for forty days, but
if her child is female, eighty days.

44. Unmarried Women and Prostitutes, Paris, c.1200

Thomas of Chobham (d. c.1233) was educated at Paris under Peter
the Chanter (d. c.1199). He was one of a group of secular clergy who
became concerned about the spiritual welfare of outcasts, including
prostitutes. In the following text Thomas of Chobham refers frequently
to two sources: the Bible, in particular St Paul's letter to the Corinthians, and Gratian's *Decretum*. The latter, written around 1140 by
Gratian, a monk at Bologna, became (from the mid-twelfth century
onwards) the standard handbook for ecclesiastical (or canon) law.

Translated by Dr Keiko Nowacka from Thomas de Chobham, 'De
penitentis: Questio VIa. De meretricio' in his *Summa confessorum*, ed.
F. Broomfeld, *Analecta namurcensia* (Louvain: Éditions Nauwelaerts,
1968), 25, pp. 346–51.

We thank Dr Keiko Nowacka for allowing us to use her translation. Passage numbers have been added by editors for the purpose of
easier cross-referencing with the Latin text.

1. It remains that after this we should speak about prostitution.
In a woman it is called prostitution and in a man fornication,
because just as a woman is called a prostitute, so a man is called
a fornicator. Therefore the same penance which is owed by the
prostitute, should be also owed by the fornicator.

2. A prostitute can be described in a number of ways. Indeed
the apostle [St Paul] called a prostitute any woman who gives
herself to lust within marriage as can be read in the first letter

to the Corinthians: 'Know ye not that your bodies are the
members of Christ? Shall I then take the members of Christ and
make them the members of a harlot? God forbid [1 Cor. 6: 15].'
And again, 'Who is joined to a harlot is made one body [1 Cor.
6: 15]?' But according to this meaning, any simple female fornicator can be called a prostitute, which we pass over for the
present since we have spoken already about simple fornication.
Moreover according to canon law, which we accept and use
here, one would describe a prostitute from this description: 'A
widow is a woman whose husband is dead; a cast-off woman is
a woman who is renounced by her living husband; a prostitute
is a woman who makes herself available to the lust of many
men.' The stress is placed however on this word 'patet', since
this type of woman is said to open herself to the lust of many
men. Unable to deny any of the many men, and being dissatis-
fied with one, she makes herself available to many and thus, as
the scripture says: 'spread on your [i.e. her] feet to all passing
by'. Therefore, of such scandalous behaviour is written and
read: 'sons of a woman who wantonly takes a man [Ezek. 16:
25].' Elsewhere in canon law it is said in this way: 'The Lord
forbids women to become prostitutes and men to go to prostitutes. The prostitute is a woman who sells her depravity in
public.' If, however, a woman were to sell herself secretly, she
could not therefore be called a prostitute. And, moreover, if she
were to sell herself only to one, she would not be labelled a
prostitute. This description moreover agrees in all aspects with
the earlier definition, except that she cannot be called a prostitute unless she sells herself, even though she opens herself to
the lust of many, as has been said above. Each of these two
types, she who follows a rampant lust and she who sells her
body publicly, commits a grave sin. Indeed she who uses her
body in such a way, that even a savage animal himself would
recoil in horror to use his body in this way, perverts the faculty
of reason in human nature.

   3. However, it is noteworthy that of the one who gives herself to many for the satisfaction of lust, and of the other who
does so out of need, the first is worse and yet well-deserved
penitence is not enjoined upon this one, since she did not

profess publicly her status as a prostitute. Indeed, professing herself leads to well-deserved penitence.

Chapter 2: Why the Church Should Support Prostitutes

4. One may ask why the Church should tolerate prostitutes, since it is bound to extinguish all public and infamous sins and to force sentencing on all who persevere. Why then does the Church punish usurers more than prostitutes? Especially since the Lord said in the Law: 'There shall be no fornication in Israel [Deut. 33: 17].' Indeed, the canon says: 'The Lord prohibits women from becoming prostitutes and men from visiting prostitutes.' How can the Lord forbid what the Church allows? Besides, as it was said above, if a woman remains for a long time with one man without marrying, she would be excommunicated unless she were to renounce him or marry him. Why then is a woman not excommunicated who adheres to many, and remains unmarried for a long time? It thus seems not to be a sin, but something that is tolerated by the Church, especially since such women not only are sentenced by the courts of the secular princes, but also by the courts of bishops.

5. And it is manifest that the carnal fragility of our time inclines strongly towards lust and hardly anybody can be persuaded or forced to be continent. Prostitutes and fornicators are tolerated by the Church in order to avoid a worse lust, just as Moses did when he saw his people contemplating the murder of their wives; in order to avoid murder, he allowed them to be given a bill of divorce. That is, he allowed a man to separate from his wife, who suffered from nasal tumours or chronic disease, in order that the husband should not kill his wife. He who is separated in this way from his wife sins mortally. And, similarly, the Church allows, that is, it tolerates prostitutes and fornicators in order that not even more base acts of lust are performed. However, it must be upheld by the Church that they ought to be always forbidden from taking the Eucharist unless they repent, as the canon says that prostitutes and

fornicators and actors should not be admitted to the ecclesiastical communion. Indeed they ought 'not eat the riches of the earth' unless they worship. However, those who do not worship are those who commit a crime publicly, and who continue without penance.

6. Indeed it is the custom of many good and educated men to say that priests should not receive at the altar gifts [from prostitutes], since the Lord says 'do not offer to my altar the gifts of fornication or of a dog [Deut. 23: 18].' And thus, though prostitutes and actors should not be denied access to the Church, yet they should be denied access to the altar.

7. Nevertheless there is a custom in Paris, in its main church [Notre Dame], that on Saturdays, at Vespers, many women offer candles to the altar, and mingling among them are prostitutes. For this reason it used to be said that this was allowed because at that time of day they were not sacrificing the Body of Christ at the altar. However, in no way should prostitutes be allowed to make an offering to the altar during Mass lest they carry with them the stench of the brothel to the perfume of the sacrifice.

8. However, we saw that in that city prostitutes wanted to donate a stained-glass window to the main church and the Bishop of Paris [Maurice de Sully, d. 1196] did not permit this to be done, lest it be understood that by accepting the money from them, he approved of their life.

Chapter 3: On the Penance of Prostitutes

9. If, however, prostitutes and fornicators do come to do penance, priests should make clear their baseness to them so that they understand how much they have offended God by selling their bodies, which God made for service to Himself, to the service of the Devil. Nor can there be a viler piece of merchandise than selling one's own baseness. Moreover, they put so many sinners in danger, as they cause the guilt of as many of them. Indeed, since they accept any unknown person that they do not know to lie with, they do not know whether he is a

husband, an excommunicate, a priest, a monk, a Jew, a father or brother or a relative of the person with whom they had previously slept. And since they maintain that they avoid mortal sin with all care, nevertheless, they still do that which they can strongly assume to be criminal and wicked, and from which crime they are not immune.

10. For this reason prostitutes should be encouraged to perform penance for adultery, for incest and for all impurity and wantonness that they may incur in such acts. And they should receive absolution as if they were excommunicated, since perhaps they may have liaised with an excommunicate in such a liaison, and by chance, been the cause of murder, theft and pillage. Indeed, they must perform penance for all such sins, and since they have sinned publicly, they ought thus to repent publicly. We saw, however, certain prostitutes who, in their penance, tore their hair out and wore hairshirts, since they were not able to purge such sins of the flesh without much affliction of the flesh. Yet they are allowed, because of fear of relapse, to be joined in matrimony to anyone unless it is proven that they have committed flagrant incest by sleeping with a father and son or with two brothers, in which case the canons say that they who commit such crimes with prior awareness should never in the future be able to contract marriage.

11. However, they ought to be advised earnestly to be chaste, since chastity is the greatest medicine against wantonness. If, however, they are not able to be persuaded to chastity and if there should be a great fear of a return to lust, and it is not proved that they have committed acts of incest, they should be allowed to marry, though it should be especially pointed out to them that they can never be allowed to act as a witness, or testify or perform other legal acts since they will always be considered infamous. Indeed no penance can take away infamy as far as the law is concerned.

Chapter 4: On the Price of a Prostitute

12. It is also a common practice to query the price of a prostitute or whether a prostitute can be legally paid by a fornicator.

It seems to be the case, since human law says that she acts basely because she is a prostitute, but not that she earns basely because she is a prostitute. One can also read that Judas found Thamar sitting at the crossroads in the manner of a prostitute and having made a deal on the price, slept with her and afterwards sent her payment through his boy [Gen. 38: 14–23]. However, the authorities commend him for the fact that he did what he promised. From whence it is seen that he paid legally and she earned legally.

13. The contrary to this is found in God's law, which says, as stated previously, 'Do not offer to my altar the gifts of fornication or of a dog.' However, if she had earned legally, she would have been legally able to donate money. Moreover, such a woman sells either her body or the use of her body. If her body is free, she sells nothing, since a free body has no value and for this reason she earns nothing legally: if, however, she is a servant, her body cannot be sold, unless into servitude. But if, on the other hand, she sells the use of her body, but that use is nothing but mortal sin: then, in this case, however, sin has no price, because it is worth nothing. If therefore she sells sin, she receives nothing legally. Therefore certain men say that the fornicator gives illegally and that she receives illegally, nor does she become the mistress of things owned by her own labour; but [if these things are seen as] a benefice the law of equality confers her the lordship [over them] at the expense of the fornicator, since human law says that in cases of equal sin the claim of the possessor is stronger. Others used to say that she received the price in return for the pain and suffering which she sustained and for the injury caused to her. For anyone should receive legally compensation for his or her injury.

14. It is, moreover, clear that the prostitute is able to convert the received price for her own use and to purge sin by spending money on pious causes, since one reads that Mary Magdalene had bought oil with money earned from the prostitution of her body, with which she anointed the feet of the Lord. The Lord would never have allowed this unless she had bought that ointment from money legally earned. Therefore a prostitute can

purge her sin through penance, since by purging sin, the money she earns, once purged, will become clean.

15. Nevertheless there is a distinction to be made here. For, if a prostitute deceitfully adorns herself with cosmetics and acquires a false image, thereby deceiving the eyes of the onlooker, or perhaps if she should lie that she is noble, thereby inciting another to lust, then she cannot convert to her own uses what she acquires through deceit; but she ought to make restitution to the person she deceived or to the Church or to the poor. For example, if the client were to see her in her true form, he might give her only one *obol*, but because he sees her covered in cosmetics and adornments or thinks that she is the daughter of a knight, he might give her one penny. However, in this case, she may keep the one *obol* for herself, but, on the other hand, she is obligated to make restitution of the rest, just as a player of dice, who, if he follows the rules of the game, is able to keep for himself that which he had won. However, if he were to commit fraud in a throw of a dice or in another way, he ought to make restitution for what he had acquired fraudulently.

16. Therefore it ought to be stressed to a confessing prostitute that she ought to recall to memory all that she has earned through this type of fraud, so that she make restitution for what she earned fraudulently. If, on the other hand, she has no cause to do this, she may ask for mercy.

45. Single Mother's Lament, Germany/France, c.1200

A verse translation of this text also appears in *Selections from the Carmina Burana*, tr. David Parlett (London: Penguin, 1986) pp. 127–8. In his notes, Parlett highlights the fact that commentators are divided on whether the first stanza truly belongs to the poem. We have left it as found in the Gaselee collection simply because the verse can be interpreted as an ironic opening to the maid's lament about her situation.

Newly translated from: 'The Maid Forlorn', *The Oxford Book of*

Medieval Verse, ed. Stephen Gaselee (Oxford: Clarendon Press, 1928, repr. 1937) = *Carmina Burana*, poem 88, ed. P. S. Allen, in *Modern Philology*, 6 (1909).

Blossom time is here,
The birdsong grows,
The earth gives solace,
But woe!
Such are the joys of love!

Here I am, wretched me,
I had hidden the thing well,
And loved secretly.
At last the wrongdoer suffered,
For her womb grew fuller
And the pregnant one's birth was upon her.

From here my mother called me
From there my father blamed me
Both dealt with me roughly;
Now I sit at home alone
I don't dare to go out
Nor to play in public.

When I do go outside
I am stared at
As if I were some monster.
When they see this belly
One nudges another,
And they hush whilst I pass.

They nudge with their elbows
And point at me with their fingers
As if I had done something astonishing.
With nods they point me out,
They judge me worthy of the grave
Who only sinned once.

What shall I go through as a single woman?
I am in the stories and mouths of everyone;
My pain piles up
Because my lover is in exile
On account of that tiny trifle.

Because of my father's fury
He fled to the furthest parts of France.
I suffer from his force,
Now I will die of grief
And am always in tears.

46. Marbod of Rennes, Poem to the Countess Ermengarde of Brittany, France, Early Twelfth Century

Marbod was Bishop of Rennes (1096–1123), and left works of poetry, hagiography and encyclopaedic compilations. Countess Ermengarde of Brittany (d. 1147), daughter of Fulk of Anjou (d. 1109) was married to Count Alan Fergeant of Brittany (d. 1112), but even during his lifetime she wished to retire early to the community of nuns at Fontevrault. Marbod's poem is a typical eulogy, but also reflects his clerical background in his exhortation that, despite her marriage and having given birth to a son, Conan III, provided she lived chastely the Countess could still consider herself to be a virgin.

Newly translated from: F. J. E. Raby, *A History of Secular Latin Poetry in the Middle Ages*, 2nd edn (Oxford: Clarendon, 1957), p. 333.

Daughter of Fulco, ornament of the region
    of Brittany
Beautiful, chaste, comely, radiant, distinguished,
    and young,
If you do not submit to the marriage bed, and
    the labours of birth, you can be Cynthia,
    in my opinion.

But because a wife cannot compare to the chaste,
    The honour of virginity is better,
In the company of wives believe you can be
    one of the goddesses,
The first among the first, O very beautiful one!

47. A Wealthy Heiress, England, 1137/8

The text is written in the technical language of medieval feudal land-holding, which is difficult to interpret. Emma held land (formerly that of her father, Grimbald) in 'seisin', which means that she was given the right to hold that land (presumably after her father's death) from the legal title holder (the king). It seems that what is at issue is a disputed claim to the lands in question. Walter Martel is the claimant and Emma is in possession of some of the disputed land (as Grimbald's daughter and heir). Emma has conceded Walter Martel's right to the land and in order to put that claim beyond doubt has surrendered the land to the king, so that the king can grant it to Walter Martel as a fief [land held under certain conditions] and as an inheritance. Emma also guarantees to defend Walter Martel's right to hold the land in any legal proceedings and she binds herself to help him in his lawsuit claiming the other lands of which she is not seised (but to which she does have a hereditary claim), at Walter Martel's own cost.

The probable reason why the dispute came about is this: Emma's father, Grimbald, was presumably seised of all the land, but only some of it came to Emma; part of it was kept by Grimbald's widow, Atselina. In this agreement, Emma is surrendering the land of which she is seised to her lord (the king) and giving up her claim to the land which has not yet come to her. Emma is almost certainly single, as there is no mention of a husband, but probably of full age and out of ward since she is able to give up the land (which minors could not do). The reference to Emma making a promise 'in the hand' of one *William* Martel (he presumably being a relative of Walter) refers to the fact that she held his hand when she solemnly asserted that she had not kept Walter out of his lands fraudulently.

Newly translated from: *English Lawsuits from William I to Rich-*

ard I, Vol. 1: *William I to Stephen nos.* 1–346, ed. R. C. van Caenegem (London: Seldon Society, 1990), p. 247 and *Regesta regum Anglo-Normannorum* 1066–1154, Vol. 3, *Regesta regis Stephani ac Mathildis imperatricis ac Gaufredi et Henrici ducum Normannorum* 1135–54, ed. H. A. Cronne, R. H. C. Davis and H. W. C. Davis (Oxford: Clarendon Press, 1968), no. 579, p. 211.

Stephen, king of the English, greets the archbishops, bishops, abbots, earls, justices, barons, sheriffs, ministers and all his faithful men of all England. May you know that Emma, daughter of Grimbald the physician, has before me and with my consent, quit claimed and handed back to me all the land that belonged to her father, that of which she was seised, as well as the land that was hers by right and of which she was not seised. And, in her presence and with her consent, I have given and granted all that land to Walter Martel in fief and as inheritance for him and his heirs after him, and she pledged that she will warrant it for him everywhere as far as possible; and as far as those lands are concerned of which she is not seised, and which Walter will claim, she will support him as far as is possible to deraign that land, at Walter's expense. She confirmed in the hand of William Martel that she and her heirs held [the land] without guile. And in return for this grant Walter gave Emma in my presence one ring of gold, and John Marshal, on whose advice she did this, confirmed for his part that she held this without guile, and Grimbald's wife, Atselina, will hold the land which she holds in peace from Walter as long as she lives, and afterwards the land will return to Walter's demesne. I therefore will and firmly command that he shall hold it well and in peace and freely and quietly in all things and places with soke, sake, toll, team and infangthief [a technical formula for the handing over of various rights that come with the holding of land] and all the freedoms belonging to it, with which Grimbald ever most freely held it or somebody else before him.

Witnesses: Waleran, Count of Meulan; Robert, Earl of Leicester; William Martel; Aubrey de Vere; Robert de Vere; Hugh Bigod; Geoffrey de Mandeville; and Eustace FitzJohn. At Worcester.

48. *Single Women's Business Transactions, Crete, 1301*

Whether all the women here were single is not certain, but their use of patronyms, rather than identifying themselves as wives, suggests that they were, or that their transactions related to property they owned and managed separately from any spouse. See the introduction to text 31 above for more information about these business transactions and how they were written down.

Newly translated from: *Benvenuto de Brixano, Notaio in Candia, 1301-2*, ed. Raimondo Morozzo della Rocca, Fonti per la Storia di Venezia, sez. 3: Archivi Notarili (Venice: Alfieri Editore, 1950), pp. 16, 26 and 65.

Entry 34: 16 April 1301

I, Bonaventura, daughter of Mistress Diamantis, once of Acco [Acone], make clear that I and my successors have received from you, Lady Flora, wife of Peter Rinier, inhabitant of Candia, and your successors, seven *perpera* which I must give back to you when you demand it in any future occasion. This etc.

Witnesses: N. Prizolo and Comes.

To be completed and dated.

Entry 61: 23 April 1301

I, Viola Ovetaro, inhabitant of Candia, make clear that I received from you, Maria Natale, inhabitant of Candia, one pound of silk which you sold to me, for which I owe you three *perpera* and four *grossi* in Cretan currency, and I must pay you this within six months. This documents etc.

Witnesses: Paul and John Ruzero.

To be completed and dated.

Entry 173: 8 June 1301

I, Flordelice, daughter of the late Jacob Bolano, inhabitant of Candia, and my successors, make a full and irrevocable agreement with you, all the executors of my father [name above], and your successors, about the four *perpera* and all that you have to give to me from the goods of my above-mentioned father and my brother, whether through bequests or through succession or any other means in money and goods. Now etc.

Witnesses: Nicoletus de Scribana from St Peter's Church and Nicoletus Belo.

To be completed and dated.

49. A Single Woman: Liutberga, Germany, Ninth Century

Liutberga (see above, texts 23 and 26) lived in the ninth century in northern Germany. She became a servant of Countess Gisla (daughter of Count Hessi in Saxony), and looked first after Gisla, then became housekeeper of Gisla's son, Berhard, and also acted as nurse to his two sets of children. After the extract quoted, the story continues, to say that, nevertheless, Liutberga pursued her intention to become a recluse. After that she retired to Wendhausen, where she died between 860 and 865. See S. F. Wemple, *Women in Frankish Society. Marriage and Cloister* 500–900 (Philadelphia: University of Pennsylvania Press, 1981), pp. 99–100, 173–4.

Newly translated from: *Das Leben der Liutbirga. Eine Quellen zur Geschichte der Sachsen in karolingischer Seit*, ed. O. Menzel, Deutsches Mittelalter, Kritische Studientexte des Reichsinstituts für ältere deutsche Geschichtskunde, MGH, 3 (Leipzig: Verlag Karl W. Hiersemann, 1937), c. 7–9, pp. 14–15.

But then the time came when the venerable matron Gisla reached her mature old age and fell ill. Sensing that the day of her death was coming close, she called her son Berhard and said: 'My son, do not neglect your mother's words, but follow freely my final wishes. I will bequeath you ample wealth, various lands and houses as well as moveable wealth, which should be sufficient for your present life, if God wishes. As far as other things are concerned, may you always remember to restore churches, and care for those left behind [i.e. widows and orphans], and thereafter strive to take care of your sisters and provide them with your protection and with brotherly love in a just and good manner, because the care of women easily suffers a little if male vigilance reduces its support at times. Moreover, there is one more thing that I commend to you; something your mother commends to your trust and which she demands with special pleading and with maternal affection. That is, that you may provide worthy honours for my beloved daughter, Liut-birga, whom I, with faithful promise, adopted as my daughter, and that you may accept her lovingly as an additional sister and that you listen to her advice as well as theirs, and that you may commit to her care all your precious furnishings because she has in all things always been faithful to me.' And, taking her hand, Gisla commended Liutberga to her son's trust and having kissed her son and said farewell to all, she ended her life in peace. She was buried with honours at the time of Emperor Louis [the Pious, 814–40], father of Lothar, Pippin, Louis and Charles. She left her son Berhard as her heir.

The venerable Liutberga remained at the home of her lord, and according to his mother's wishes, she took care of all his neces-sary [household] arrangements as much as she could, so that the rule of the house fell entirely on her; and her lord loved her with sincere respect as a mother, and she was revered by all other domestic servants of both sexes as 'Mother of the house'. Ber-hard took as his wife, Reginhild, daughter of Count Lothar, a well-known man, and she bore him two sons. One was named after his father, the other was called Otwin. And Reginhild loved the venerable Liutberga so much that during her time [as Berhard's wife] she could not easily avoid noticing the obvious truth that Liutberga, as an experienced and loving mother, in sincere honesty adorned the family with the great quality of her honesty each day. After a long period of illness and still at a young age, Reginhild, loved by all, came to her life's end, and left behind her husband and sons in a whirlwind of intense grief.

Berhard, however, was unable to bear this life as a young man without the consolation of a wife, and thus took another girl of the same well-known people from his native soil, very beautiful and pretty, as his wife, and with this treasure reduced the painful wound of his first marriage. Called Helmburg, she bore him four sons, of whom the eldest was Unwan, the second Adalbert, the third Asic and the fourth Ediva, all named after her kinsmen, and two daughters. The two girls were called Gisla and Bilihild. The venerable Liutberga showed mother and children the strength of her trust, and in everything the greatest love of her deep devotion, so that they called her 'Mother Nurse' rather than 'Nurse'.

CHAPTER 3

MARRIED WOMEN AND MOTHERS

Introduction

The question of marriage in the Middle Ages has received a significantly larger amount of attention from historians than almost every other life stage.[1] Only widowhood has generated more interest, largely because it has been cast by generations of feminist historians as the moment at which a woman gained her 'freedom'. But freedom from what? What did marriage in the Middle Ages actually constitute? And was the absence of a husband really a cause for celebration? Before we can make a judgement on the latter question – which is in any case more properly dealt with in the next section on widowhood – we need to explore the nature of medieval marriage.

This section of sources is by far the largest in the book, because medieval authors, lay and clerical, took an active interest in marriage, and because the vast majority of women spent a significant proportion of their lives married, whether once or several times in succession, and as mothers. Some of the sources in this section look at the processes of making a marriage, but most feature married women going about their daily lives. On one thing historians are largely in agreement: in the early Middle Ages 'marriage' took a number of forms. A marriage could be contracted between families betrothing their children and agreeing property transfers for their future support (as we saw above in text 34); it could be precipitated by the prior seizure and rape of the girl or woman (which assault might be compensated for by the assailant agreeing to take the victim as his wife – her views seemingly unasked-for and unimportant); it could be the mutual agreement of a man and woman to live together and have children; or it might be constituted by a formalized ceremony and/or feast in the presence of family, friends and/or a cleric. Not all of these choices were viewed as licit marriages: the social status of the partners might debar them from becoming a married couple, even if they wished to be together (texts 50 and 51), and expectations of the ideal spouse were often unrealistic or downright misogynistic (text 52). The emphasis on marriage as an occasion for lavish feasting and celebration among the wealthy, however, remained strong throughout the period, an opportunity for the families to display their wealth ostentatiously (texts 53 and 54). Although the Church is present in some of these transactions, and early medieval clerics were concerned to ensure the durability of marriage and the consent of the parties involved, it is in the eleventh and twelfth centuries that the emphasis on marriage as a holy sacrament really began to be emphasized. This did not stop other forms of marriage existing, but a declaration of willingness to be joined together in the presence of the Church became the litmus test for a valid Christian marriage, and the Church became involved in several rituals during the wedding day itself (text 55). Marriages were also expected to be public, not private or clandestine.[2] At the same time, the Church increasingly insisted that disputes about marriage be heard in episcopal, rather than secular, courts (in Jewish culture, the validity of marriage had always been tested against Talmudic law and decided by rabbinical courts, but this could be disrupted by secular intervention, as in text 81).

Although this change over time affected the ways in which marriage was upheld, one constant factor throughout its history was the exchange of property which accompanied the union, and this is one reason why marriage is so heavily documented in medieval sources. It has been argued that there was a shift in the balance of such exchanges between the early Middle Ages and later centuries, with a payment by the husband or his family for the woman – brideprice, perhaps having its origins in the compensation paid in the case of rape – losing ground against the payment by *her* family of a dowry to support her.[3] The supposed purchase of the bride owes much to clauses in early medieval law codes, such as that of King

Rothari of the Lombards in Italy, which specifically speak of a payment for control over a woman who became the purchaser's wife.[4] The dowry was an important element in the marriage – it remained the property of the wife, despite often being managed by her husband (e.g. texts 56–8), and was the focus of considerable legislation – if the Church set down the rules for legitimate marriage, it was secular rulers who tried to regulate dowry payments (text 59). The dowry functioned not only as an insurance policy to support the wife and any dependent children in case of widowhood, but also as a marker of her social status, as demonstrated by two very different documents concerning dowry from thirteenth-century Marseilles (text 60). Wives also had redress against husbands who failed in their management of the dowry: after all, many dowries amounted to substantial sums.[5] Indeed, dowry inflation became a notorious problem in the later Middle Ages, as families struggled to meet the going rate for daughters of certain social classes, and non-payment became a major issue. And, as we have already seen, the lack of a dowry was seen as a problem, even a barrier to marriage, which philanthropic donors sought to solve by providing poor girls with the means to marry (see above, text 41).

The legal status of wives determined how much say they might have in the management of their own property and the running of the family finances. Early medieval law codes drew upon the Roman idea of guardianship, where the head of household, the *paterfamilias*, controlled all aspects of the family's life. This supervision, termed *mundium* in Germanic culture, envisaged a woman moving from her father's control to that of her husband, rendering her legally incapable. The degree to which this was enforced varied geographically, even within regions. Within Spain and southern France, for example, we see relatively little evidence of the *mundium* in the central Middle Ages (texts 61, 62 and 66), despite it having existed in early medieval Francia (i.e. modern-day France, parts of Germany and the Low Countries), whilst in Italy, the fragmented political nature of the peninsula meant that women in different parts enjoyed very different rights over the disposal of their property (texts 63–5).[6] To some extent the enforcement of *mundium* offered protection: as we shall see, the assumption that a woman was under her husband's control – later termed *couverture* in England and France – rendered her immune to prosecution if she had collaborated in his misdeeds. It also rendered husbands responsible for the actions (and misdemeanours) of their wives (e.g. texts 67 and 68).

This does not mean that wives were kept away from the running of their households – far from it – but the degree of autonomy which they had in doing so was strictly limited by their status vis-à-vis their husbands. Two alleged rape cases from medieval England also underline the view that the assault of a wife could be viewed as a theft from the husband as much as, or possibly more than, an assault upon the woman (text 69).[7] A husband's supposed protection did not always mean that wives were safe. Nowhere is this more clearly demonstrated than in the ill-treatment which wives might suffer at the hands of their husbands' enemies, whatever their social status might be. Soranza Soranzo of Venice found that being the Doge's daughter did not protect her from practical incarceration when she returned from exile after her husband's rebellion against her father (text 70). Slightly earlier Venetian records show how fragile a woman's reputation could be and how quickly she might become entangled in disputes which were in reality her husband's (text 71). Elsewhere Christina, wife of William Nymhithalf of Southampton, found herself held hostage with her children, nailed into the house which her husband was alleged to have been forced to hand over to Thomas White when she refused to give the house up to him. Her incarceration lasted over twelve weeks during 1460.[8] Their treatment was nothing, however, compared to the cruelty shown to female members of Robert Bruce's family by Edward I in 1320 (text 72).

Married women's level of independent action may also have been influenced by their age relative to their husband's – as we have seen in the previous section, a period of singledom in their teens was a less realistic prospect for girls than it was for boys, and so there might be a considerable difference in age between husband and wife on their marriage (text 73 reveals a bride who seems hardly out of girlhood). Research has shown that this differential was dependent on social class – less well-off and peasant couples being closer in age to each other – and on geographical location – the tendency towards much older husbands was more marked in southern Europe than in the north.[9]

So was marriage oppressive? Was widowhood really the point at which a woman gained some kind of freedom? Perhaps a better question would be to ask what marriage provided for women. For most it offered economic and social security, and husbands and wives worked in partnership with each other, and when that partnership was disrupted, it caused distress (texts 74 and 75), and as we shall see, widowhood could be a time of vulnerability rather than self-determination. There was also a strong expectation that women *would* marry; the fear of sexual promiscuity leading families to ensure that daughters and sisters did find a suitable husband. Such pressure may have led to mismatches. Certainly we can find instances of unhappy marriages (texts 76–7), and examples of wives convinced by others that their husbands did not love them (text 78), but it is easy to focus on these because they, like other dysfunctional elements of medieval life, are the moments at which a marriage would make it into the medieval record. The thousands of couples who got on with their everyday lives without conflict are far less likely to attract attention (although penitential texts (text 79) were keen to regulate just what they did as a couple, as James Brundage has memorably shown).[10] When a marriage did go wrong, divorce was an option, but it was wellnigh impossible for a woman to initiate. Rather, men put aside their wives, to varying degrees of disapproval, utilizing the excuses of consanguinity (text 80), or infertility (text 81), or the wife's adultery, to do so.

Acting this way, husbands were able to call upon the heightening of concern with proper marriages, and to exploit the Church's attempts to prevent incestuous unions. Such regulation went hand-in-hand with the Church's reforming efforts – with varying success – to discourage clerical marriage (texts 82 and 83), and its continued celebration of the celibate life for priests and those whom it classed among the saints. Hence we find numerous exhortations in clerical writing to spurn marriage and sexual intercourse altogether (texts 84 and 85).[11] The persuasive, sometimes shrill, language used to advocate this path, however, should not be taken to mean that the Church wished to undermine marriage totally. Indeed, the Church's increasing concern to sustain and regulate marriage is another reason why the subject is so richly documented. In cases heard by the papal court, marriages were upheld even if one of the couple converted to a different faith, provided that both partners still wished to remain married, and neither was permitted simply to leave the other (text 86). Such was the strength of commitment to the sacrament of marriage by the thirteenth century.

Just as most medieval women married, so most married women would go on to have children. The issues of pregnancy and birth have been discussed above, as has the fact that most of the blame for non-productive marriages was laid on the woman's inability to conceive.[12] In this section, however, we include mothers in action. Motherhood could cover a wide range of roles. Apart from looking after their own children, the possibility of remarriage meant that women might also be responsible for stepchildren, and the complications this led to with regard to inheritance may be at the heart of early modern fairytales of wicked stepmothers. Women might also act as godmothers (as in the case of Maria Salbaconsa, below, text 65, or the Empress Judith, below, text 87), and more generally as a moral compass for their offspring.

Of course, within the Christian world it was easy to idealize mothers along the model of the Virgin or, more usefully, that of her mother, St Anne. Numerous male authors hold up their mothers as paragons of virtue, no doubt partly to emphasize their own attributes and qualities.

The reality of motherhood might be quite different, dependant on the woman's status. As we have seen in Chapter 2, the children of unfree mothers were a commodity in themselves, and a mother might have little or no say in the fate of her children. The unfree peasants of text 88 probably experienced the same lack of choice. At the other end of the spectrum, noble mothers might expect to keep their children by them in the early years of their lives, but then might suffer separation, particularly from their sons, from an early age. The young Prince Charles' eagerness to join his father and stepbrother at the hunt, and his mother's refusal to allow him to go, speaks of this tension between maternal protection and the pressures to enter the world of men (text 89).[13]

Nonetheless, it was often to a mother that the task fell of ensuring her children's education. Again, this role is visibly idealized in biographical works, such as the life of Queen Margaret of Scotland excerpted below (text 90), but at the heart of such images lay a didactic message – good mothers saw to the socialization of their offspring. The purpose of such education, according to most of our clerical authors, was to bring up the next generation of good Christians – and the mother's influence over the moral and religious education of her children might be brought starkly into focus in cases of disputed custody (text 91).

At the heart of all the literature was a recognition of a mother's unconditional love for her children, which is why infanticide is treated with such horror in text 79. Even the most formal and public letters between mothers and children contained expressions of affection (text 92). It is unclear whether the Muslim mother documented in text 93, protecting the rights of a young disabled boy and other underage children, is their mother or stepmother – and Rohais in text 94 had clearly fostered the disabled boy featured in the text, despite not being related to him – but their solicitousness underlines that mothers often had to care for the economic well-being of children as well as their social role. Hence we see a mother in Crete in 1301 placing her son as an apprentice (text 95, and compare text 28 above). More directly, women of means would ensure that their children were provided for in their wills, many of which we have already included (and see text 96). In some cases, mothers and children collaborated economically, especially if the latter were of age (text 97). And whilst the issue of remarriage might mean a family consisting of children born of different partners, stepmothers were not always seen as a threat, and may have been a more regular feature of day-to-day life than they are now (text 98).

Marriage and motherhood did not always represent a continuous, linear progression for women from girlhood to middle and old age. Sometimes they were punctuated by unexpected events. Children might die, or a young woman might find herself widowed early, whether through war, sickness or perhaps the advanced age of her husband. When widowhood occurred, it represented a break which opened up new possibilities in a woman's life. The next section, however, will reveal how such choices were not always positive.

50. Letter of Einhard's Wife, Imma, on an Illicit Marriage, France, 828–36

The legal background to this letter indicates that the husband named, Wenilo, would be liable to the death penalty for having 'married' a free woman, hence Imma's urgent intervention.

Newly translated from: *Epistolae Karolini Aevi III*, ed. K. Hampe, MGH, Epp V (Berlin: Weidmann, 1878/9, 1974), no. 37, p. 128.

To her dearest sister, Blidthrut, Imma, her aunt, sends greetings in the name of the eternal Lord.

A certain slave of yours from Mosbach, named Wenilo, took a certain free woman in marriage; and now feeling your anger and also that of his lord, Albuin, he has sought refuge within the boundaries of [the Church of] Saints Marcellinus and Peter. On account of which I ask your charity that you will agree to intercede with him [Albuin] instead of me, so that he [Wenilo] is allowed with Albuin's and your grace to have that woman whom he has accepted. I bid you fare well always.

51. Barriers to Licit Marriage, Milan, 20 May 822

The decision in this case effectively dissolved the couple's marriage, as Dominicus no longer had control over the futures of his wife and children. Note the apparent requirement in the record that the wife, Luba, be questioned as well as her husband.

Newly translated from: C. Manaresi, ed., *I Placiti del Regnum Italiae*, Fonti per la storia d'Italia, 92 (Rome: Istituto Storico Italiano, 1955), Vol. 1, no. 34, pp. 106–8.

There came together Dominicus, with his wife, Luba, inhabitants of Valtellina in the place called Circiuno, and on the other side Nonio, monk and Deputy of the Monastery of St Ambrose sited outside the wall of the city of Milan, in the presence of: Gausarius the gastald, Aribert's representative in the city of Milan, John Scabinus, Rachibert the priest, Tholomeo and Auperto from Porta Argentea, Marchadraxo, Oldelfrit de Calvariate and many others in that assembly. At this [assembly] St Ambrose's party said that they would confirm by an oath, that the above Luba, wife of Dominicus (called Camonno), along with her descendants, were the property of the Monastery of St Ambrose. When both sides joined in over this issue, which they had placed in the presence of the above hearers, to demonstrate the liberty of his wife, Luba, as best they could, so the above hearers asked the above Dominicus (called Camonno) whether he could prove the liberty of his wife, Luba, or not. And the above Dominicus said and demonstrated that he could not prove or bring [documents to the court which would show] either her liberty or that of her descendants, Urso, Martin, Bonello, Lubo, Arasuronda and Laurentius, and so he said and demonstrated in the presence of the hearers that Luba and her children must belong to the Monastery of St Ambrose. After this declaration and manifestation, it appeared to the above hearers, and thus they judged, that according to the profession and manifestation of the above Dominicus, the above Luba and her children should be returned to Nonio, Monk, and Deputy of the Monastery of St Ambrose. And thus Dominicus (called Camonno), with his own hand invested the above Nonio, monk and Deputy of the Monastery of St Ambrose with the ownership of his wife, Luba, and her children. And the dispute was ended in this way, and just as these things were done and deliberated, the hearers ordered me, Iona, to write this notice for the permanent use of St Ambrose, and it was read by them.

Done at Milan in the ninth year of the Emperor Louis' reign, on the twentieth of May, in the fifteenth indiction.

And what we did not record above, we add below. That Luba was asked by the above hearers whether she could produce anything about her liberty; she said and demonstrated just as her husband Dominicus did, that she could do or prove nothing about her own or her children's liberty, and so they must be St Ambrose's.

+ Gausari the gastald, who was present at these acts.
+ I, Aribert.
+ I, Auperto.
+ Marchardiraxo, who was present at these acts.
+ I, John, was there.

52. The Ideal Wife Described: Bonizo of Sutri, Italy, Late Eleventh Century

Bonizo of Sutri (c.1045–c.1095) wrote in the late eleventh century. Although his *Liber de Vita Christiana* was not extensively copied or circulated, it distils many of the predominant ideas of the clerical patriarchy of the time. The target of his text was Countess Matilda of Tuscany (1046–1115), who broke almost all his rules by her repudiation of two husbands and her very prominent role commanding armies during the papal–imperial conflict in Italy. (On Countess Matilda as military leader, see David J. Hay, *The Military Leadership of Matilda of Canossa, 1046–1115* (Manchester: Manchester University Press, 2008).) Although originally a supporter of the countess, Bonizo later turned against her, and the *Liber* is the product of that reversal.

Newly translated from: Bonizo of Sutri, *Liber de vita Christiana*, ed. Ernst Perels (Hildesheim: Weidman, 1998), Book 7, c. 29, p. 251.

If a woman is married, let her love her husband and tremble under his authority; she should bring up their children, and take care of her house; she should be terrified of wars, dread soldiers and love peace. Let her carry in her hands loom weights and a comb, spindles and threads, linen and wool and silk. And she should not trouble herself greatly with leading military expeditions.

53. A Marriage and Wedding Feast, Flanders, Twelfth Century

In this excerpt, Arnold II ('Arnold the Old', Lord of Ardres (1094–
c.1138)) marries Gertrude, sister of Lord Baldwin the Fat of Aalst. But
this text was written retrospectively, approximately eighty years later
(c.1200), by Lambert, the chaplain of Arnold V, Count of Ardres
(c.1178–1220) and II, Count of Guînes (1206–20). (In the 1170s the
two families of Guînes and Ardres had formed a dynastic marriage
and merged to become one. See texts 55 and 131 for accounts of the
family later on.) One confusing aspect of the text is that the chronicler
Lambert quotes extensively in the first person a man called Walter,
who was the illegitimate grandson of Arnold the Old of Ardres. Thus
the text refers to the latter as 'my grandfather', although of course
Walter was not the chronicler Lambert's own grandfather.

Newly translated from: *Lamberti Ardensis historia comitum Ghisnensium*, ed. J. Heller, MGH, SS 24 (Hanover: Hahn, 1879), pp.
550–642, at 622.

How Arnold the Old Took Gertrude to be his Wife

When Lord Arnold of Ardres, my grandfather, nicknamed
the Old, frequented the court of Flanders and his fame reached
all the barons of the realm of the French, who with true voice
reported and spoke much good about him, his reputation, military prowess and splendour reached Lord Baldwin the Fat of
Aalst. One day, on the occasion of a famous and glorious tour-
nament which was held within the borders of Tournai, where
Arnold obtained and acquired for himself the whole weight
and glory of that warlike day of tournaments, with the agreement even of the envious, Baldwin the Fat of Aalst invited him
and solemnly entertained him and his men with the most splendid food and drink. The next day, after many and varied
discussions, Arnold was betrothed to and lawfully married
Gertrude, the sister of the noble man. Arnold received with her
the hereditary lands which Baldwin held: the castle of Bergues
and its lands at Aardenburg and Oostburg, and around Yzen-
dijke, Vulendick and Gaternesse. Then, Arnold with his wife,

Gertrude, arrived at Ardres, and, with the bells tolling solemnly, he was welcomed in his church by the clergy and people, and then, after a brief prayer, he was joyfully welcomed at home in his castle. There, over a period of three days, as if they were at Bacchus' festival, they celebrated the wedding feast, indulging themselves in food and drink as well as in games and merriments, with pleasure and delight.

54. The Marriage of Urraca, Spain, c.1082

Urraca was King Alfonso's daughter by his concubine, Gontrada. The most striking thing about this account of her wedding to King Garsia Radimir of Pamplona is Urraca's relative anonymity in the whole proceedings.

Newly translated from: *Chronica Adelfonsi Imperatoris*, ed. A. Maya Sanchez, in *Chronica Hispana Saeculi XII, pars* 1, ed. Emma Falque, Juan Gil and Antonio Maya, Corpus Christianorum Continuatio Mediaevalis, 71, (Turnhout: Brepols, 1990), Book 1, c. 92–5, pp. 191–4.

The king ordered messengers to be sent out to all his own soldiers, counts, princes and dukes throughout his kingdom, so that each of them should be prepared to come to the royal wedding with all his noble militia. Hearing this pleased everyone, especially the Asturians and Tinianis, who, just as the king had ordered, were very ready to come to the wedding. So the king came, and with him his wife, the lady Queen Berengaria, and the greatest crowd of powerful men, counts, dukes and soldiers of Castile. King Garsia also came, with a crowd of not a few soldiers, all prepared and dressed just as they should be to come to the wedding of their king.

Then the most serene infanta Lady Sancha [Alfonso's sister] entered Leon by the Cauriensem Gate, and there came with her her niece, the infanta Lady Urraca, wife of King Garsia, with a great crowd of nobles, soldiers and clerics, and women and girls, the daughters of all the great men of Spain.

The marriage bed was placed in the royal palaces, in St Pelagio, by the infanta Lady Sancha, and around the marriage bed there was the greatest crowd of old women and women and girls singing with instruments and flutes and cytharas and lutes and all kinds of musical instruments. Then the two kings sat down on a royal throne in a raised place in front of the doors of the king's palace, and bishops and abbots and counts and princes and dukes sat down on benches placed in a circle about them.

Other powerful men, chosen from all of Spain, spurred on their horses to a gallop in the way of their country, threw their lances and pierced a board set up to show off their skills as well as the virtues of their horses. Others, provoking bulls to anger through the barking of dogs, killed them with long hunting spears. At the end of the hunt they placed a pig, which they wished to kill, in the middle of the field, and, wanting the pig to fight, they took turns to strike it and to drive it to anger, to the amusement of all those around. Thus was great joy celebrated in that city, and they gave thanks to God, who always made them prosper in everything. The wedding happened in June 1082.

The king gave to his daughter and to his son-in-law, Garsia, great gifts of silver and gold and horses and mules and many other riches, and blessed them and dismissed them honourably to return to his country. But the infanta Lady Sancha gave to her niece many dishes of gold and silver, and male and female mules loaded with royal riches. Then King Garsia set out from Leon with his men in great glory, and he had Count Roderick Gomez and Lord Gutierrus Fernandiz in his train, who went away with the king and his wife to Pamplona, his city. King Garsia held a great and royal feast for the Castilians who were with him, and for all the soldiers and princes of his kingdom, and for many days the royal wedding was celebrated and the king gave great gifts to the counts and dukes of Castile, and each returned to his lands.

And the aforementioned mother of Garsia's wife, the queen, whom we have named above as Gontrada, when she saw what she had hoped for above all, the great honour to her daughter, who had become a queen through both royal unions, lost all worldly desire and laboured as hard as she could to reach heaven [became a nun].

55. The Blessing of the Marital Bed at the End of the Wedding Day, Flanders, Twelfth Century

Arnold V, Count of Ardres (*c*.1178–1220) and II, Count of Guînes (1206–20), married Beatrice, the heiress of Bourbourg, before 1198. The author of this piece was Lambert of Ardres, Arnold's chaplain. (For an account of the chronicler Lambert and the family relationships, see texts 53 and 131.) Lambert's eyewitness account of the count's blessing of the marriage bed, in particular his blessing of his son, narrated in a style heavily influenced by biblical imagery, is a unique testimony in its time, and thus not easy to verify.

Newly translated from: *Lamberti Ardensis historia comitum Ghisnensium*, ed. J. Heller, MGH, SS 24 (Hanover: Hahn, 1879), pp. 550–642, at 637–8.

How Arnold Married Beatrice, the Lady Castellan of Bourbourg

After some time had passed, a period of almost four years, the young castellan of Bourbourg, Henry, son of the noble Walter, who had not yet reached adolescence, died without an heir around Michaelmas Day and was honourably buried in the Church of St Mary of Bourbourg, as was fitting. Then Arnold of Guînes rejected Eustacia, daughter of Hugh [IV, 1174–1205] Count of St Pol, called Candavène, to whom he had first been betrothed, and on the advice of his father, Baldwin, Count of Guînes, who was still alive, he married a young woman of powerful nobility as his lawful wife and in legitimate marriage. A virgin of a most noble lineage and origin, deeply learned and skilled in the liberal arts, as glorious in spirit and life as befitted her young age, envied by Cassandra or even Helen for the stunning beauty of her well-shaped body, similar in wisdom to

Minerva, equal to Juno in the wealth of her possessions, she [Beatrice] was the sole and most rightful heiress of the castle and lands of Bourbourg, sister of that most noble, but now dead and buried, Henry, castellan of Bourbourg, indeed the lady castellan of Bourbourg herself. The noble advocate, William of Béthune, and his brothers, Lord Cono, Count Baldwin of Aumale and John, afterwards venerable Bishop of Cambrai, were present, as was Henry of Bailleul, whose agreement for the disposal of the castle and lands of Bourbourg was required. The venerable rectors of the holy mother church, William, Archbishop of Reims, and Lambert, Bishop of Thérouanne, gave their consent. As dower, Arnold gave her Ardres and Colvida, with all their rights and dependent properties there. [. . .]

Betrothed to his noble wife, Beatrice, the lady castellan of Bourbourg, Arnold of Guînes celebrated the wedding at Guînes in such a way as we never have seen or heard of before or after in the whole of Guînes. On the first evening, with the bride and groom in one bed, the count [Baldwin], filled with the zeal of the divine spirit, called us and our brethren, Baldwin, William and Robert, the priest of Audruick, indicating that he wished us to sprinkle the bride and groom with holy water, while walking round the bed wafting aromatic gums and unguents which had been prepared for this; he also wished us to bless them with incense and commend them to God. We did all this and everything else at the most devout wish of the count, with the greatest care and devotion to detail. And then when we were ready to go, the count, still persevering in the devotion of divine love and with the grace of spiritual virtue, lifted his eyes and hands to heaven and said: 'Holy Lord, omnipotent Father, eternal God, you who blessed Abraham and his seed and granted them the grace of benediction, bestow your mercy upon us and deign to bless the couple – your servants – joined now by the law of holy intercourse and by the rite of marriage, so that they may live in your divine love and persevere in concord and so that their seed may be multiplied in the length of days and for as long as the infinity of time.' And when we replied 'Amen', he went on, 'But to you, my most dear and first-born son, Arnold, most beloved of all other sons, if there is any grace in a father's blessing of his son, if any wealth and grace of benediction has been left to me by the ancient fathers, I give to you the same grace of benediction that God the Father once granted our father, Abraham, that Abraham gave to his son, Isaac, that Isaac then gave to his son, Jacob, and his seed, insofar as our faith allows me [as this would have been a lay person's rather than a priest's blessing].' When Arnold joined his father's hands and bent his head towards his father and invoked God the Father in a devout whisper, the count added, explicitly expressing and confirming his benediction, 'I bless you, except for what belongs by right to your brothers, and I leave you my benediction, if I have any power of benediction, here and forever.' All present then answered 'Amen' and left the room, all returning to their own homes.

56. Donation by Bernard of Narbonne to his Wife, Ermengarda, Narbonne, 27 August 1031

Although this is ostensibly a gift, it appears that Bernard might in fact be handing over property in exchange for Ermengarda's dowry, a fairly common practice. Bernard is making Ermengarda a 'gift of dower': financial assets given by a husband to a wife to support her after his death.

Newly translated from: C. Devic and J. Vaissete, *Histoire générale du Languedoc*, Vol. 5, 2nd edn (Toulouse: É. Privat, 1872–5), no. 197, p. 398.

I, Bernard, in God's name give to you, my sweetest spouse and wife, Ermengarda, a piece of vineyard in the place called 'ad Instagno', within the boundaries of the Villa Locajaco in the county of Narbonne, which I received from my parents. And this vineyard borders to the east that of Bernard de Cucuciaco, and to the south that of Nantieso, which is being improved, and to the west and north my vineyards. And I give you, in another place called Roca de Utza, a half-vineyard, which I obtained through planting it. And this borders to the east the land belonging to the Church of Saints Justus and Pastor; to the south, the public road; to the west, my land; and to the north, the public road. Everything which is within these boundaries I give to you in order that whilst you live you will hold and possess them; after your death, if you have children by me, it shall go to them; if not, then it shall revert to my nearest relatives; and on top of this I give you gold and silver. And if I, the donor, or any man or woman should come to break this agreement, then let them pay to you three pounds of gold, and let this charter of gift of dower remain firm and stable for all time. This charter of gift was made on the sixth Kalends of September, in the first year of the reign of Aiagrico [Henry I of France] the King.

+ Bernard, who had this charter written and asked the witnesses to sign it.

+ Baronus. + Ebrardus. + Bellus. + Nantidis. + Recondinda. Sigarius, the priest, wrote it on the day and year above.

57. Managing a Dowry, France, Before 1148

This charter illustrates the close cooperation between monastic institutions and local families in the cultivation of land. It seems that the Abbey of La Roé made available the manpower to clear a piece of land to enable cultivation of the whole of it, for which the monks received one half of it in return. For the first seven years of cultivation the monks would hand over half the amount of grain they produced. The whole plot had been given as a dowry by Rainald to his son-in-law, Geoffrey, upon marriage to his daughter. Also, as is common in medieval legal documents recording deals about land ownership and use of land, more people are involved in these transactions than the record allows us to explain. In this case, there are tantalizing references to other members of the local community, e.g. Raymond of – and his sons, or Gaudemerus, about whom we do not know anything more than is mentioned here.

Newly translated from: Cartulary of the Abbey of La Roé (Mayenne), Archives Départementales Mayenne H 154, no. 84, published in

Exploiter la terre. Les contrats agraires de l'antiquité à nos jours. Actes du colloque de Caen (10–13 septembre 1997), ed. G. Béaur, M. Arnoux and A. Varet-Vitu, Bibliothèque d'Histoire rurale (Rennes, 2003), pp. 521–2.

Rainald of la Roche gave his daughter in marriage to Geoffrey Peleit, together with the bordage [land held by a tenant] of La Bellière, which the couple would never have been able to cultivate themselves because it had been abandoned a long time ago. That is why they had talked to Michael, then Prior of that place [the Abbey of La Roé], and they agreed that Michael would clear the whole bordage and cultivate it for seven years, giving Geoffrey half the harvest of grain for his portion during that time. And [they also agreed] that the bordage would be divided into two parts; the one chosen by Michael for the Church of La Roé and the canons would remain with them, as the perpetual alms of Geoffrey and his wife. This was approved and agreed by Raymond of – and his sons. The agreement was witnessed and guaranteed by the lords of the land, namely: Guiol Chotart, Suhard de Méral, John Chaorein, who acted as guarantors in front of various of their men, who watched and witnessed [the agreement]: Jean the weapon-bearer, William the baker, Robert Constance; for the canons: Bernard the bearded, together with a large part of the parishioners, because this was done in front of the Monastery of Saint-Pierre-de-Cosmes. In return for this land, the canons owed to Gaudemerus the service of one horse, and to Suhard de Méral and John Chaorein, their taillages [taxes].

58. *Regularizing of the Property Surrounding Marriage, Genoa, 1159*

For the details of the cartulary from which this document comes, see above, Chapter 1, text 7.

Newly translated from: *Il Cartolare di Giovanni Scriba*, Vol. 1, ed. Mario Chiaudano and M. Moresco (Turin: S. Lattes & Co., 1935), document 552, p. 296.

Witnesses: Oto of Milan, Baldezon Ususmaris, Amicus Grillus, W. Astanova, John Graina and John Lercar. I, Peter Clericus, declare that before I had any children by you, Mabilia, I married you and took you as my legitimate wife, but, because at that time I did not have the patrimony which I received from you recorded in a public document, nor the counter-dowry which I gave to you, I now declare that I received ten Genoese pounds from you and give you back the same amount as a counter-dowry, to have and hold according to the custom of the city. Done in the Church of St Mary de Vineis, 1159, eighteenth Kalends of September, sixth indiction.

59. Customs on the Dowry, Amalfi, Thirteenth Century

A set of customs is documented in the independent city-state of Amalfi as early as 1007, but it was probably not until the twelfth century that they were compiled and written down. The customs set out here, therefore, reflect a consciousness of change over time. The currencies used reflect the change from Amalfitan independence to its existence under Norman rule, when its coinage was replaced by Sicilian currency, and there was more emphasis on the weight of coins (measured in pounds, ounces and grains). The text itself demonstrates the complexity of the monetary system, the differing value of coins and the need for established exchange rates to be written down – and, despite this, some of the text's calculations are still wrong.

Newly translated from: *Consuetudines Civitatis Amalfie*, ed. A. de Leone and A. Piccirillo (Cava de Tirreni: Di Mauro Editore, 1970), pp. 28–36.

1. On the Dowry
    This once consisted of *solidi*, in the form of *tari*, which were minted in the city, with five ounces of gold and five ounces of silver in each pound. Each *solidus* was worth four *tari*. Each *tari* weighed twenty grains, and was worth twelve grains in Sicilian gold money.

2. How Dowry Used to be Given

Each ounce of Sicilian gold was worth twelve and a half *solidi*. For the moveable goods: if [the total value of the dowry] was worth a hundred *solidi*, it could not be given as a hundred *solidi* in cash, nor as any more than two ounces of Sicilian gold; for two-hundred-*solidi*-worth [of dowry] no more than four ounces in Sicilian gold; each ounce was valued at twenty *solidi*, which was the equivalent of one ounce or eighteen *tari* in Sicilian money. If forty *solidi* (or three ounces or six *tari* in Sicilian money) [of the dowry] was paid in cash, the rest of the hundred-*solidi*-worth was paid in silk cloths, silver, cloaks and other moveable goods. If those goods included a belt of silver worth twelve *solidi*, it was counted as being worth fifteen.

3. How Dowry is Given Today

Now [the dowry] is given in Sicilian *tari*, as there are no more Amalfitan [*tari* produced], but still in the proportions given above: twelve and a half *solidi* for each ounce of Sicilian gold, so a hundred *solidi* is valued as eight ounces of gold. If the equivalent of eight ounces of Sicilian gold is given in goods, then only two ounces of that can be given in actual gold (worth three ounces and or six *tari* [in Sicilian money].) The nobility of Amalfi give [as dowry] the bed, linen, cloths with and without silk borders and vases of bronze, but all these latter items are not counted if the bed has silk covers. If a curtain is given [as part of the dowry], it is counted. Among the common people, however, the bed, linen and bronze dishes are all counted.

60. *Dowry Payments, Marseilles, 1248*

These documents are preserved in a notarial cartulary like that of Giovanni Scriba from Genoa (see above, Chapter 1, text 7). The interest of the first document is that it acknowledges that a dowry has remained unpaid, whilst in the second a mother draws partly upon her own dowry to provide for her daughter.

Newly translated from: J. H. Pryor, ed., *Business Contracts of*

Medieval Provence: Selected notulae *from the Cartulary of Giraud Amalric of Marseilles, 1248* (Toronto: Pontifical Institute of Medieval Studies, 1981) nos. 26 (p. 135) and 51 (pp. 159–61).

24 April

I, Raimundus Morrucus, confess and acknowledge to you, Berengario de St Paul, my son-in-law, that I owe to you twenty pounds of royal crowns as dowry, which I promised to you for my daughter, Peirona, your wife. I promise and stipulate to give and pay to you the above twenty pounds on the next feast of St John the Baptist [24 June]. And all costs and expenses and damages that you may have or incur through the above debt to the end of this term, I promise and stipulate to make reparation for. I make this obligation to you and your present and future heirs. Renouncing my right to any delay of twenty days and four months, or any other delays and laws and exceptions that may prevent me from doing this. This public instrument of it was made.

Witnesses: Hugh Simon, Guillelmus Bernardi, Hugh Pansa.

5 May

In the name of the Lord. In the year of His incarnation, 1248, sixth indiction, the third of the nones of May. Let it be noted by all present and future [readers of this note] that we, Andrivetus Andree, son of the deceased Guillelmi Andree, and Maria, his wife, both spouses and citizens of Marseilles, both together and in good faith and without any grief, give, constitute and consign to you, Raimund Montanee, here present, as dowry and in the name of our daughter, Marieta, your future wife, on account of the marriage which you will legitimately celebrate, the possessions and property and quantity of money here below listed, which are: all the vineyards and lands, cultivated or uncultivated or scrubland, which we the above spouses have and hold in the territory of Marseilles in the place called Val Corte, under the dominion of the Church of St Mary, the [episcopal] seat of Marseilles, which vineyards are held there by the following [list of tenants follows] for us to work. These vines and lands are bordered on one side by those of Aubert de Cuiacis, and on the other by those of Raimundi Andree, deceased, with a path in the middle, and by the vineyard of Hugh Barreti. Also, three houses joined and one plot adjoining the three houses, which are in Marseilles, in the upper town next to Castrum Babonum, the boundaries of which are on two sides two public roads, and on the other side the houses of Raimund Maurelli and the house of the freedmen of the deceased Peter Bernardi, and then the house of Badini and Peter Andree the Catalan, deceased. Also, half of the house site which was once Stephen Johannis's, in the lower town of Marseilles towards St Saviour, under the dominion of the Monastery of St Saviour, Marseilles; and this borders on one side the house of the deceased Roso de Sancherio, and on the other the houses of Raymund de Cavalleria, Petronella Simbaude, Ruodolfi de Parisiis and Raymund de Cavalleria [sic], and on the other two sides by two public roads. Also a hundred pounds of royal crowns which I, Maria, wife of the above Andree, give and donate, constitute and consign from my dowry to you, Raimund Montanee, here present, in the name of and to give a dowry to my daughter, Marieta, on top of the goods which my husband and I have given above, out of the dowry which my husband had from me and received from someone else for me. Also, we give, constitute and consign, both spouses together and each of us to you, Raimund Montanee, here present, in the name of and on account of the dowry of our daughter, Marieta, your future wife, three hundred pounds of royal crowns on top, which is the damages from the court case which we both have against the Genoese. Which three hundred pounds of money we wish you, Raimund, to have and to take, on account of the dowry, from the first money which we shall have and receive from the men and citizens of Genoa on the occasion of the verdict given and conceded to us against them. Also we constitute, consign and promise to give to you, Raimund, from the above cause, two pairs of wedding clothes for the above Marieta and other nuptial ornaments. We the above spouses, citizens of Marseilles, give, constitute and consign to you, Raimund Montanee, all the above vineyards and cultivated and uncultivated lands and their rents and fruits and dues and whatever rights we have in them, and the above houses and plots of land and the above quantities of money on account of the dowry and on behalf of our daughter, Marieta, your future wife. We constitute all this in your name to possess the property and whatever and whomever belongs to it, and you can enter and take them, and we give you licence to enter and seize your property bodily and have your own authority, and you will not need any other authority or permission or request from us. [A lengthy restatement of Raimund's possession of the property follows.] And should you be evicted from any part we promise to compensate you for any damages or expenses you may meet or incur by this stipulation. [A restatement of their obligations to him to protect the dowry.] Done at Marseilles, in the house of Bernard of Carcassonne, deceased.

Witnesses: Peter Andree, John Marinus, Marinus de Sala, Gausbertus de Podio Bressano, Vivaudus de Jherusalem, Ancelmus Andree, Peter de Parente, Guillelmus Martini.

61. A Wife Gives all her Property to her Husband, Barcelona, 3 March 981

Like most of the documents from Spain, there is little sign that wives here required their husbands' permission to transact property agreements. This text explicitly declares its author's autonomy, whilst the next shows a wife representing her own and her husband's interests.

Newly translated from: Àngel Fabreca i Grau, ed., *Diplomatari de la Catedral de Barcelona Documents dels anys 844–1260, Volum 1: Documents dels anys 844–1000* (Barcelona: Capitol Catedral de Barcelona, 1995), no. 131.

In the name of the Lord. I, Saborela, am a female donor to you, my spouse, Marcuco.

It is recorded because it pleased me and still pleases me, not ordered by anyone nor persuaded by deceit, but by my own spontaneous will, that I choose with God's will to make a charter of donation to my husband Marcucco of anything I have, and so I do it here; so I give him houses with upper storeys and

MARRIED WOMEN AND MOTHERS

a courtyard, and a piece of land which is above the road, with the oak trees which are there: all my property which came to me from my deceased parents. And all the above is in the county of Barcelona, in Vallensis, in the village of St Eulalia. And the boundaries of the houses with upper storeys and the courtyard are: to the east, the road; to the south, the house of Eroigio and his heirs; to the west, the land of Eroigio; and to the north, the pasture land of Count Suniarius. And the boundaries of the piece of land with the oak trees are: to the east, the road; to the south, the land of Auroco and his children; to the west, the land of Marrazino; and to the north, the land of St Eulalia. All within these boundaries I give to you as written above and completely, without the permission of any man. And I give to you a black bull, and 4 sheep, and 7 breeding sows, and a beehive, and 2 geese, and a packhorse, and a paddock, and a *velada*, and a tub, and a large barrel, and a chest, and a *lito escandale*, and 2 sheets of linen and hemp, and 2 chickens with a cockerel, all completely, [and the land with] entry and exit, and as is made clear.

And I transfer all of the above from my possession to yours, and whatever you might wish to do with it, you will have the power from this present day and for all time. And if I the donor or anyone comes to break this agreement, may they incur the wrath of God, and share the fate of Judas Iscariot, and pay a penalty of double the value of the property; and may this donation remain from now on firm and stable, now and for all time.

The charter of donation was made on the fifth of the nones of March, in the twenty-seventh year of the reign of King Lothar, son of Louis [of France, which at that date incorporated the Spanish borders].

+ Saborella, who made this charter of donation and asked for its confirmation.
+ Eroigio.
+ Teudericus.
+ Undila.
Unifredus, Priest, wrote it on the day and year above.

62. A Wife Defends the Property Rights of herself and her Husband, Barcelona, 17 October 987

This document is written against the background of the aftermath of Al-Mansur's sacking of Barcelona in 985. Such disruption was often used as a pretext to claim property, whether or not rightfully, and court cases frequently increased in its wake.

Newly translated from: Àngel Fabreca i Grau, ed., *Diplomatari de la Catedral de Barcelona Documents dels anys 844–1260, Volum 1: Documents dels anys 844–1000* (Barcelona: Capitol Catedral de Barcelona, 1995), no. 172.

In the year of our Lord, 986 [sic], in the thirty-first year of the reign of Lothar, on the Kalends of July, fourth feast day, Barcelona was besieged by the Saracens and, God permitting it through the impediment of our sins, it was captured in the same month on the second of the nones, and all the inhabitants of that city and its county, who had entered the city by the order of Count Borrell to guard and defend it, were either killed or captured; and there perished all their substance, whatever they had brought with them, including books and royal decrees and all their charters, however they had been drawn up, through which they held all their allodial land [i.e. land free of obligations to a lord] and possessions among themselves and from their relatives up to two hundred years and more previously.

Among these were lost the charters of a certain man, named Adam, and of his wife, named Dulcidia. And so the aforementioned Dulcidia came and sought advice from Judge Aurutio as to what she could do about these charters; and the above-mentioned judge asked whether she could bring witnesses who could say they had heard or seen these charters; and the aforementioned woman produced witnesses who had heard and seen them, who were: Daniel, Bellido and Pasquale. [There follows a list of fifteen documents, including a sale to the couple by a Jew, which the witnesses testify about.] And to this, we, the above-mentioned witnesses, swear, first by God, the Almighty Father, and by Jesus Christ, His son, and by the Holy Spirit, who in this

Trinity is the one and true God, and [they swear] by the place of
veneration of St Clement, the martyr of our Lord, whose church
is situated in the suburb of Barcelona, in the street of St Mary
which is to the west, above whose sacrosanct altar in this foundation we placed our hands and touched it as we swore; [we
swore] that we, the above-mentioned, heard the above charters
read out, and saw others of them written down, and by these
charters the above-mentioned Adam and his wife hold allodial
land firmly and undisturbed; that on the day of Barcelona's sub-
mersion these charters were lost there, and today, according to
the law, the same text which was in those above-mentioned charters is renewed, and we testify that to our knowledge it is done
so rightly and truly, and we swear by the above oath in the Lord.

And I, Dulcidia, female, swear that everything to which
these witnesses have testified in this judgement is true, and
there is no fraud nor evil deceit in this case, but this page renews
our just properties by order of Judge Aurutio.

Written down on the sixteenth of the Kalends of November,
in the first year of the reign of Hugh the Great, King.

+ Daniel + Bellido + Pasquale, we are witnesses and have
sworn this oath.

+ Dulcidia, female, who asked for this judgement to be made
and sworn to by the witnesses, and asked the witnesses to confirm it.

+ Sesenandus + Salomone + Paul, who all heard it.

+ Aurucius, judge.

+ Seniofredus the priest, who wrote this on the above day
and year.

63. Controls over Wives in Northern
Italy, Bologna, 1016

Unlike their contemporaries in certain parts of the south, northern
Italian wives were subject to their husbands, although the latter were
not permitted to dissipate their wives' property when managing it.

Newly translated from: Giovanni Feo, ed., *Le carte bolognesi del secolo XI*, 2 vols., Vol. 1, Istituto Storico Italiano per il Medio Evo, Regesta Chartarum Italiae, 53 (Rome: Istituto Storico Italiano, 2001), no. 19, pp. 41–2.

In the name of God and of our saviour, Jesus Christ. In the time of Benedict the Apostle, and the fourth year of his pontificate in God's name, and the third year of the rule of King Henry [of Germany], 16 January, fourteenth indiction, Bologna. I, Gasperga, wife, in the presence and with the consent of Vuinibaldo [her husband], son of the late Arardo, it pleases me with a free will to make this charter of concession, with which I, Gasperga, daughter of Teberto, spontaneously and willingly make, give and concede to you, Richizo, my dear brother-in-law, and to your heirs in perpetuity, half of what belongs to me, which I bought with a charter of purchase from Arardo above and Ana, his wife, your mother and father, my father- and mother-in-law: lands, vineyards, fields, meadows, pastures, woodland, willow orchards, vines, apple trees and fruit trees of many kinds, and all in this city of Bologna; lands and sites, both with houses and empty, and all in the suburb of Bologna; both in the hills and plains, cultivated, uncultivated – half of everything. And all the above half, as is set out above, I, Gasperga, concede and give to you, Richizo, and your heirs to have and hold and possess in perpetuity by this charter, on condition that wherever it is required you pay the taxes on it. And if it happens that you, Richizo, should die, if you have no sons or daughters, then your portion shall revert to the above-mentioned Vuinibaldo, your brother, and to his heirs. And neither I, Gasperga, nor my heirs shall attempt any molestation or dispute with you, but I, Gasperga, and my heirs promise to defend your right to the above half, Richizo, and to your heirs. And if we cannot defend it, or we go against this charter of concession at any time, by whatever means which human nature is capable of, or we presume to dispute with you any of the above, then I, Gasperga, and my heirs promise to compensate you, Richizo, or your heirs with a penalty of a hundred *mancusi* [gold coins of approximately the same value as *solidi*], and after the penalty is paid, let this charter remain firm as stated above. Done in the city of Bologna, in the above fourteenth indiction.

+ Gasperga who asked for this charter of concession to be made and read out to them [the recipients and witnesses].

+ Vuinibaldus [. . .] consented and signed with his own hand.

+ + Borningo, son of Rimingausi, and Rainfredo, son of the deceased Adarto, asked to witness.

+ This charter of concession was written by the hand of Everardo, Notary, asked by the above woman, then witnessed by witnesses, and handed over. I witnessed, completed and dated it.

64. Sale of Land by Elica of Verona, Verona, 5 December 1127

This document is interesting for the specific statement of the legal framework under which Elica lives and makes her transaction. This is not uncommon in twelfth-century Italian documents, as notaries became more aware of the competing traditions of Roman and Lombard law. A *mundoald* was a male guardian.

Newly translated from: E. Lanza, ed., *Le Carte del Capitolo della Cattedrale di Verona (1101–1151)*, Vol. 1 (Rome: Viella, 1998), no. 58, pp. 117–19.

In the name of the Lord God eternal, 1127 years from the incarnation of our Lord, Jesus Christ, the fifth day of the month of December, fifth indiction.

I, Elica, wife of Crescentius the weaver, inhabitant in the city of Verona, near the Church of St Anastasius, declare that I live according to Lombard law, and with my husband and *mundoald*'s consent and confirmation, and, according to the same law, having notified my nearest relatives, that is Toto and Tebaldo, in whose presence as witnesses I declare that no man has done any violence to me, nor has my husband and *mundoald*, and that of my own free will in the presence of the witnesses I accepted from you, Tedisio, Deacon of the Church of Verona and son of Obizo, inhabitant of the chapter house in the above city of Verona, through your servant, Enverardum, who comes from Monteaurio, eight pounds in weight of good Veronese *denarii* as the price for a piece of arable land which I own in the valley of Fontense, at Monteaurio, in the place called Vigoscolo, near the Church of St Anne. [Clauses defining the boundaries of the land follow. Elica confirms that she hands over the land, and that a penalty of double the price will be payable if she fails to honour the sale.]

Done in the city of Verona.

+ of the hand of the above Elica, who asked for this charter of sale to be made, as above.

+ of the hand of the above Crescentius, husband and *mundoald* of the same woman, who agreed to everything written above.

+ + of the hands of the above Toto and Tebaldo, father and son, the closest relatives of the same woman, who were asked by her to be witnesses and consented, as above.

+ + + of the hands of John Zoco, Weaver, and Odo, and Nigro, living according to Lombard law, witnesses.

I, Albericus, called Bonifacius, Notary, wrote this charter as asked and completed it after the payment and transfer of the land.

65. Will of Maria Salbaconsa, Naples, 1076

Whilst most women in southern Italy were governed by the strictures of Lombard law (see below, Chapter 4, text 99, for an example), those who lived in the coastal duchies of Gaeta, Amalfi and Naples enjoyed the less restrictive boundaries of Roman law. Hence Maria makes her will without her husband's active intervention.

The coinage used here reflects Naples' position as a major centre of trade – gold *solidi*, *tremissi* (worth a third of a *solidus*) and *tari* (worth a quarter of a *solidus*) are all mentioned in the will.

Newly translated from: B. Capasso, ed., *Monumenta ad Neapolitani Ducatus Historiam Pertinentia*, Vol. 2.1 (Naples: Giannini, 1885), no. 523, pp. 314–17. Capasso's editing means that some of the content is not reproduced in his volume. His interventions in the text are marked here as 'Capasso'.

On the fifteenth of November, fifteenth indiction, at Naples. In the ninth year of the reign of Michael and Constantine Porphyrogenitus and Andronicus [Byzantine emperors].

An order made by Maria, honest woman, daughter of Sergius Salbaconsa and his wife, Marenda, both deceased, currently wife of John Gaytanus, about how she has willed her inheritance and property both here and abroad, to remain firmly and permanently, in perpetuity, as set out below.

First of all, she wills that if she dies, all this inheritance worth five hundred Amalfitan gold *solidi*, made up of [worked] gold, silk cloths and charters of security [debts owed to her], and other *solidi*, which are to be collected from diverse persons, should be directed for the good of her soul; and these should be directed for the good of her soul via the hands of Master John, Archbishop of the Church of Naples and via those of the venerable Peter, the priest and administrator of this same church, her spiritual father, and via the hands of Master John, the venerable priest and *cimiliarch* of the same church, all of whom are her executors, and via the hands of her husband or those of whomever's hands this will should appear in; and they should distribute these [*solidi*] in this way: first, if God wills that she should enter the Monastery of St Gregory the Great to become a nun, this monastery should be given a hundred *solidi*; the above-mentioned Master John, the archbishop, should keep fifteen *solidi*; the above-mentioned Peter, the venerable priest and her executor, should keep five *solidi*; then give to the Monastery of St Vincent six *tari*, and to the Monastery of St Andrea at Iscule six *tari*, and to the Monastery of St Archangel in Baiane six *tari*, and to St Maria at Platitia six *tari*, and to St Archangel Sicule eight *tari* for candles, to St Maria de Domina Regina twenty *tari*, to St Menna six *tari*, to St Ciprianum six *tari*, for the cross and to light the altar which she has in the Church of St Apaciri twenty *solidi*, and for her tomb in the Church of St Lucia, twenty *solidi* to take her inherited burial place there, to St Maria at Pugnano eight *tari*.

To Leones, truly, twenty *solidi*; to Maria, her servant, fifteen *tari*; to her [Maria the servant's] children twenty *tari*; to Landulf, her servant, six *tari*; to Stephen and to Guidelmo four *tari* each; to Maria, her servant, eight *tari*; to Tanda Amalfitana, her servant, four *tari*; to Maria, the nun, two *tari*; to John, whom she and her husband raised from the basin [are godparents to, but clearly they had adopted him in some way too, as the will makes further reference to him below], seven *tari*; to Maria Calafata, the nun, four *tari*; to Cesarius and John and Ursus, her nephews, sons of Peter Gaitani, her brother-in-law, four *solidi* each; to Maria Salbacovesa, her sister-in-law, twenty Amalfitan *solidi*; and ten *solidi* should be returned to Stephen Bulcano, her relative.

Whatever remains of the money should be distributed for the good of her soul wherever the executors should see fit.

She also wills that after her death the above-mentioned John, whom she raised from the basin as her son, as above-mentioned, should be given all her lands at Clium; and a cauldron, a pan, a stand and a good box, and a large cask, and another cask, and a bed with all its bedding, all of this to be held by John and his heirs; but he must serve and protect her above-mentioned husband all the days of the latter's life, just as is stated in the charter which she had from the Church of St Maria Maioris.

She wills that all of her land in Pausillipo should be offered to the Monastery of St Sebastian after the death of her husband [the text goes on to state the permanence and comprehensive nature of the gift]; and her land in Euple where the fortress of Lucullanum stood is to go to the monastery on the Saviour's island, to have [Capasso: etc.]; and her land in Porclanum is to go to the Neapolitan church.

Item: She wills that after her death all the portions she has in churches within and outside the city with all their appurtenances [Capasso: etc.] should be given to the Church of Naples, to have [Capasso: etc.], and they should be under the stewardship of whoever is the archbishop at the time.

Item: Her house called 'de Nido' in Fistola Fracta Vico should be offered to the Church of St Dionysius, which she owns half of.

She wills that Altrudula, daughter of the above-mentioned

Stephen Bulcani, should be given the whole strip of land on Caput de Monte, which is at the top of the close of land which she left to her husband, and, if [Altrudula] dies underage or without heirs of her own, this should revert to Maria, mother of the above-mentioned Altrudula, wife of the above-mentioned Stephen Bulcani.

Item: Her husband should be given her whole house in which she lives, in Regio Furcillense, with its lower and [Capasso's cut: the clause would have included upper floors and all appurtenances]; and another house with a garden, similarly placed at Albini; also all her moveables, small and great, of great or small value; the remainder of her inheritance and all her different groups of bondsmen and women, with all their goods [Capasso: etc.] should revert after her death to her husband; after his death, the goods should all be donated to the church for the good of their souls via the hands of the above-mentioned executors or whoever [holds this will].

Item: She wills that after her death, Master Aligernus Buccaplanula should be given as much as belongs to him of the destroyed bath at Capuano, with houses and courtyards and all its appurtenances [Capasso: etc.], a portion of which belongs to him, along with other owners.

She wills that after her death that whatever property she holds from the Church of Naples should be returned to it. Let the Church of Naples also have, without fail, one *tremissus* coin for candles, and let the penalty [for not executing the terms of the will] be six Byzantine pounds of gold.

Written by the hand of Stephen the scribe, disciple of Master John the scribe. Done by Stephen, once Scribe, now Head Scribe, in this twelfth indiction.

+ Maria above.

Witnesses: John, son of Ursus the judge, witness; Gregory, son of Master Saductus, [Capasso: . . .] also a witness; and John Primarius, witness.

This is a copy of the will, made authentically from it at the order of Master Jacob, venerable abbot of the Monastery of

St Sebastian, and read separately by Bernard primarius and Cesarius tabularius of the court of the city of Naples, in the twenty-second year of the reign of our Lord Alexius and the [Capasso: . . .] of his son, John, born to the purple, on the first of June, eleventh indiction [1103].

66. Will of Dulcelina Gomberta, Marseilles, 6 July 1248

Newly translated from: J. H. Pryor, ed., *Business Contracts of Medieval Provence: Selected notulae from the Cartulary of Giraud Amalric of Marseilles*, 1248 (Toronto: Pontifical Institute of Medieval Studies, 1981), no. 93, pp. 230–31.

I, Dulcelina Gomberta, wife of Peter Gomberti, sane of mind but sick of body, but in good and sane memory, I make and order my will announcing it as written below. First, I choose to be buried in the cemetery of St Maria de Accuis, and let me take ten pounds' worth of silver in mixed money from my goods for the benefit of my soul and the redemption of my sins. From which I leave for works to the said Church of St Maria twenty *solidi*; for the works of the friars preachers, ten *solidi*; for the works on St Michael belonging to the nuns of St Poncius ten *solidi*; and for the works of St Martin Marseilles, ten *solidi*; to Hugue Estoperie, twenty *solidi*; to Juliana de Podio Pucinier, twenty *solidi*; from the remainder of the ten pounds I wish to pay my funeral expenses, and if there is anything left let it be distributed for the love of God to the poor, orphans and widows and in other works of mercy identified by my husband, Peter, whom I appoint executor. Also, of my other goods I will by law to my daughter, Guillelma, nun of Molege, twenty *solidi* in money current in Marseilles for each year that she lives. I will the use and profits of all my moveable and immoveable goods and payments and rights to my husband, Peter, whilst he lives. After his death I wish and order that a hundred *solidi*-worth of money current at that time should be given to my daughter, Alamanna, wife of

Hugh Danielis, and I will those a hundred *solidi* to her by law, and I wish and order that she be content with those one hundred *solidi*, because she may not seek anything further from my moveable or immoveable goods. In all the other goods, both moveable and immoveable, and rights and future transactions, I constitute as my heirs John and Aicardus equally, after the death of my husband. If it happens that either of my sons should die without legitimate heirs from his body, then let the other inherit instead. And I wish that this should be my will and that it be valued legally, and if it is not valued as a legal will, then let it be a codicil or some other last will and testament.

Done at Marseilles, in the house of the above Peter Gomberti. These witnesses were called upon and present: Peter Vetulus, John Giraudi, Hugh Daniel, Amaudus de Sancto Jacobo, Hugh Pansa, Peter Aiscardi, Guillelmus Nielli, Guillelmus Danieli, Bertrand de Narbonne.

67. A Married Woman in Charge of Cash, Normandy, Late Eleventh Century

This text provides us with an interesting glimpse of life at Pont Saint-Pierre in eastern Normandy, an area that frequently suffered from frontier warfare. The story can be dated to the late eleventh century, as we know the dates of death of two of the participants: Gerard de Gournay died during the First Crusade (1096–9) while William of Breteuil, son of William FitzOsbern, lived until 1103. The miracle story highlights the villagers' vulnerability in times of violence and warfare, and their local church (dedicated to St Nicholas) as its safest place for storing moveable wealth. The story shows an early example of the circulation of money in village communities. The village reeve was the person responsible for the collection of local taxes and judicial fines. Here, the wife of the village reeve was clearly in charge of safeguarding the cash she and her husband usually kept at home.

Newly translated from: *Miracula sancti Nicolai conscripta a monacho Beccensi*, Vol. 2, ed. A. Poncelet, *Catalogus codicum*

hagiographicorum Latinorum Bibliotheca Nationali Parisiensi, ed.
Hagiographi Bollandiana (Brussels: 1890), c. 24, pp. 419–21.

It is said that another happy miracle took place in the same
church [at Pont Saint-Pierre] that is worthy to be remembered.
It happened at the time of the war between William of Breteuil,
lord of the village of Pont Saint-Pierre, and Gerard of Gournay;
the war had been caused by William, who had given shelter to
one of Gerard's rebellious knights. With both men being at war
and each wishing to damage the other as much as possible, the
villagers, out of fear that their possessions would go up in
flames, began to bring their belongings to safer places. Amongst
them was a lady called Reimburga, the wife of the village reeve,
Geoffrey, who as a parishioner of St Nicholas took to the
church two sacks full of clothes and other things. She asked the
clerk whether he would hide the money she had with her somewhere in the church; he was called Roger, the churchwarden
second after the priest, and who next was subdeacon, but several years later became a priest and monk of Bec (when he told
his story to the author of this account). Roger willingly did
what the lady asked him and he put the sacks in a hidden space
of the church's loft in the hope and belief that nobody would
look there. However, it so happened that some young men in
search of birds' nests – for birds were nesting there – noticed
the sacks full of money hidden in the loft space. They spurred
each other on to this end, that they would return in the dead of
night, having made plans to steal the sacks and take them away.
When night had fallen the conspirators climbed the stairs to
where the sacks were and secretly took them from their hiding
place and fled in the direction of Rouen. In the hope that they
had travelled far enough they found themselves nearby a church
dedicated to St Nicholas. Full of amazement, they wondered
how this might have happened, but without any sense of guilt –
for those imbued by malice do not easily feel penitent – they
again took the road, this time to the Forest of Lumbuel. When
they arrived at the spot in the wood, which they knew and considered safe, they found themselves in the garden next to a
church of St Nicholas. Although they were greatly amazed,

they nevertheless persevered in their crime. With a spade they dug a hole into which they emptied the money from the sacks. They then covered it with ground pine, which in turn they overlaid with earth, level with the surrounding ground. Thereafter, the robbers resumed their flight with the sacks and some leftover money. When they considered that they had been away long enough, and with dawn approaching, they found themselves in front of the door of the Church of St Nicholas [at Pont Saint-Pierre]. Stricken with fear, they fled, leaving the sacks under a stone near the door. In the morning the warden [Roger], who had received the sacks in custody, arrived at the door with his keys. Spotting the sacks at the door, he recognized them and became rigid with fear and anxiety as he was in no doubt that the sacks entrusted to him might not any longer be there [in the loft]. He entered the church where he had hidden them, and when he found them gone he was deeply distressed that the money was missing. While standing forlorn and deep in thought in front of the church door, the lady [Reimburga] joined him. The warden showed her the sacks and told her where and how he had found them. Recognizing the sacks instantly, the woman wrung her hands and exclaimed with great lament: 'Alas, I, miserable woman, have lost everything.' After much wailing, as the female sex is wont to, her husband came along. And when he was told what had happened to his wife, he accused the warden who had been entrusted with his wife's possessions. But the warden excused himself on oath that he knew nothing except that he had truly received her money for safekeeping and that he had put it in such-and-such a place, yet that he had only just discovered the empty sacks at the church door. After they had discussed the matter between them, the warden said to Reeve Geoffrey that the money had probably been stolen: 'Yesterday two notorious youths from the village had walked round the church with a ladder saying that they were looking for birds' nests.' And the reeve replied: 'And where are they now? I just saw Duel' – the name of one of the two youths – 'at home drying his breeches in front of the fire.' Having heard this, the village reeve rushed to the young man's house, where indeed he found him drying his breeches near the fire. He caught him and with great anger and force ordered him to own up, for otherwise he would be severely punished, at worst with the death penalty. What more? Willy-nilly, the youth revealed what he and his mate had done and where the money was hidden. Upon hearing this, the reeve went to the site and when he had found the money where it had been said it would be, he returned all the money to the woman, thanking God and his most clement confessor Nicholas for having returned the money to her.

68. Female Workers in City Regulations, Pisa, 1287

Although it was perfectly possible for single women and widows to work as laundresses, the interest of this text lies in the fact that male launderers were held accountable for the actions of their wives if the latter were also laundresses.

Newly translated from: A. Ghignoli, ed., *I Brevi del commune e del popolo di Pisa dell'anno* 1287, Fonti per la Storia d'Italia Medievale, Antiquitates 11 (Rome: Istituto Storico per il Medio Evo, 1998), pp. 206–8.

On the Launderers

We shall recognize or have recognized by ourselves, or our assessor, or the notary of the assessor, all male and female launderers of Calci and Asciano and all others of the city and district of Pisa; also an oath to the worthy guarantors of the city of Pisa shall be had from them to save and take care of all the cloths which are given to them, or any one of them to wash by anyone, and they shall not take away these cloths on their backs, nor cause them to be taken, nor use these cloths themselves or cause them to be used by anyone, nor to carry and bring back these cloths in their goods, bundles or bags, nor to make bundles of any linen cloth or any other cloth which are given to them to wash, and they will come back to Pisa and bring back the washed cloths to return and restore within eight days in the summer and fifteen days in the winter, making no fight or deceit, but washing for all who ask and want it. And if they should lose or not return any cloths given over to them to wash, and the person reclaiming it is in good faith, or that the cloth should be soaking wet, then they will be held responsible and fined up to ten *solidi*, but if they swear before judges [that they could not help the loss or damage] the fine may be reduced. And we the podestas [appointed leaders] and the captains [of the people] will be held personally responsible for seizing and detaining all and individual launderers and laundresses, both male and female, for all matters on which they are convicted on account of the cloths, and for the debts contracted on account of the cloths, until a whole payment and satisfaction is gained. And let these things be done and permitted, and done without any conflict with other chapters of this law code or that of the Pisan Popolo [i.e. the people's representatives]. And if anyone should transgress the above, let us take them and theirs and penalize them up to forty *solidi* for a single offence, and the accuser will have half. It should be understood that any male launderer will be held [responsible] for his wife, a laundress, or anyone of his family.

69. *Alleged Rape of Wives, England,* *Mid-fifteenth Century*

In the first case below, that of the alleged rape of Marion by the priest Richard Benet, the wording of the indictment is unusual, in that the rape is alleged to have been committed against the consent of both the wife and the husband. In a criminal prosecution for rape, the consent of the husband was irrelevant, as it was an offence against the woman. However, in a civil action of trespass, a husband sometimes complained of a violent assault upon his wife (which had been, in actual fact, a consensual act of adultery), since a trespass against the wife was a trespass against the husband as well, and therefore the husband was entitled to damages. It seems probable that the husband here is attempting to use criminal law for a similar purpose, since it is also alleged – again, unusually – that the defendant, a beneficed cleric, was in the habit of committing adultery with married women against the will of their husbands. In the second case, the defendant William Swayn, another cleric, is presented as a 'common rapist', and this case appears to have been a straightforward criminal prosecution. However, in the last case, the defendant produced a pardon and was discharged (William Swayn did so with the help of six 'sureties' (persons who would guarantee his good behaviour).)

Translated by John Baker from National Archives, KB 27/779, Rex, m. 21d, and KB 27/778, Rex, m. 9.

We thank Professor Jonathan Rose for drawing our attention to these records. We also thank John Baker for his translation.

The twentieth of September, in the thirty-fourth year of Henry VI's reign

Heretofore, namely on the Tuesday following after the feast of St Faith the Virgin in the thirty-third year of the reign of the present lord king, at Blandford Forum, before Sir William Stourton and his fellows, keepers of the lord king's peace and justices assigned to hear and determine various felonies, trespasses and other misdemeanours in the aforesaid county, it was presented by the oath of twelve jurors that Richard Benet, late of Wareham, Rector of the Church of the Holy Trinity of Wareham aforesaid, in the county aforesaid, Priest, on the Wednesday before the feast of St Bartholomew the Apostle in the thirty-second year of the reign of the said lord king, feloniously broke and entered the house of Giles Jackemaker at Wareham aforesaid and assaulted Marion, wife of the same Giles, found then and there, and then and there feloniously raped her and lay with her carnally, against the will of the said Marion and Giles, and against the peace of the lord king. – And that the same Richard on the fourth day of August in the above-mentioned thirty-second year [of the king's reign], at Wareham aforesaid, assaulted Joan Pystell, against the peace of the lord king, and then and there feloniously lay with her in her own house, against the will of the said Joan, and that the same Richard in the night of the Thursday after the Decollation [beheading] of St John the Baptist in the aforementioned year, at Wareham aforesaid, gathering with him a number of wrongdoers and disturbers of the lord king's peace in warlike array, feloniously lay in wait to kill John White of Wareham aforesaid, and then and there assaulted him and beat, wounded and ill-treated him so that his life was despaired of, and would have then and there killed him if he had not been prevented, and that the said Richard is a common night-walker and disturber of the king's peace, as a man living suspiciously and holding and taking the wives of various men in adultery against the will of their husbands, which indictments the present lord king afterwards caused to come before him to be determined in certain cases.

The eighth of October, in the thirty-fourth year of Henry VI's reign, Warwickshire

Heretofore, namely on the Wednesday before the feast of St Bartholomew the Apostle, in the thirtieth year of the reign of the present lord king, at Kenilworth, before Edmund, Duke of Somerset, James, Earl of Wiltshire, John, Viscount de Lisle, and Richard Byngham, the lord king's justices. [. . .]

It was presented by the oath of twelve jurors that William Swayn of Solihull, in the county of Warwick, Chaplain, on the Monday before the feast of the Assumption of the Blessed Mary in the above-mentioned thirtieth year, with force and arms, namely, bows and arrows etc., assaulted Margaret, wife of William Carpenter, in a certain meadow called Holywell Meadow at Solihull, and beat and wounded and ill-treated her, and tied the hands of the same Margaret behind her back, and there feloniously raped her against her will. – And that the aforesaid William Swayn, on the Thursday following after the feast of St Michael the Archangel in the twenty-ninth year of the reign of the said king, with force and arms, namely, staves and knives, broke [into] the house of Margaret Rower at Solihull, and then and there feloniously raped her. – And that the aforesaid William Swayn, on the Tuesday following after the feast of the Epiphany of the Lord in the above-mentioned twenty-ninth year, with force of arms, namely knives and daggers etc., assaulted Margaret Bekenessale at Solihull, and then and there feloniously had carnal knowledge of her and raped her. – And that the aforesaid William Swayn, on the Thursday following after the feast of Corpus Christi in the twenty-eighth year of the reign of the said king, with force and arms, namely staves etc., broke [into] the house of Thomas Grossby at Solihull and assaulted Alice, wife of the aforesaid Thomas, and then and there feloniously raped her. – And that the aforesaid William Swayn, on the Wednesday before Christmas in the above-mentioned thirtieth year, with force and arms, namely staves etc., broke [into] the house of John Rank at Solihull and assaulted Agnes, wife of the selfsame John, and feloniously had carnal knowledge of and lay with her, and that he is a common ambusher of ways where women walk about their business, and a common rapist.

Which indictments the aforesaid justices afterwards delivered before the lord king [i.e. in the crown court].

70. A Rebel's Wife in Custody, Venice, 1326–8

The Venetian Council of Ten was charged with all kinds of public order responsibilities in early fourteenth-century Venice. Among the entries in its register are several dealing with the Doge's daughter, Soranza [Latin: Superancia], who had gone into exile when her husband had been involved in a plot against the Doge, her father. Returning to Venice, Soranza found herself confined to the Nunnery of Santa Maria de Virginibus, her residence there renewed roughly every six months by decision of the council, and exits being granted only at times of illness. On Soranza's history, see Eleni Mahaira-Odoni, 'Venetian colonialism in the Aegean: Sifnos in the thirteenth century', *Harvard Center for European Studies Working Paper Series*, 144 (2007), at www.ces.fas.harvard.edu/publications/docs/pdfs/MahairaOdoni.pdf, accessed 27 August 2009.

Newly translated from: *Consiglio dei Dieci: Deliberazioni misti, registri III–IV, 1325–1335*, Vol. 2, edited by Ferruccio Zago, Fonti per la Storia di Venezia, sez. 1, Archivi Pubblici (Venice: Il Comitato Editore, 1968), pp. 31, 53, 76, 80, 117 and 151.

Entry 72 (12 February 1326)
Agreed that a licence be given to the lady Superancia Super-

ancio, that she may go to stay in the house of Lady Iacobina Dandulo, who is ill, for fifteen days, going and returning in a covered boat at night after the third bell, and not leaving that house.

Entry 137 (14 May 1327)

Agreed that a licence be given to the lady Superancia Superancio, that she may come to the feast of the Ascension at night, in a covered boat, and may come to the quay of the palace. And when she has seen the Blood of Christ, she must go up into the palace and stay there to visit her father, the Doge, for eight days, but she must not come out of the palace, nor descend its steps, by any means. And when she does, she must go by night, in a covered boat.

Entry 205 (12 November 1327)

Agreed that Lady Superancia, on occasion of her illness and for the consolation of the Doge, may come and stay in the palace for fifteen days, not descending from the palace. And when she comes she must come in a covered boat and leave the same way.

[On 26 November of the same year her stay was extended by fifteen days (Entry 211).]

Entry 219 (7 January 1328)

Conceded to Lady Superancia that she can come and stay in the palace for ten days in order to advise her sister, Lady Fantana, who wishes to enter the Monastery of the Minoresses, and to accompany her there, and then to return to the palace on the same day to visit the Doge.

Entry 336 (30 December 1328)

That Lady Superancia, daughter of the Doge, may come and stay here in the palace for eight days on account of the Doge's illness. And if in the meantime the Doge should die, she may go to the funeral and return home with the ladies [...] and stay only one day, and then go back to St Maria de Virginibus to serve the usual order etc.

Entry 446 (24 May 1329)

It is conceded to the lady Superancia Superancio that she may come to the next Feast of the Ascension, and on the day of the vigil she may come to her brother's house, and may come to see the Blood of Christ on the morning of Ascension Day, and then return to her brother's house. And the next day she must return to her place in the monastery, coming and going by covered boat.

71. Impugning Female Honour, Venice, 1290

The incomplete tale here starts with rude words being spoken about a married woman, whose honour is defended by her friend, only for the friend to become the victim of assault and insults. We should note, however, that there seems to be a 'history' between the assailant and the initial victim's husband. The outcome of the case is unknown.

Newly translated from: *Podestà di Torcello, Domenico Viglari (1290–1291)*, ed. Paolo Zolli (Venice: Il Comitato Editore, 1966), pp. 14–16. On the power of evil speech, see the essays in *Fama: The Politics of Talk and Reputation in Medieval Europe*, ed. Thelma Fenster and Daniel Lord Smail (Ithaca: Cornell University Press, 2003).

On Monday 8 May:

Bertholota Paduana de Maiorbio, ordered by the lord to swear and put on oath to tell the truth about the assault on her by the parish priest of Burano Maris, replied and said that, when she was going together with Maria, wife of Vitalis, along the road, Bertucius Cortessius spoke rudely about the above Maria. Which when the said Bertholota heard it, she began to speak to him, intending to say: 'You are speaking badly.' Then the above parish priest raised his hand and hit the above Bertholota with his hand below her left eye, and then twice with his fist on her head: that is, on her face by her nose, so that blood began to flow from her mouth and nose, and another way by her ear, and afterwards he injured her, saying: 'You shameful and vile whore, now I have given you a little punishment, go, and take the bastards you had by Valentio with you, for I am grieving and sad that I did not throw her [Maria] in the water.' Questioned by those present: the priest, Silvester; the priest, Nicolas Mazaporco; the priest, Dominicus Marinus; the priest, Bartholomew de St Peter; Biellus, Deacon; and Victor, Deacon, she replied that the said Maria, wife of Vitalis, when the said priest hit her . . . [The text is crossed out here in the original document. The next six lines are blank.]

The same day:

Maria, wife of Vitalis, ordered by the lord to swear and put on oath to speak the truth of what she knew about the above assault, replied and said that, when Belzufus, on the one side, and Bertucius Cortessius and Benevenutus Sulimanus, on the other, were disputing with each other, and when this case was spoken about, the above Vitalis with several other men went to St Stenum in order to make peace between them, then she, Maria, wife of the above Vitalis, realized that the above Bertucius had said something shameful to her husband. For this reason she called the above Bertholota, saying that she must go with her, and, whilst they were going together along the road, she said that she heard the words which were being said, and that the above Bertucius said that this rumour was about her, and then she said that the above Bertholota Paduana wanted to say she did not know what, and when she went to speak, the said priest of Burano Maris went towards the same Bertholota and hit her with his fist upon her face. And she said that she could see and saw that he took her and wanted to throw her in the water, but the priest stopped him, saying, 'You are acting like a peasant.' And she said also that the above priest called her a mule and other injurious things, and afterwards she went away and went further on towards St Stenum to find her husband, and what they did afterwards she does not know.

The same day:

Benedicta Cavatorta and Nicolota Marino said that they heard the priest saying of the above Bertholota, 'She is a filthy whore; now I have done what I wanted to do, and had it not been for the priest who defended her, it would have gone badly for her.'

72. *The Incarceration of the Bruce Women, Scotland/England, 1306*

In 1306 several women connected to Robert Bruce, namely, his wife, Elizabeth, his daughter, Marjorie, aged approximately twelve; his sisters, Mary and Christian; and his friend, Isabel, Countess of Buchan, were incarcerated (with varying degrees of severity) on the orders of King Edward I (1272–1307). The poignant documentation below is for Isabel, Countess of Buchan, and Mary, who were kept in their cages for a year or so, and for Marjorie, who was spared similar treatment in the Tower of London and instead was sent to her widowed Aunt Christian, and held in captivity in Sixhills Nunnery in Lincolnshire.

Newly translated from: *Documents and Records Illustrating the History of Scotland and the Transactions between the Crowns of Scotland and England Preserved in the Treasury of her Majesty's Exchequer*, Vol. 1, ed. F. Palgrave ([London], 1837), no. 155, items 6–9, pp. 358–9.

It is ordered and mandated by letter of the Privy Seal to the Chamberlain of Scotland or, in his place, his deputy at Berwick-on-Tweed, that in one of the towers of the castle in the same place [Berwick], in a spot which he thinks is most appropriate he is to prepare a cage of strong, latticed timber, well reinforced and strengthened with iron, in which he is to put the Countess of Buchan, whom he will ensure that she be so securely guarded in that same cage that she cannot by any means leave it. And that he will assign to her one or two women of the same town of Berwick, an English woman or women – about whom there is no suspicion whatsoever – to attend her, to serve the said countess with food and drink and other things which may be needed in that place. And that he has her so well and closely guarded in that cage that she shall not speak to any man or woman who belongs to the Scottish nation and that nobody attempts to come near her except the woman or women who shall be assigned to her and those who shall guard her. And that the cage shall be made so that the countess shall have the convenience of a privy, but that it shall be so well and securely put in place that it will not disadvantage the custody of the countess. And that he who has her custody shall be charged to answer body for body [pay with his life if she were to die] and that he shall have an allowance for costs.

And in the same way it is ordered that Mary, sister of Robert of Bruce, previously Count of Carrick, shall be sent to Roxburgh to be kept in captivity there in a cage in the castle.

The same: that Marjorie, the daughter of Robert of Bruce, shall be sent to the Tower of London to be put in a cage in the said manner and that she shall not speak to anyone nor anyone to her, except for the constable of the Tower, who shall be assigned to have custody of her.

[This order was revoked and instead it was decided that:]

The same: that Marjorie, the daughter of Robert of Bruce, shall be sent to Mr Henry of Percy, in order to be delivered to the safety of her Aunt Christian, sister of the said Robert, widow of Christopher de Seton [and Abbess of the Nunnery of Sixhills, Lincolnshire] in order to be kept in captivity in England in the same manner.

73. A Young Married Woman: Petronilla, Lady of Ardres, Flanders, c.1138–9

Newly translated from: *Lamberti Ardensis historia comitum Ghisnensium*, ed. J. Heller, MGH, SS 24 (Hanover: Hahn, 1979), pp. 550–642, at 629.

His [Arnold the Young's] wife, Petronilla, was a young woman, pleasing to God, simple and God-fearing, and either she served God with serious application in church, or amongst her maids put her youthful mind to childish jokes and dancing, and similarly to games and dolls. Often in the summer, inspired at least as much by her simple nature as by the agility of her body, she took off her clothes, except for her shift, let herself go and went into the fish pond, not really to wash or bathe, but rather to cool off and to stretch herself out. Here and there in the streams and bends of the water she was swimming, now face down, now on her back or now disappearing into the water, now whiter than snow she showed herself or her white shift dry above the water in full view of the knights, no less than her maids. Behaving as amicably in these and similar ways and manners, she showed to her husband, to her knights, as well as to her people, how pleasing and just lovable she was.

74. A Couple Rent a House, Bologna, 1071

Newly translated from: G. Feo, ed, Le Carte Bolognesi del secolo XI, Vol. 1, Regesta chartarum Italiae, 53 (Rome: Istituto Storico Italiano, 2001), no. 192, pp. 392–3.

In the name of the Lord. In the year of our Lord's incarnation, 1071, in the fifteenth year of the reign of Henry, son of Henry the Emperor, the ninth of December, ninth indiction. We pray to you, Bononia, daughter of the deceased Bonifanti, that you deign to concede this day in the name of the law in long lease to us, Martin, son of Floro de Orbisi, and Guinichilda, my wife, and our heirs, a piece of your property which is in the suburb of the city of Bologna, next to the road which goes to Castelloni, which is a plot of land with a house, with its entrance and exit on to the public road and with all above and below it, measured in legally defined feet as 24 feet long and 15 feet wide. Its boundaries are as follows: on one side, [the land] is owned by Floro the priest, and on the other side, [the land] is owned by Leo, son of Martin; at one end is the alley between this plot and that of Floro the priest, and at the other end is the alley to the above-mentioned road to Castelloni, and these are the other boundaries. On this present day, I, Bononia will give all the above land and house to you, Martin and Guinichilda, spouses, and your heirs, to have, hold and possess and do with as you please, provided that you pay the due taxes; and after the completion of your – the above petitioners – inheritance, this lease will be renewed by the giving of lime. And thus, on account of this, you, the petitioners, and your heirs, will owe to me, Bononia, and to my heirs, a rental of one silver Venetian *denarius* each indiction, which you will pay to me as rent. And I, Bononia, and my heirs, promise to defend and authorize the above-mentioned property for you, and your heirs, against all men. And if anyone attempts to go against this document of the above lease and does not respect all that is contained there, then let them pay as a penalty a hundred *solidi*-worth of silver *denarii* of Verona, and after the payment of the penalty let the lease in the charter remain firm. Done in the suburb of the city of Bologna, in the above ninth indiction.

+ + the above Martin and Guinichilda, spouses and petition-ers, who asked for the above lease document to be written.

+ + + + + Ugo, son of Girardo de Sichinulfo; and Peter, son of Martin Raviniano; and John, son of Teucio Strilla; and Peter de Richilda de Peter Russo; and Dominico, son of Fusculo del Guascuniano, who were asked to be witnesses.

+ This instrument of lease was written by my hand – Ezo, Notary, son of Arardo, Notary – asked as above, I completed and finished it.

75. A Wife's Account of her Sick Husband, Cured by John Cacciafronte, Martyred Bishop, Verona, 1224

The account translated here is one of many witness testimonies gath-ered by the ecclesiastical authorities as evidence of the sanctity of this murdered bishop. Such inquiries often only reproduce the parts of the testimony that the inquirers felt would serve their case, but they never-theless purport to record the voices of ordinary men and, in this case, women. Berta's 'spoken' words are reproduced here within quotation marks.

Newly translated from: Franco Scarmoncin, ed., *I Documenti dell'Archivio Capitolare di Vicenza (1083–1259)* (Rome: Viella, 1999), no. 34, p. 86. On the process of seeking witnesses to John's miracles, see G. Cracco, 'Ancora sulla *Sainteté en Occident* di André Vauchez (con un appendice sul processo Cacciafronte del 1223–4)', *Studi Medievali*, third series, 26 (1985).

Berta Nicolai of Planeciis of the district of Lacu said under oath that her husband, Nicholas, had lain in bed on account of illness for twelve years, so that he could not raise himself in any way: neither by a low belt, nor by a cord hung where he could take hold of it, nor any other way by himself unless he was turned, and when he heard how God, through the merit of the Blessed John, once Bishop of Vicenza, was performing miracles, he very much wanted and carried on wanting to come to his tomb, and he made a vow to come to the tomb, and next he decided to come to that which he had chosen, and thus he was put on a beast, because he could not come on foot, and was led to the saint, and his children came with him and they spent the night there at the tomb with him for two nights, and thus it happened by God's mercy that he, remaining in prayer at the tomb, by the merit of the Blessed John, was liberated and stood freely for two years (less a week), 'While living with me and I with him,' thanks to the glorious liberation of the Lord God Himself, and the Blessed John, once Bishop of Vicenza, testifying to this, until by the will of God he was taken from this world to the other; and the same Berta said that after this Nicholas was liberated he would go to the fields with her and their children and work, a thing he could not do for twelve years; and she saw that he was liberated at the tomb from Good Friday onwards, and she believed there were three years to come, and thus on that next Wednesday after Easter Sunday he came to the village of Planeciis, in control of his body and freed, and she said that she firmly believed that he had been freed by the merits of the Blessed John, and of this there was public knowledge as there had been many witnesses present.

The priest Avancius of the same village and district said on oath and confirmed that everything which Berta there present had said about the infirmity of the said Nicholas was true, how he saw him thus infirm after he had been priest in that territory for close on two years, and afterwards he came to the tomb of the Blessed John, the bishop, and he returned to the village, and how he saw him well, and coming and going and doing business just like everyone else; on account of which he was very happy and believed firmly that he had been freed by the merits of the Blessed John: and the public knowledge of this and three witnesses prove this miracle.

76. Royal Marital Troubles, France, 1149–50

John of Salisbury's account of the troubled marriage of King Louis VII and Eleanor of Aquitaine during their participation on the Second Crusade is well known. Note how John does not mention Eleanor by name and omits any reference to her after her release from captivity during their visit in Sicily. John's reference to Louis' childlike passion for Eleanor is as famous as it is puzzling.

Newly translated from: *John of Salisbury's Memoirs of the Papal Court*, ed. and trans M. Chibnall (London: Thomas Nelson and Sons Ltd, 1956), pp. 52–3, 60–62.

In the year of grace, 1149, the most Christian King of the French, after the break-up of his forces in the east, arrived at Antioch, where he was honourably welcomed by Prince Raymond, brother of the late William, Count of Poitou [d. 1137]. He was the queen's paternal uncle who owed the king loyalty, love and respect on many grounds. But while they stayed there in order to console, heal and restore the rest of the wrecked army, the closeness of the prince and the queen during their intense and almost endless talks raised the king's suspicions. These became even stronger when the queen wished to remain in Antioch while the king made preparations to leave; the prince endeavoured to keep her with him if he could do so with the king's consent. But when the king hastened to take her away, she mentioned their kinship and said that it would be unlawful for them to remain together any longer, because they were related within the fourth and fifth degree [distant cousins]. Even before their departure word about this had circulated in France, where the late Bishop of Laon, Bartholomew, had calculated the degree of their kinship, but it is uncertain whether the results were right or false. The king was much shaken by this, and although he loved the queen with almost excessive affection, he would have acquiesced in sending her away [i.e. divorcing her] if his counsellors and French noblemen had allowed it. Amongst his secretaries was Thierry Galeran, a knight and eunuch whom the queen had always hated and whom she used to make fun of, but who was loyal and very close to the king, as he had been to the king's father before him. Audaciously he persuaded the king that the queen should no longer remain at Antioch both because 'guilt under kinship's guise could lie concealed' [Ovid, *Heroides*] and because, according to him, a perpetual shame would threaten the kingdom of the French if, amongst all other disasters, the king was to be reported as having been robbed of the queen or left by her, either because he [Thierry Galeran] hated the queen or because he really did think this, perhaps moved by widespread opinion. As a result she was forced to depart and taken on the journey to Jerusalem with the king, and in their hearts mutual anger grew stronger and however much they tried to conceal it, the harm was done. [. . .]

In the year of grace, 1150, the King of the French returned, but on his return journey the galleys of the Emperor of Constantinople [Manuel Comnenus, 1143–80] laid an ambush, during which the queen and all those who were with her on board were captured. The king was advised that he should return to his brother and friend at Constantinople, and a force was already being prepared for the journey, when the galleys of the King of Sicily [Roger, 1130–54] came towards them, set the queen free, freed the king and escorted him back to Sicily, rejoicing in fame and triumph. This was achieved on the orders of the King of Sicily, who feared the tricks of the Greeks and wished very much to display the respect in which he held the king and the kingdom of the French. He came to meet the King of the French and with great honour and sufficient display of horses he escorted him to Palermo, where he honoured him and those who were with him with many gifts. With all the necessary provisions, he accompanied him all the way through his land to Ceprano, the final stop on the frontier between the principality of Capua and Campania, which is part of the lord pope's domain.

There, the cardinals and ministers of the Church met the king and, providing him with all he needed, took him to Tusculum to the lord pope [Eugenius, 1145–53]. The pope received the king with such humanity and respect that it seemed that he was welcoming God's angel rather than a mortal being. He dissolved the disagreement between the king and the queen which had started at Antioch, having listened to each of their stories, forbidding them to raise the matter of consanguinity any more and, confirming their marriage orally and in writing, he ordered them under punishment of excommunication that they not raise any objection against the marriage, nor indeed dissolve it. The king was clearly enormously pleased with this outcome, because he loved the queen in an almost childish fashion. The pope made them sleep in the same bed, which he himself had had decorated with the most precious cloths. And each day of their short visit he endeavoured to bring them together in love through close talks. He honoured them with gifts, and when in the end they departed, although he was a stern man, he could not prevent his tears and he bade them farewell, blessing them and the kingdom of the French, which he thought better than all the kingdoms of the world.

77. A Young Woman Excommunicated for Leaving her Husband, England, Late Twelfth Century

During the twelfth century bishops increasingly became involved in the regulation of marriage and its breakdown. As most of our

documentation comes from episcopal sources, which almost invari-
ably were meant to uphold canon law, it is hard to find evidence
illustrating the feeling of the 'wronged' party. In this excerpt it is
interesting to note that the girl who had left her husband had done so
with her mother's support.

Newly translated from: *Magna vita sancti Hugonis: The Life of St
Hugh of Lincoln*, 2 vols., Vol. 2, ed. D. L. Douie and D. H. Farmer,
(Oxford: Oxford University Press, 1985), Book 4, c. 6, pp. 31–2.

An adolescent girl from Oxford, the daughter of a burgher,
already legitimately married to a young man there, left him in
order to live with another young man (with whom she had
become strongly infatuated) as if she was his wife. Impeached
by her first husband and proven guilty, the bishop [Hugh of
Lincoln, 1186–1200] warned her very sternly indeed to return
immediately to her first husband. Dissuaded by her mother,
who revealed herself as another Herodias by the criminal
advice she gave her daughter, the girl proclaimed shamelessly
that she would rather die than live with him as his wedded
wife. The Lord's man [i.e. the bishop] then took the right hand
of the husband and, mixing persuasion with threats, said: 'If
you want to be my daughter, obey my order and accept your
husband with a kiss of peace, with God's blessing. If you do
otherwise, I shall spare neither you nor your pernicious counsellors.' He ordered her husband too that he give her a kiss of
peace. When he was about to do so, that unhappy girl shamelessly spat at him in the face, even though he was near the altar
in the presence not only of many most reverend men but also of
the bishop himself, and of a great throng of the faithful, who
were there in the church. When all those present felt deeply
ashamed by such insult committed to her husband, the bishop,
with a terror-inspiring voice, said: 'Because you have spurned
my blessing and instead preferred my curse, my curse shall hit
you.' And he instantly excommunicated her. She returned home
obstinately, where, during the few days allowed to her by heavenly mercy to deliberate a more profitable course of action, her
feelings hardened even more and on no account did she repent,
when, suffocated by the evil enemy [i.e. the Devil], she suddenly

exchanged her forbidden and transitory delights for the sufferings that are as just as they are perpetual.

78. The Suicide and Miraculous Revival of an Unhappy Wife, Normandy, Early Twelfth Century

This miracle story was written down by Abbess Marsilia of the Nunnery of St Amand in Rouen (Normandy) and sent to the Abbey of St Amand in Flanders in order that it should be added to its miracle collection despite the fact that the miracle had been witnessed by women (nuns) only. The actual story is a rare account of a married woman's depression and attempted suicide, first in Lisieux and then later in the Nunnery of St Amand at Rouen, where she had been taken by her husband to be cared for by the nuns. For a discussion, see E. van Houts, *Memory and Gender in Medieval Europe 900–1200* (Basingstoke: Macmillan, 1999), pp. 56–7.

Newly translated from: *Historia mulieris suspensae ad vitam revocatae descripta a Marsilia abbatissa Rotomagensi ex mss Elnonensi, Insulensi aliisque, Acta sanctorum*, Vol. 1, Febr., c. 902–3, and previously published in E. van Houts, ed., *The Normans in Europe* (Manchester: Manchester University Press, 2000), no. 23, pp. 80–83.

In the year of the Lord's incarnation, 1107, in the district of Lisieux, a certain distinguished woman incurred such great cruelty from the ancient enemy, not so much because her own sins required it, but rather so that the glory of God through his holy bishop [St Amand] might become more widely known – so that at first she was disturbed by malignant and varied illusions of thoughts. Then, when she had lost her normal perception, she deliberated on what she might do on her own when everyone was absent, namely, that she might lay hands on herself and cut short her life in some way, whether by hanging from a noose or by self-submersion in a river. And she would have done that, except that her husband's unexpected arrival more than once prevented her from doing so. For she had been led astray by a certain foolish woman, who was restless and talkative and approached her with deceitful speeches indoors, outside and in the street, reporting that her husband regarded her with hatred and that he esteemed another woman more and preferred her in carnal union. Soon the woman believed in the lie, just as once Eve believed the serpent, and she fell into a depression which worked towards death. And unmindful of God and the Christian faith, she was always contriving and labouring towards this in all ways that she might put an end to her miserable life by any kind of diabolical act. But divine compassion, which wishes no one to perish, prevented her, so that this deed might not happen in order to multiply the praise and glory of His holy confessor, Amand. And when her husband learned of such a great disgrace, he consoled her repeatedly with pleasant words and consolations, so that she might come to her senses from this diabolical thought, and that she might cheer herself and her relatives, who were saddened by her troubles. Her response to the words of encouragement was full of miserable desperation when she said: 'This won't help me, but direct me to go to hell with the Devil, to whom I am predestined and given.' No compliments, no promises, no threats could prevent her from uttering such worthless words from her mouth.

Then, when beneficial counsel had been sought, they brought the sick woman to the Nunnery of the Blessed Amand, to whom this type of virtue is believed to be especially conferred by the saviour, that no demonic strength may be able to resist him ... Yet, when several people of sound faith and of either sex, who gathered to her for the sake of visiting and encouragement, urgently asked her that she might protect herself with the sign of the salutary cross, she did not agree. Repeating that which is related above, the statement of unhappiness, she but complained more intently. Why should she prolong the delay in going to the pitfall of death? When certain religious men and men of wiser intelligence approached her more directly and comforted her more privately, she responded, with adequately composed speech, that she was completely delivered to the infernal flames and sulphurous punishments, and while detained in this world she would experience that just part of these punishments, and she expected the remainder not long afterwards. Then it was decreed by these men, who were of complete faith and keen in intellect, that she should be blessed by water poured from a chalice and that the next day she would be delivered at once through the hands of priests via the invocation of the name of Christ and His virtue and power. She was immensely astounded when she consciously heard and understood these things, and she began to be more intensely oppressed and to draw frequent breaths. Then with everyone looking on, with diabolical cunning she pretended to behave modestly on the outside, although on the inside she raved with devilish insanity.

And so when evening had come, she was brought beyond the choir and she stood before the altar on which St Amand had been accustomed to celebrate masses. Then when the darkness of night was coming on, those who had brought her and who were appointed to watch over her as her guardians withdrew. O cunning of the Devil, O guile of the ancient serpent in the destruction of the human race. For immediately, the unhappy woman, when she discovered an opportune moment to kill herself, deceitfully suggested to her guardians that from this time they might rest after the guard duty and the labours which they had devoted to her, and that they, exhausted by such great inconvenience, might now yield to sleep. She even pretended to them that she was very much weary and wished to rest with them. Indeed, already seven days and just as many nights had passed since she had been brought there. And when a bed had been prepared and arranged decently enough, she had given herself as if to sleep for a little while, and, looking around, she perceived that no one would be at hand. Wearing only her smock, she furtively climbed up a wall which seemed high. And she twisted part of her head-veil around the top of a column in the wall. Indeed, from the remaining part she prepared an ordinary noose in an amazing manner. Putting her neck into it and jumping straight down, she bent her neck with such great force that a spurt of blood poured forth from her throat and stained a part of the facing wall. Midnight had already passed when one of the guards woke and got up. She did not find the woman in her bed, and after she had checked the whole church she discovered the spot where she was hanging. Shocked by the great horror of it, she realized that the body was rigid and thoroughly lifeless.

On the spot she made noise with a great clamour, announcing by shouting what had happened. When these things had been heard, all the nuns were called together and with a clamour arising from all sides they lamented the miserable dead woman. St Amand was invoked with many sighs and tears, that he should not allow the dignity of this place to perish, but compassionately would think it worthy to come to the aid of those who were running to him. Then, when a light had been lit, the neck of the hanging woman was pulled from the noose, and the lifeless cadaver was thrown down on the floor of the church. Three of the sisters, who were bolder and more experienced, went for the archdeacon – since it was night – and in tears they asked him what to do. He gave the following response and advice to them: that before dawn might break the body should be removed from the church and thrown into a pit in any manner whatever. And the archdeacon followed closely after those women, who returned, and with the nuns crying out and standing there, he stood nearby, wondering at the great cunning of diabolical deceit. Meanwhile, when some of the nuns came nearer, one of them noticed renewed breath quivering in the woman's chest, and saw the face slowly regaining colour, and, indeed, the eyes slowly opening; and then the woman drew a deep breath. The nuns standing there examined this most diligently yet, and, with a huge clamour, they called for the help of St Amand, their patron, and beating their breasts, they multiplied the wishes of their prayers. While these things were being done, they recognized immediately that by the virtue of the omnipotent God and by the intervention of their glorious and admirable Bishop Amand, the soul had returned to the body. Yet on that day and on the following night after the woman had been resurrected she remained without the service of her voice and such was the force of her great strength that four people could scarcely hold her down.

At the dawn of the next day her first words were truthfully:

'Holy lady, pious mother of God, Mary, help me.' And then her mouth opened to the praise of our saviour and His esteemed confessor, and with manifold congratulations to the omnipotent God, she rendered prayers of thanks. Thus, after this had happened, a certain priest was summoned and she made a full confession concerning her past sins and she humbly received absolution. Then she added: 'I give thanks to you, Lord Jesus, you who resurrected me by your favour, by the merits of my lord St Amand, you freed me from the hands of the most pernicious enemy and from the infernal abyss. I believe faithfully in you, with the Father and the Holy Spirit, I adore you and I renounce all displays and traps of Satan.' When this wonderful miracle resounded far and wide, the glorious and wonderful God was magnified in His holy bishop, through whom He worked so many signs miraculously. For just as formerly when placed in the world he resurrected a robber by prayer, who was fixed to a gibbet and was dead, so now in heaven, living with Christ, He recalled to life by His precious merits the miserable woman who had died by hanging, for the praise of our Lord, Jesus Christ, in whom alone and everywhere, with the Father and Holy Spirit, God lives and reigns through infinite ages of ages.

79. *Penitential Texts on Sexual Intercourse, Spain, Ninth to Eleventh Centuries*

On these penitential texts, see above, Chapter 1, text 20.

Newly translated from: *Paenitentialia Hispaniae*, ed. Ludger Körntgen and Francis Bezler, Corpus Christianorum, Series Latina, 156A (Turnhout: Brepols, 1998), pp. 25, 29, 36 and 65.

C: VIII, 135: If a woman should conceive in adultery and should kill her child either in the womb or after it is born, she should never again receive communion, for she has doubled her crime.

S: VI, 92: Women who fornicate and kill their children should do 15 years' penance.

S: VI, 93: If a woman should conceive in adultery in the absence of her husband, and kills the child after the deed, she should never again receive communion, as she has doubled her crime, and should do penance for 17 years.

S: VIII, 129: If a wife is sterile, both she and her husband must abstain from pollution.

S: X, 200: If a woman takes her husband's semen in her mouth or mixes it with food, she must do 3 years' penance.

80. A Dubious Consanguinity Case, Sicily, Twelfth Century

The case documented here is notable for the flimsiness of the husband's case – Hugo's treatment of the story underlines the scepticism with which he viewed the episode, but the chapter heading still imputes blame, rather bizarrely, on to women!

Newly translated from: *La Historia o Liber de Regno Sicilie e la Epistola ad Petrum Panormitane Ecclesie Thesaurium di Ugo Falcando*, Fonti per la Storia d'Italia, 22 (Rome: 1897), chapters 29 and 30. An English translation of the entire work, with introduction, is *The History of the Tyrants of Sicily by 'Hugo Falcandus'*, trans Graham A. Loud and Thomas Wiedemann (Manchester: Manchester University Press, 1998).

On the Changeability of Women

[. . .] At this time Richard of Say came to Palermo, bringing with him his wife, the sister of Bartholomew de Parisio, so that he might send her away and marry the niece of the Archbishop of Capua [Alfanus, 1153–80], a most noble harlot for whom he had long been seized with love. This man stood out for a long time as captain and master constable [regional representative of royal power] of Apulia, when all the others rebelled so many times, and retained his faith unbroken and never broke away from the king. The queen [Margaret of Navarre, widow of King William I of Sicily] welcomed him and gave him the county of Richard of Aquila, Count of Fondi, who was in exile in Roman territory with no hope of return. On the matter of the marriage dissolution, she ordered the courtiers of the court to assemble bishops and other clerics to hear the claims of both sides and come to a fair conclusion. They called the cardinals to attend the examination of the matter, because they had more knowledge of these things, the Roman court frequently dealing with such cases. John of Naples willingly agreed to their request. When the Bishop of Ostia [Hubald, 1158–81, as Pope Lucius III, 1181–5], a man whose honesty was not in doubt, saw his colleague corrupted by money and favours (so that his freedom to judge properly was taken away), he could not be persuaded by their appeals to take part in the case.

The aforementioned Richard thought his marriage should be dissolved on the following grounds: he said that long before he had married, he had had an affair with a cousin of his wife; two soldiers came forward as witnesses to say they had most certainly seen this. The other side denied this, and said that they would prove that this testimony was false, not because they believed that such testimony, even if it were true, could be enough to dissolve the marriage, but because they wished to protect their cousin against the injury of such accusations; the cardinal, anxious to decide the matter speedily, ordered the above witnesses to swear an oath. And thus he dissolved the marriage, ordered both sides on their oath not to cohabit in future, and allowed Richard to proceed to a second marriage; but he ordered Richard's wife to remain without hope of another marriage.

The Sentence of the Cardinal Unjust in Part

The clerics who were present had no doubts that [the cardinal, John of Naples] had done this as a favour to Richard of Say and his friends, but they nevertheless wondered still more that the man who had sinned had been forgiven, whilst his wife, who was blameless, was sentenced to perpetual continence. When they had secretly found fault with his shamelessness, they asked him as a test whether they should make the same order in similar cases; he replied that he was permitted to do things they were not, and that he had not done this now to create a precedent.

81. Infertility? A Jewish Divorce Upheld by the King, England, 1242

The divorce of the prominent Jew, David of Oxford, from his wife, Muriel, and subsequent marriage to a wealthy widow, Licoricia of Winchester, was of interest to King Henry III, due to the wealth of the parties involved, and because Muriel had apparently appealed to the Jewish court (Beth Din) in Paris. The case is discussed in Suzanne Bartlet, *Licoricia of Winchester: Marriage, Motherhood and Murder in the Medieval Anglo-Jewish Community* (London: Vallentine Mitchell, 2009).

Newly translated from: *Close Rolls, Henry III, 1237–1242* (London: PRO, 1911), p. 464.

[Henry III to members of the English Beth Din.]

To the Masters Mosse of London, Aaron of Canterbury and Jacob of Oxford, Jews, greeting. We forbid you from henceforth holding any plea concerning David of Oxford and Muriel, who was the wife of the same. You are not to force him under any circumstances, either to take or retain her or any other woman as his wife. Know for a certainty that if you do otherwise, you will incur grave punishment.

[Written by William, Archbishop of York, Regent in Henry III's absence.]

Whereas by the counsel of the venerable Archbishop in Christ, W[illiam] of York, and sundry of the king's council, it was provided that henceforward no tribunals might be held concerning the Jews in England. And therefore the justices assigned to the custody of the Jews are firmly enjoined on the part of the king to see with regard to all the Jews of England that no courts should henceforth be held throughout England. Consequently, Peytevin of Lincoln; Muriel, who was the wife of David of Oxford; Benedict, son of Peytevin of Lincoln; Vaalin; and Moses of Banbury, Jews, are to appear before the aforesaid archbishop and others of the king's council on the octave of St Michael, wheresoever they may be in England, to show cause why they sent to France to hold a court concerning the Jews of England. And the aforesaid justices are ordered not to suffer David of Oxford to be coerced by the Jews to take or hold any woman to wife except of his own free will.

82. Clerical Celibacy, Lisieux, Normandy, Late 1170s

Amongst married women, priests' wives formed a distinct category for much of the Middle Ages. Priests were supposed to lead celibate lives, especially since the Reform Movement in the eleventh century. That in practice the canon law was very difficult to enforce becomes clear from the following text. In c.1178–9 Bishop Arnulf of Lisieux (1141–81) wrote to Pope Alexander III (1159–81) with a report on one of his canons, Hamo, who had been living in concubinage for more than thirty years and refused to give up his wife. The problem with married priests was that they used ecclesiastical property to provide inheritances for their children. Moreover, as one of the canons working for the Bishop of Lisieux, Hamo would have had significant status; he would have had several priests working under his authority, and the power to assign new priests to churches within the diocese. As we see from the last paragraph of the excerpt below, all these posts were to be reassigned to priests who had not been corrupted by his influence.

Newly translated from: *The Letters of Arnulf of Lisieux*, ed. F. Barlow, Camden third series, 61 (London: Royal Historical Society, 1939), no. 115, pp. 177–8.

To the same [Pope Alexander III]

It has been reported to you that the priest, Hamo, has a public concubine and that he has had her in his house, at his table and in his bed for more than thirty years and that he has had by her many children. And this has always been the case so manifestly and notoriously that it was never even hidden by any veil of sorts to the extent that his rejoicing in the weddings of his daughters acts as the best evidence for this.

As far as he is concerned, when I received the letters from Your Eminence that I should warn him to make amends as well as stop him [cohabiting], I advised him of this in the presence of the chapter meeting of all the brothers many times in addition to your terror-inspiring holy proclamation. But I have not been obeyed at all, because he refuses to leave his spouse's side by day or night. I have several times sent [men] to investigate if he ever shows God or yourself any due respect, but the mother and daughters stripped the two priests I sent, by attacking them cruelly with their hands in a heinous crime; with God's mercy, however, the two were set free by passers-by, as delighted that they had escaped from their hands as from wolves' teeth. The priest, however, presumed that he could defend his crime as if by precedent [i.e. the relationship had been long established] and did not wish to separate from her for one moment. We, however, joined by venerable men, namely four abbots, three archdeacons, a precentor and the furniture-keeper of our church, as well as many canons and religious monks, having read your letters in public, and having observed all lawful proceedings as ordered, we have taken care to seize his property, and we have decided to hand over to you, without any doubt, the evidence of the judgement with the signatures of the witnesses so that no one can deny by anyone's false suggestion on this subject what is so clearly established by your authority and reason. It is surely correct that the punishment of one will lead to the discipline of many, so that it can be said that under your guidance ecclesiastical honesty has triumphed over men with concubines. May your zeal impose silence on the guilty man [i.e. Hamo]. May you assign his churches to more suitable people, which in the diocese of Séez he had handed over to the son of one of his own priests (chosen through a foreign bishop), rather than through the bishop who removed the evil [i.e. Bishop Arnulf himself]. For there are many churches, and what has been accumulated by the evil greed of one can be of use to many honest persons.

83. *An Irregular Liaison, Bologna, 1092*

Unaldus may well have entered the church *after* he fathered Cristina, but the document does not make this clear!

Newly translated from: G. Feo, ed,. *Le carte bolognesi del secolo XI*, document 411, pp. 826–7.

In the name of the Lord God and our saviour, Jesus Christ, and in the year of our Lord, 1092, in the eighth year of the reign of Emperor Henry, the day before the Kalends of March, fifteenth indiction. I, Ermengarda, offer in God's name for myself and for my daughter, Cristina, both from fear of God and for the sake of the souls of Unaldi, Priest, and ourselves, and all our relations living and dead, to you, Gandulf, Abbot of the Monastery of St Maria in Strata, and to your brethren and successors in the same monastery, to have and hold and possess according to the law, all that belongs to my daughter and I, and which belonged to the above-mentioned Unaldi, Priest, whose daughter Cristina is, in the place called Vacarise and in Melitulo and Campo Cauci, and it measures, at the lawful perch of twelve feet (which is called the measure of Liutprand [i.e. a measure set out in the Lombard Laws of the seventh and eighth centuries]), four *staria*, and if there is anything else there which is ours, then let it remain in this charter. We give the above property with its top and bottom and its entrances, and promise according to the law to defend it against all men. And if we do otherwise, then let us pay double the value of the property, whether it has improved or remains of similar value, and after the penalty is paid let the charter of donation remain firm. Done in the above monastery.

+ Ermengarda, who asked for this charter to be written and confirmed.

+ + + Sassolo and Carbone and Zanto, who were asked to witness.

+ Cristina, daughter of the above Unaldo, who asked for this charter to be confirmed and signed.

In God's name, Fredulfus Tabellio wrote it, completed it and confirmed it.

84. A Clerical Portrayal of the Miseries of Marriage, Italy, c.1200

This text is also useful for its opinion on dissolving a marriage.

Newly translated from: *Lotharii Cardinalis (Innocenti III): De miseria humane conditionis*, Vol. 1, ed. Michele Maccarrone (Lucca: Thesauri Mundi, 1955), 17, c. 4–5, p. 23.

On the Misery of the Continent and the Married

A wife competes to have the most expensive dresses and accoutrements, so that the upkeep of the wife always exceeds her husband's fortune; in general, she sighs and cries, day and night, and gossips and grumbles. There are three things that a man should not allow to remain in his house: smoke, rainwater and a bad wife. She'll say, '*She* is better dressed and can go out in public, and is honoured there by everyone; whilst *I* am the most miserable, the only one to be looked down upon in the gathering of women, and am disparaged by all.' Only she wishes to be loved, only she to be praised: praise of another is treated suspiciously as a disgrace to herself. Everything she loves is to be loved, everything she rejects is to be hated. She wishes to win, but her victory is worthless. She cannot bear to serve, but strives to dominate. She wants to be allowed to do anything and not to be prohibited from anything. If she is beautiful, it is easy to fall in love with her, and if she is ugly she will willingly do her best; but it is difficult to keep hold of what is loved by many, and troublesome to possess what no one wishes to have [. . .]

*

You can try it out before you buy a horse, an ass, an ox or a dog, clothes or a bed, even a cup or a jug; but a wife is only glimpsed with difficulty, so that she might not displease before she is taken; whatever might come about in the end, she must be kept by necessity, even if she is fat, stinky, ill, idiotic or proud or irascible, or if she has any corrupted blemish. Only if she is a fornicator can a wife be sent away from her husband. But he, having sent her away, cannot marry another, nor can she marry anyone else. For whoever sends away his wife (unless it is for fornication), and marries another, sins; and whoever marries a sent-away wife also sins. But if a wife leaves her husband, she must either remain unmarried or be reconciled with her husband; the same is true for the husband if he leaves his wife.

85. Christina of Markyate's Heroic Struggle against Marriage, Huntingdon, Early Twelfth Century

Although Christina had been married off by her parents to Burthred, she was still living at home, where they did everything possible to persuade her to have her marriage consummated. In order for a marriage to be lawful it was necessary for consummation to have taken place. However, Christina preferred to visit churches and monasteries. See also Chapter 2, text 37.

Newly translated from: *Vie de Christina de Markyate*, 2 vols., Vol. 1, ed. and trans. P. L'Hermite-Leclercq and A.-M. Legras, (Paris: CRNS, 2007), c. 8–11, pp. 84–9.

[. . .] Instead [of visiting monasteries], they [Christina's parents] forced her to come with them to parties, where an exquisite variety of chosen food alternated with drinks of different kinds, where the music of cythars and harps accompanied the seductive lyrics of singers, in order that they might weaken the strength of her resistance and lure her at last to worldly debauchery. Their tricks, however, completely failed and instead provided proof that in her wisdom she gained the upper hand.

Hear now, at last, what she did and how she behaved at the guild, called 'the merchants' guild', at the greatest and most famous feast of traders. One day, a large crowd of noble people had congregated, presided over by Autti and Beatrix, the most noble of them. It pleased them that at this honourable occasion their eldest and most worthy daughter, Christina, would act as cup-bearer. They ordered her to get up, to take off the gown that covered her, to fasten her dress round her waist and her sleeves round her arms, and to graciously serve the cup to honour the nobles. They counted that the praise of those present on the one hand and her drinking a little on the other would gradually force her heart to agree and her body to be corrupted. Executing her parents' command, she raised her well-placed shield against these two lances. Against the flatteries of human praise, the Mother of God was constantly on her mind and in this effort she was aided by the hall where the feast took place, for due to its enormous size there were various entrances, one of which Christina passed regularly and through which she could see the Monastery of the Holy Mother of God. [Text corrupted in ms.] And she opposed the incentive of drunkenness with the burning shield of her thirst. No wonder that she felt thirsty. During the whole day that she had served the drinkers, she herself had not taken a drop. Late in the evening, however, equally afflicted by hunger and thirst, she drank a little water and so quelled both.

But then her parents, whose plans had been foiled, tried something else. At night they secretly allowed her husband [Burthred] into her room, hoping that if he found the virgin fast asleep he might take her suddenly by force. But by the very providence to which she had commended herself, he found her awake and dressed. She cheerfully welcomed him as a brother and sat with him on her bed, where she presented him with examples about saints and strongly urged him to lead a chaste life. [. . .] Having spent most of the night being regaled with stories of this kind, the young man finally left the virgin alone. When they who had led him to her had heard this they called him a weak and useless man. And, strongly reproaching him, they pressed him again, so that another night they ushered him into her room with the warning not to let himself be weakened by her endless evasiveness and talk of purity. Instead, he ought to achieve his goal, either by request or by force. And if none of this worked, he should know that they were close by and ready to help; he just had to remember to act as a man.

When Christina realized what was going on, she immediately jumped out of bed and with both hands grabbed a peg fixed to the wall, and, trembling, hung on to it, between the wall and the curtains. Meanwhile, Burthred came towards the bed, but when he did not find her as he had expected, he at once notified those waiting by the door. They rushed into the room, and with lights lit they ran around everywhere, acutely conscious that they knew for sure that she had been inside when he had gone in and that she could not possibly have left without them having noticed. Now, I ask you, how do you think she felt at that moment? How she trembled amidst the noise of those who 'were looking for her' [Ps. 34: 4]. Was she not deeply shocked by fear while she imagined herself being drawn in their midst, surrounded on all sides, watched and being threatened to be handed over to her rapist-seducer? Then, one of them, tapping, touched her dangling foot by accident, but because the curtain hung in between it deadened his touch, and, not knowing what it was, he let go. Then Christ's servant regained her courage and prayed to the Lord: 'Let them be turned backward that desire my hurt' [Ps. 69: 4]; and at once they left in disgrace so that she was safe again.

Nevertheless, for a third time, similarly aggressive, Burthred returned to her again. But while he entered through one door, she fled through another, only to discover ahead of her some sort of fence, the height of which, and the razor-sharp spikes on top, didn't allow anyone to climb over it. Behind her, the young man seemed just close enough to be able to grab her, when, incredibly she jumped across it. Safe on the other side, she turned around, and, watching him standing there unable to pursue her, she said: 'Just now I have really escaped from the devil I saw last night.'

86. Religious Conversion Not an Excuse for Separation: Papal Opinions, Rome, Twelfth Century

The Jewish and Muslim communities of medieval Europe came under increasing pressure to convert to Christianity from the twelfth century onwards, a pressure which increased further in the following century. Nevertheless, both popes featured in these texts underline the central tenet that a freely contracted marriage, based upon consent, should not be broken up because of the conversion of one party to another religion. However, some practices were clearly forbidden, such as that of Levirate marriage, practised by Jews, whereby an unmarried brother might marry his late brother's widow (i.e. his sister-in-law), in order to spare her shame (which would have been incurred because she had lost her husband before bearing him children). In practical terms, however, couples of different faiths would have found it difficult to maintain a marriage or agree upon the upbringing of children, as we shall see below, text 91.

Newly translated from: Shlomo Simonsohn, *The Apostolic See and the Jews: Documents 492–1404* (Toronto: Pontifical Institute of Medieval Studies, 1988), documents 62 and 68 (pp. 65 and 72).

Pope Clement III to Gundisalvus, Bishop of Segovia [1187–91]

You asked whether Jews or Christians converted to the Christian faith could live with their wives whom they had married within the second, third or fourth degree [as closely related cousins] whilst infidels, or whether it is permitted for those converted to leave their spouses and enter other marriages. And we responded to Your Eminence, that just as long as those converted to the faith of Christ wanted their wives to remain with them, whether they [the wives] converted or not they should have permission if they want to keep them; they are not, however, to be forced to do so. These [i.e. the wives] living and wishing to remain with them, they [the converted] should not marry others; but if they receive [spouses] in hatred of the Christian faith, as in the text of Gregory, [i.e. Gregory VII, whose letters show him intervening in several irregular marriages], the condemnation of the Creator [shall be] on the one left [i.e. the abandoned spouse, who is now technically married to a bigamist]. Let the law dissolve the marriage [i.e. that of the convert to his original spouse], and she should not be prohibited from taking another in marriage. Nor should they marry within the second or third degree as they did in an alien faith, as was prohibited in the old law, in order that they do not reveal their sisters' shame.

Pope Innocent III to Joscius, Archbishop, and the Cathedral Canons of Tyre, 30 December 1198, Rome

You wished to consult us about infidels converted to the faith and whether, if before their conversion they had married, according to their old laws and traditions, and within the grades of consanguinity set out in canon law [i.e. that they were not too closely related], they should be separated after baptism. On this we gave this response to Your Worship, that a marriage contracted thus before conversion should not be separated after the baptismal font; just as the Jews asked the Lord whether it was permitted to leave a wife for any reason, he responded to them, 'Whom God joins, let no man separate'; because of this, let the marriage remain permitted between them.

Done at the Lateran, the third Kalends of January, first year [of Pope Innocent III's pontificate].

87. Empress Judith as Godmother, France, 826

The poem by Ermoldus Nigellus for Emperor Louis the Pious (814–40), here called Caesar, to celebrate the occasion of the baptism of Harold Klak, a Danish prince, with his wife and children at Ingelheim in 826 presents a splendid portrait of the emperor and his wife, Judith, acting as godparents for Harold and his wife and children. Note that Harold Klak's followers were baptized as Christians too, as Emperor Louis felt that he could only enter into negotiations with the Danes if he could rely on their promises, which as Christians they were not supposed to break, which is also why Emperor Louis is mentioned as being a father (godfather) to Harold. Also present, wearing festive clothing and decoration, were many of Louis' nobles, such as counts (Matfrid of Orléans and Hugh of Tours), abbots (Helisachar of Saint-Aubin and Fridugisus of Saint-Martin), clergy (Hilduinus, the royal chaplain) and army leaders, such as Gerung.

Translated by Lucy McKitterick from *Ermold le Noir. Poème sur Louis le Pieux et Épîtres au roi Pépin* (Paris: Société des Belles Lettres, 1964), ed. E. Faral, pp. 170–75, 176–7 and 180–81.

We are most grateful to Lucy McKitterick for allowing us to use her translation.

With these orders given, and the holy preparations completed, Caesar and Harold make their way to the church. Caesar, in God's honour, receives Harold as he comes up from the waters and, with his own hand, clothes him in white robes. The fair Empress Judith raises Harold's queen from the sacred font and covers her with robes, and Lothar Caesar, son of the venerable Louis, lifts Harold's son from the water. The nobles of the court raise up and dress the king's lords, and the mass of the people does the same for those of the other race. O mighty Louis, what great throngs you give to God! How splendid a perfume rises to Christ from what you have done! The benefits, Prince, of what you have done will long remain with you: you have snatched a nation from the mouth of the wolf and made it a people of God.

Clothed in white and reborn at heart, Harold now approaches the gleaming palace of his illustrious father. Mighty Caesar gives him magnificent presents, all such as may come from Frankish lands, a purple tunic with a jewelled belt, bordered with gold, and a sword for his side which Caesar himself has worn, neatly hanging from golden straps, golden bracelets for his arms, a jewelled baldric hanging at his thigh, and a splendid

crown for his head; golden spurs are set upon his heels, a golden
cloak is splendid on his broad back, and his hands sport shining white gauntlets.

Judith, meanwhile, gives to the prince's wife queenly gifts and
due honour: a golden tunic, indeed, stiff with jewels, such as
Minerva might have woven; a golden headband set with gems
encircles her head, a broad necklace covers her young chest, a
circlet of twisted gold winds about her throat and a lady's
bracelets clasp her arms; upon her firm hips lies a belt wrought
with gold and gems, and upon her back a golden cloak.

    [. . .]

Caesar goes rejoicing through the vast halls to his palace,
zealous as always in sacred matters. Splendid with gold and
glittering jewels, he makes his way happily in the midst of his
court. Hilduinus is at his right hand, Helisachar at his left,
Gerung walks behind the king's footsteps, bearing his accustomed staff, his head crowned with a circlet of gold. Good Lothar,
along with Harold in his robes, follows behind them, splendid in
the gifts they have been given. The handsome young Charles
walks happily in front of his father, glorious in gold, rejoicing at
each step upon the marble floor. Judith, meanwhile, is advancing,
magnificent in queenly glory and splendid dress, accompanied in
great honour by two nobles of the court, Matfrid and Hugh,
both crowned and venerating the goodly queen, each of them
tall and shining in golden clothes. Then follows close behind
the wife of Harold, happy and dressed in the gifts which the
good empress has given her, and Fridugisus is there, too, followed by the learned company of his disciples, white in their
garments and white in the faith, then, in due order, the rest of
the people, arranged in the clothes which Caesar has given
them.

    [. . .]

As soon as the religious ceremony is over, Caesar in his golden
finery prepares to depart, and with him depart his wife, children and all the golden crowd, followed by the clergy in their

white robes. The good emperor reaches his palace, where, in the imperial manner, the feast has been prepared. He lies down happily, with the fair Judith at his side in accordance with his wishes, kissing his knees with her lips. Lothar Caesar and Harold as guest take in their turn the places which the king has appointed them. The Danes are astonished at the feast, astonished at the emperor's weaponry, at his servants, at his fair youths. Justly is this day for the Franks and for the reborn [i.e. baptized] Danes a happy one and one which they will long remember.

88. Peasant Mothers and their Children, France, c.820

Monastic inventories are important sources of information about medieval peasants; they list the names of parents, children and servants; they also give the exact servile status of the peasant. The polyptych of the Monastery of Saint-Germain des Prés, near Paris, drawn up on the order of Abbot Irmino in c.820, lists the landholdings and peasants owned by the abbot and monks of the monastery. The document is partly written in note form: when the inventory states 'the rest is the same', it means by that the same conditions, those which applied in the previous entry. Blank spaces have also been left by the scribe, indicated here by –, presumably names and lists of duties which were to be filled in later on.

In the excerpt below the section on the abbey's lands at Gagny (Val-d'Oise) follows. Most of the peasants listed here are *coloni* ('colons'), that is, hereditary landholders or serfs. But the degree of servile status could differ enormously. These peasants were attached to their landholdings ('manses'), which are described as 'servile' or 'independent', indicating the various conditions allied to the peasants' particular status. The peasants could be acquired or sold with the manses. In return for the right to the land the peasants had to perform duties of various kinds, often on demand. These duties are spelled out in the text: sometimes, the peasants had to sow summer or winter grain, at other times provide horse- and manpower to the abbot and monks if they needed transport, or even to supply the monastery with cash to buy food and provisions for the military when required.

As for measurements: a *bunuarium* or *bonnier* is a land measure of approximately a quarter of an acre, an *arpent* is a length of 120 feet and a *modius* is a land measure as well: i.e. an amount of land which could be sown with grain, or grapes to make wine. *Modius* is also used to indicate a measure of liquid.

Newly translated from: *Polyptique de l'abbaye de Saint-Germain des Prés rédigé au temps de l'abbé Irminon*, ed. A. Longnon, 2 vols., Vol. 2 (Paris: Société de l'histoire de Paris and de l'Isle de France, 1886–95), pp. 41–2 and 44–5.

1. There is at Gagny a demesne manse with a house and other lodgings in sufficient number. There are 4 pieces of arable land, containing 48 *bonniers*, where one can sow 192 *modii* of grain; 66 *arpents* of vineyard, where one can harvest 400 *modii* [of wine]. There is also a forest with a circumference of 2 leagues, providing food for 150 pigs. There are also 14 *arpents* of meadow land, where one can harvest 30 carriages of hay.

2. Ansegarius, colon, and his wife, colon, named Ingalteus, have with them two children, named Ansegildis and Ingrisma. He holds an independent manse, comprising 3¼ *bonniers* of arable land and 3 *arpents* of land for growing grapes for wine. For the army, he pays four *solidi* one year, two *solidi* on alternate years; for pannage [the right to feed pigs on the land or in the forest] he pays 2 *modii* of wine; he works 4 perches [of land] in exchange for doing the winter sowing and 2 perches in exchange for these duties, when one requests them from him: carriage service, hand labour, woodcutting, plus 4 chickens, 15 eggs and 50 shingles.

3. Aldricus, colon, and his wife, colon, named Agentrudis, people of Saint-Germain, have with them two children, named Godinus and Senedeus. He holds an independent manse, comprising 3½ *bonniers* of arable land, 1 *arpent* of vineyard and one half-*arpent* of meadow land. The rest is the same.

4. Richardus, colon of Saint-Germain, possesses an independent manse, having 3½ *bonniers* of arable land, 2 *arpents* of vineyard and 1 *arpent* of meadow land. The rest is the same.

Ditfredus, colon, and his wife, colon, named Waltgudis, people of Saint-Germain, have with them two children, named Ragenteus and Waltgaudis. He possesses an independent manse with 3 *bonniers* of arable land, 2 *arpents* of vineyard and one half-*arpent* of meadow land. The rest is the same.

[. . .]

21. Aregius, colon, and his wife, colon, named Blitgildis, people of Saint-Germain; Ingelhaus, colon, and his wife, colon, named Erlindis, have with them two children, named Rectrudis and Aclevolda; Amalgaudus, serf, and his wife, colon, named Frotbolda, have with them two children, named Frotberga and Lotberta; Lontgaus, colon of Saint-Germain. These four men possess one independent manse, which has 4 *bonniers* of arable land and 2 *arpents* of vineyard. The rest is the same.

22. Baldricus, colon, and his wife, colon, named Ragambolda, have with them three children, named Hiltberta, Gamaltrudis and Hildricus; Adalboldus, colon. These two men possess one independent manse, which has 4 *bonniers* of arable land, 3 *arpents* of vineyard and 1 *arpent* of meadow land. The rest is the same.

23. Gunthardus, colon, and his wife, colon, people of Saint-Germain, have with them three children named —, — and —; Framberta, colon of Saint-Germain; Berengaus, colon of Saint-Germain. These three men possess one independent manse with 4½ *bonniers* of arable land and 2 *arpents* of vineyard. The rest is the same.

24. Stradidius, colon, and his wife, colon, people of Saint-Germain; Bernehaus, colon. These two men possess one independent manse, which has 3½ *arpents* of arable land, — *arpents* of vineyard and one half-*arpent* of meadow land. The rest is the same.

25. Bertradus, colon, and his wife, colon, named Waldina, people of Saint-Germain. They possess one half-manse, which has 1⅓ *bonniers* of arable land and one half-*arpent* of vineyard. The rest is the same.

*

The Serfs:

26. Alaricus, colon, possesses one servile manse, which has 3 *bonniers* of arable land, 2 *arpents* of vineyard and one half-*arpent* of meadow land. He pays for pannage with 4 *modii* of wine; he cultivates 4 *arpents* in the vineyard; he has 2 perches to work in exchange for doing the winter sowing and in exchange for these duties when one requests them from him: carriage service, hand labour, woodcutting, plus 7 *facula* [probably candles], 1 sester [an indeterminate amount] of mustard, 4 chickens and 15 eggs.

27. Dominicus, colon, and his wife, colon, named Ercantrudis, people of Saint-Germain, have with them three children, named Ragenoldus, Hardradus and Hildradus. He possesses one servile manse, which has 3 *bonniers* of arable land and 1 *arpent* of vineyard.

28. Gislemarus, serf, and his wife, colon, named Bertrada, people of Saint-Germain, have with them three children, named Winemarus, Winulfus and Gisledrudis; Wandalfridus, serf of Saint-Germain. These two men possess one servile manse, which has 5½ *bonniers* of arable land and 2 *arpents* of vineyard. The rest is the same.

29. Ansfredus and his wife, colon, named Ermengardis, people of Saint-Germain; Gislebertus, serf of Saint-Germain. These two men possess one servile manse, which has 3½ *bonniers* of arable land and 1 *arpent* of vineyard. The rest is the same.

30. Ingalbertus, colon, and his wife, colon, named Wandelindis, people of Saint-Germain, have with them one child, named Baltadus. He possesses one servile manse, which has 4 *bonniers* of arable land, 1½ *arpents* of vineyard and one quarter of it is meadow land.

31. Adalmodus, colon, and his wife, colon, named Goda, people of Saint-Germain. He possesses one servile manse, which has 3 *bonniers* of arable land and 1 *arpent* of vineyard. The rest is the same.

32. Johannes, colon, and his wife, colon, named Oliva, people of Saint-Germain, have with them four children, named Ingbolda, Ermbradus, Johanna and Ermbolda. He has one

servile manse, which has 2 *bonniers* of arable land and 1½ *arpents* of vineyard. The rest is the same.

89. A Mother's Refusal to Let her Son Hunt, France, 826

The poem by Ermoldus Nigellus for Emperor Louis the Pious (814–40) to celebrate the occasion of the baptism of Harold Klak and his wife and children at Ingelheim in 826 (see text 87 above) also reveals a splendid portrait of the emperor, his wife and their children at a royal hunt. Note how Empress Judith forbids her son, Charles, later known as Charles the Bald (King, 840–77; Emperor, 875–7), to join his father and older brother. Charles' famous grandfather (mentioned in the last sentence) was Charlemagne (768–814), King of the Franks, who conquered most of western Europe and was crowned emperor in 800; the Carolingian dynasty was called after him.

Translated by Lucy McKitterick from *Ermold le Noir. Poème sur Louis le Pieux et Épîtres au roi Pépin* (Paris: Société des Belles Lettres, 1964), ed. E. Faral, pp. 182–5.

We are most grateful to Lucy McKitterick for allowing us to use her translation.

Louis the Pious at the Hunt

At the hounds' clamorous baying the entire wood resounds with the uproar of men's cries and blast after blast on the horn. The wild beasts bound away, flee into the thorny wilds; for them flight holds no safety, nor do the woods and the stream. Among the antlered stags is slain the baby doe; transfixed by the spear, the tusked boar falls too. Joyously, Louis the Emperor takes many a wild beast as game, with his own hand striking them down; while Lothar, swift and strong, in the flower of youth, lays low many a boar. As to the rest of them, his thronged retinue in the meadows all about slays many a beast of every kind. The hound-pack in dire pursuit, the little doe flees through the shady glades, leaping over the willows, until, of a sudden, she comes to the spot where stands a mighty throng, the Empress Judith and young Charles. Determined, she presses on, her only hope is flight, for if fleeing does not save her, then doomed she is. Charles catches sight of her. He longs to course the doe, like his father. Afire with excitement, he demands, he begs for a horse. Earnestly he asks for arms, a quiver and swift arrows; he longs to ride in the chase, as his father does. He pleads and pleads again, but his lovely mother forbids him to go, will not let him have his way. Had not his tutor and his mother held him back, the boy would have raced off on foot, as boys will. Other young lads speed away, capture the little doe as it flees and bring it back to Charles, unharmed. Then, taking up arms suited to his tender years, he strikes the beast in the back as it stands there, trembling. A paragon of boyhood was Charles in every respect, endowed with his father's virtue, ennobled by his grandfather's fame; like Apollo, resplendent in progress through the heights of Delos, bringing great joy to Latona, his mother.

90. Queen Margaret of Scotland's Care for her Children's Education, Scotland, Eleventh Century

The care of Queen Margaret of Scotland (d. 1093), wife of Malcolm III (1058–93), for her children's education is well described by her biographer, who is known only as T. (probably Turgot, Prior of Durham (until 1107/9) and Bishop of St Andrews (1107/9–15)). Her children were Edward (d. 1093), Edgar (d. 1107), Edmund and Aethelred (no dates of death known), Alexander (d. 1124), David (d. 1153), Matilda (d. 1118) and Mary (d. 1115).

Newly translated from: *Vita s. Margaretae Scotorum reginae auctore ut quibusdam videtur Turgoto monacho Dunelmensi*, ed. H. Hinde, in *Symeonis Dunelmensis opera et collectanea*, Vol. 1 (Durham: Surtees Society, 1868), pp. 234–54, at 240.

*

She lavished care on her children no less than on herself, in order that they be nurtured with all diligence and brought up as much as possible in honourable ways. And because it is written in the scripture that 'he who spares the rod hates his son' [Proverbs 13: 24] she had ordered her household steward to punish the children with threats and slapping whenever they were naughty, as young children often are. As a result of their mother's religious care, the children's behaviour was much better than that of other, older, children. They happily and peacefully got on with each other, and the young ones always respected their older siblings. For this reason, during holy Mass, when they followed after their parents to bring offerings [to the altar], the younger children never tried to bypass the older ones, but they went up in order of age, the eldest first. Margaret had her children brought to her frequently, and she herself taught them about Christ and faith in Christ in words appropriate for their age and understanding. She exhorted them diligently: 'Fear the Lord, my children', she would say, 'for those who fear Him will know no need [Psalms 34: 9], and if you love Him, my children, He will give you prosperity in the present life and eternal happiness with the saints in the next.' This was the mother's desire, this her exhortation, this her tearful prayer for her children day and night in order that they should know their Creator through faith, which manifests itself through love; and by knowing, they worship Him, and by worshipping, they love Him, in and above everything, and by loving they will reach the happy glory of the heavenly kingdom.

91. Pope Gregory IX Pronounces on a Custody Case, Strasbourg, 16 May 1229

This case is also commented on and translated by Elisheva Baumgarten, *Mothers and Children: Jewish Family Life in Medieval Europe* (Princeton: Princeton University Press, 2004), pp. 160–61.

Newly translated from: Shlomo Simonsohn, *The Apostolic See and the Jews: Documents 492–1404* (Toronto: Pontifical Institute of Medieval Studies, 1988), document 124.

From your letter we received the question raised at your synod about a certain man who had been led from the blindness of Judaism to the true light of Christ and the true path, and had demanded urgently in your court that his four-year-old son should be assigned to him to be brought up in the Catholic faith, which he himself had accepted, declaring that with the support of the Christian religion and because the boy was below the age of discretion, it was better that he follow him and his faith rather than his mother and her error. To which she responded that since the boy was as yet an infant (on account of which he needed maternal rather than paternal care all the more, and that it was recognized that she had had the onerous and painful labours at his birth and afterwards, and from this legitimate joining of man and woman, it should all the more be called matrimony than patrimony), so the said boy should more appropriately remain with his mother than go across to his father, newly led to the Christian faith, or at least follow neither inclination before he reached the legitimate age; and from this point there were many other dispatches [i.e. pleas submitted by both sides in the dispute to the synod, which sat in judgement and had referred the case to the pope]. You, in the meantime, kept the boy in your power as you wished to consult with us about what should be done. Since truly a son should be in the power of his father, whose family he will follow, not his mother's, and [since] at such an age he should not stay with persons of whom there could be suspicion that they might plot against his health or life; and [since] a boy should thrive and stay with his father, who is not suspect, for three years, whilst the mother of the boy, if he stayed with her, could easily lead him to the error of infidelity, so I responded to Your Fraternity in greatest favour of the Christian faith, assigning the boy to his father.

Done at Perugia, on the seventeenth of the Kalends of June, in the third year of our pontificate.

92. Eleanor of Provence, Queen of England, Writes to her Son, Edward I, England, 1274–85

This letter, written in the years 1274–85, to King Edward I (1272–1307) epitomizes the public language of motherhood, but does not omit to remind Edward of business matters as well.

Newly translated from: National Archives, Ancient Correspondence, SC 1/16, no 157. (We are most grateful to Dr Paul Brand for the transcription of the letter.)

Eleanor, by the grace of God, Queen of England, to our very dear son, Edward, by the same grace, King of England, greetings and motherly wishes. Know, dear sir, that we are very desirous to know good news of you and how you have been since you left us. And we let you know that we are in good heart, thank God, and we left Gillingham sooner than we expected because of the unhealthy air that we found there, and the great vapours which arose each evening, and we came to Marlborough the Friday after Michaelmas. We are in good health, thank God, and would like very much to know the same of you. Also we pray you to remember what we asked of you at Wilton, and that you send us Sir John de Lovetoft and Sir Gauter de Helyon to have their advice on some needs that we have. So we ask you to send them to us as you promised us. Send us also your will and your pleasure if it pleases you. We send you God's greetings. Done at Marlborough, 3 October.

93. A Mother Responsible for a Disabled Child, Sicily, 1138

This document is of huge interest in that it illustrates that mental incapacity did not exclude family members from their patrimonial rights, simply (as in Christian society) gave them the status of perpetual minors, to be represented by others.

Newly translated from: Salvatore Cusa, *I Diplomi Greci ed Arabi di Sicilia*, 2 vols., Vol. 2 (Palermo: Direzione degli Archivi Siciliani, 1882), no. 54, p. 709.

1138: The Christian Walter, son of Walter, buys on behalf of Henry, Archbishop of Messina, from Ali ben Abulkasem ben Abdallah the druggist, called Ibn Albaruki, and from his mother [sic: actually, wife], the daughter of Yusef Alkisi, a house in Palermo, sited behind the old castle on the small street of Ibn Chalfun, which, to the south, goes from the Alebna Gate to the Sudan Gate, and, to the north, leads to Semat Albalat: for the price of four hundred and twelve *tari*, each one missing in weight a grain of gold [i.e. these *tari* were lightweight]. The said daughter of Yusef Alkisi intervenes as the representative of the rights of Abdalla, imbecile, and Belbela, the young children of the above Abulkasem, her husband; and that with the authorization of the Cadi Abulkasem Abderrahman ben Regia [i.e. the local judge], who permits this sale according to the custom of the region, on condition that the money paid over will be spent purely on necessities, and that any spare will be used to obtain equivalent property. The above-mentioned Ali, Abdalla and Belbela each sell their portions of this undivided house: Ali, one-fifteenth; Abdalla, six-fifteenths; and Belbela, eight-fifteenths, and each will receive the price in proportion. This act was communicated to the relevant authorities and written down according to legal norms in the month of Ramadan, 532 [May/June 1138].

94. Care for a Deaf and Mute Child, Normandy, 1145

The story comes from a letter written by Haimo, Abbot of Saint-Pierre-sur-Dives, to the monks of the Priory of Tutbury in England in 1145, recording a series of journeys to Saint-Pierre-sur-Dives in the summer of that year. Following the example set by the Cathedral of Chartres, Norman people filled wagons with the sick and pulled them to the monastery, where, through the intervention of the Virgin Mary,

many miraculous cures took place. This particular miracle story illustrates the case of Rohais of Caen, who, although not the mother, had
taken on the responsibility for a deaf and mute boy.

Newly translated from: L. Delisle, 'Lettre de l'abbé Haimon sur la
construction de l'église de Saint-Pierre sur Dive en 1145', *Bibliothèque
de l'école des Chartes*, 21 (Paris: J. B. Dumoulin, 1860), pp. 113–39,
at 131–4.

But after these minor miracles, some major ones followed.
Amongst the noble women of Caen was Rohais, wife of Ranulf, who also brought a twelve-year-old boy with her. He had
been deaf since birth, and, consequently, mute as well because
he lacked a tongue, and in order to keep my account short, his
mother had given birth to him deaf and dumb; many knew
him, many often put their fingers in his mouth and could hardly
believe their senses, and therefore all that they could understand by touching they explored with their fingers or by talking
to each other. As soon as he opened his mouth he suffered the
lack of a big hole, and could not swallow, he could hardly eat
(even small crumbs given to him) through the narrow opening,
whether it was his food or whether it was his drink. Only by
nodding could one communicate with him, which he could do
expertly, and which he could easily understand. Little by little,
the Mother of God restored his health, in order that the miracle
would turn into a major miracle. For as soon as she had restored
his hearing at our place [the Monastery of Saint-Pierre-sur-
Dives] – in fact not all his hearing, but on one side only – later,
in Chartres, where the aforesaid woman [Rohais] had taken
him, his hearing was restored on the other side as well. And as
soon as he had indicated with new signs of nodding that he
could hear, so at the sound of speech or noise he shook with
fear with sudden realization. Upon his return to Caen he was
welcomed with joy and happiness by its inhabitants about the
gift of God he had received. They rejoiced in seeing that he
could hear, but they despaired that he could not speak at all
because he did not have a tongue. Who of those who knew that
Nature had denied him a tongue would have dared to think
that he might have a tongue in the future?

Meanwhile the noble people of Caen were preparing a wagon to be taken to us, and the day came that the people would take to the road. The woman, whom I mentioned above [Rohais] who had looked after the boy, went to her husband and said: 'My lord, let me bring him with me so that perhaps my Lady, who has shown him to be worthy of her mercy in part, may do so again.' And he said, 'Mad woman, are you joking? You, perhaps, may make him a tongue, but how can he speak if he does not have a tongue?' And she said, 'I am certainly not mad, neither do I make a joke, nor can I make him a tongue, but my Lady who has given him his hearing may give him a tongue. I am convinced, nay, I am sure, that with God all is possible.' Thus inspired by the constancy of her faith, she joined the people in pulling the wagon, and so did the boy whom she brought with her. I shall now recount the miracles. When they arrived at the hamlet of Le Gué Berenguer, halfway down the road to us, a tongue began to grow from scratch in the boy's throat and did so slowly, as if appearing from an abyss; it did not emerge all at once, but grew gradually, so that the miracle increased and revealed the splendour of God more fully. It is not up to us to set out how all those who were there in their gratefulness shed copious tears of joy. That night they spent in the Church of St Mary, Mother of God, holding a vigil in her praise. Meanwhile the tongue was wholly formed, even though the boy could hardly say a word. When dawn broke the following morning, a Saturday [14 July 1145], they resumed their journey to us and experienced neither difficulty nor hardship on the way due to the ardour of their faith and the depth of their joy. A large crowd came towards these noble and famous people, because they had already heard what had happened. All rushed out from the fields and the villages to see the reality of such virtue and fame. They welcomed the arrivals with much joy and praise and, joining those who pulled the wagon, they fought to pull it too. What more?

When night fell they parked the wagon in the church square, and, as was the custom, they lifted the sick and the weak off the wagon. The mute boy with the complete tongue was lifted in it, and all around lights were prepared and candles lit and a vigil was celebrated by all to pray for yet more of God's mercy. The church was full of innumerable people, as was the choir; so great was the crowd gathered everywhere there was not enough space for all. Meanwhile, the mute boy stood up, and, standing in the wagon, he raised his eyes to the top of the highest tower and nudged a weak girl lying next to his feet. She called out loudly, several times, due to the overcrowding, but when it became clear that he did not hear, in the end the priest who was in charge of the cloister approached at the shouts of the girl and began to call to him more loudly. But when the boy remained oblivious to the calls, standing immobile while keeping his eyes fixed to the top of the tower, the priest said indignantly, 'What are you doing? Are you mad and insane, looking up high while not listening to us who are talking to you?' And the boy at once, with his tongue divinely gifted, said: 'But do you not see that my Lady, the Holy Mary, is standing there?' Astonished, the priest, hearing his voice for the first time, said, 'Where is she?' And the mute boy [said]: 'There, in the opening of the tower, don't you see her holding a small boy [wrapped] in her mantle?' At the same time he pointed his finger at her, but only he saw her; he, who alone had acknowledged her virtue. And standing well because she had helped him, all was well with the boy because the boy was the Word, the Word that had become flesh, and therefore it was the boy who saw her, and he, it seemed (who had never spoken before), formed words with his mouth. At once from everywhere in the whole crowd that had gathered together there, a shout rose up to heaven, and the whole church addressed God in praise, offering to God the tokens of thanks and praise. The boy was led to the altar, no longer mute, but speaking and bringing thanks. Such a crowd stood around the boy who talked, but who before had hardly been able to bring forth a word, and saw his tongue and heard him bring forth fresh sounds, but they were not sure which of the two they admired most, the talking or the tongue. Meanwhile, he praised all about the name of his saviour, speaking fully, with sermons, which neither by man nor through man had been said before. But Rohais, who had brought him there, who had brought him up and who loved him above all others, inspired by the advice of the wise, and fearing that something would happen to him, at once took him out of the hands of those who held him and asked for him to be strengthened for the first time by the Lord's sacrament; and when this had happened, he was soon handed over to be listened to once again, for they could not stop looking at him, nor stop hearing him.

95. A Mother Placing her Son into an Apprenticeship, Crete, 1301

Like all business transactions, the placing of children into paid service was recorded before the public notary, in Candia (Heraklion), Crete. See the introduction to text 31, Chapter 2, for more information about these sorts of transactions and the way that they were written down.

Translated from: *Benvenuto de Brixano, Notaio in Candia, 1301– 1302*, ed. Raimondo Morozzo della Rocca, Fonti per la Storia di Venezia, sez. 3: Archivi Notarili (Venice: Alfieri Editore, 1950), p. 86.

16 July 1301

I, Maria, widow of Raynerii de Mutina, inhabitant of Candia, and my heirs, make clear to you, John Sclavo, inhabitant of Candia, and your heirs, that I have agreed with you in the name of God and Christ that my son, Nicolosus, must stay and be with you for five years from now in order to learn the trade of masonry. He must work to your orders, with or without you, according to his knowledge and ability; and he must not stray from your will or service, and you may chastise him with words and blows, and if he should flee from you or not do your will (except if he is ill), you may capture him, with or without help, and return him to your service. And if he does not wish to come to you and you cannot have him, and he does not obey all of your orders, he must be held to serve you for two days instead of one until his time is up [i.e. his apprenticeship would be extended for bad behaviour]. Let it be known that from now until the end of the first year any profit he may make is yours, and then from the second year onwards, half will be his and half yours, and you must teach him in good faith. And, at my expense, at the end of this term [of the contract] you must give him tools to work in his trade. All this, under a penalty of twenty-five *perpera*. [This] charter [to be] firm and lasting.

Witnesses: Comes, Thomasinus Mauro, Franciscus de Basino and Andreas Simiteculo.

To be completed and dated.

96. Will of Gentil, Wife of Jacob of Puigcerda, Pyrenees, 21 November 1306

The Jewish wills of medieval Spain are a fascinating source, giving information about a religious minority as well as evidence for the cultural interaction between Jews and Latin Christians in this region. We include this text as an example of active motherhood because Gentil's children and grandchildren are major beneficiaries of the will.

The document itself is presented in a very specific way: all the use of ellipses are as per the original Latin document, used to denote standard formulaic legal phrases which have been left out (such as those covering the executor's rights and which inbuilt protections applied to the will). The clauses which end 'and unless anything else etc.' are there to cover the maker of the will and her notary in case *they* had missed anything out – very legalistic!

Newly translated from: Robert I. Burns, *Jews in the Notarial Culture: Latinate Wills in Mediterranean Spain, 1250–1350* (Berkeley: University of California Press, 1996), pp. 180–82. The will is discussed at pp. 108–110.

Gentil, wife of Jacob Abrahe Choen the Jew, whilst etc., I make and draw up the will of my goods, ordering etc. In this will, I constitute as my representative and executor in this, my last will, the aforementioned Jacob, my husband, to whom I give etc. . . .

I apportion out to myself from my goods one hundred

Barcelonan *solidi* for the benefit of my soul, which I order to be given and distributed for my soul within one year on the order of my aforementioned husband and the heirs of everything written below.

I leave to Iudea, my daughter, wife of Fabib Salomonis of Barcelona, Jew, for the part of her inheritance by right and which is owed to her five *solidi*-worth of my goods. I institute her my heir in these goods, and the dowry or part of the dowry which I and my aforementioned husband gave to her and her husband on the day of their marriage (and is contained fully and best in the document of their marriage vows), and unless else . . .

Also, I leave to Regina, daughter of Goyo, my late daughter, for the part of the inheritance belonging or owing by right and succession of her aforementioned mother, five Barcelonan *solidi*. And I institute her my heir in these goods, and in the dowry, however much it was, which Goyo, my daughter, and Astruch Deuslosall, Jew, her husband, had and received whilst living at the time of their marriage from my goods and from my husband, just as is contained best (as to the words written therein) in the documents of their marriage vows, and unless anything else etc. . . .

Also, I leave to Goyo and to Atzero, daughters of Adzero, my late daughter, and Astruch Deuslosall, her husband, living up to this point in time, for the part of the inheritance belonging to them and owing to them from my goods through the right and succession of the said Adzero, my daughter, that is, five Barcelonan *solidi* to each of them. And I constitute each of them as my heirs in these things, and the dowry which their aforementioned mother had and received at the time of her marriage to her aforementioned husband, my son-in-law, just as is written better and more fully in the document of their marriage, and they may seek it, and unless anything else etc. . . .

And because any headers and footers to any will then institute universal heirs, I institute as universal heirs to all my residual goods wherever and whatever they may be, my sons, Abraham Iacob and David Iacob Choen, and my aforementioned husband. And I wish and order and substitute that if either of my sons and universal heirs should die at any time without legitimate heirs, let their part of my goods belonging to either of my legatees revert to and remain with the others of my surviving heirs. This all etc. . . .

Witnesses: Bernard Petri, Matheus den Bort, John Baiuli, Bernard Collati, Guido de Piritis, Arnau Ponz, Durandus Salamonis, Salamon Iuceff.

97. Two Agreements between Mothers and Sons, Crete, 1301

These brief documents largely conceal the circumstances leading up to their writing. That widowed mothers required support from their children is clear, but nothing in the legal entries gives us any clues as to whether these agreements were amicable or followed bitter disputes!

The recurrence of 'etc.' in these documents indicates standard passages that the notary would add into a full document, outlining which rights came with properties, or what penalties those contravening the contracts might face. See the introduction to text 31, Chapter 2, for more information about these sorts of transactions and the way that they were written down.

Newly translated from: *Benvenuto de Brixano, Notaio in Candia, 1301–1302*, ed. Raimondo Morozzo della Rocca (Venice: Alfieri Editore, 1950), pp. 11 and 101.

Entry 18: 13 April 1301
I, John, son of the late Teodochi the coat-maker, and my heirs, make a full and irrevocable security to Eudochia, my dear mother, and your heirs, about all that you have and hold, or may have and hold in any way, of the goods belonging to my father above in any way. From now and etc. If anyone etc.
Witnesses: Luchas de Lucha and Paduanus.
To be completed and dated.

Entry 19: same day

I, —, such a widow, make a full and irrevocable security to you, my dear son, —, and your heirs, about all that you must give to me or that which belongs to me by right of promise, bequests or in any other way from your above father, my husband, or from you. Now and etc. If therefore etc.

Witnesses: etc.

To be completed and dated.

Entry 274: 5 August 1301

I, Dominicelus Carutino, make clear to you, Agatha, my dear mother, and to your successors, that I give, donate and concede to you a full and integral half of the profits coming to me and belonging to me which were earned with the wood of Philip Bicontolo. [It is likely that Dominicelus had acted as Philip's agent in a sale of timber.] This agreement etc.

Witnesses: Paduanus and Gibertus Basilio and P. Floriamonte.

To be completed and dated.

Entry 275: same day

Dominicelus, above, made a commission to his mother, Agatha, above, to execute the above. Witnesses: as above.

To be completed and dated.

98. A Stepmother Mentioned in Passing, Venice, 1196

Court cases can often show more than simply the processes of the law – witness depositions can reveal fascinating tangential details quite unrelated to the case at hand.

Newly translated from: *S. Lorenzo di Ammiana*, ed. Luigi Lanfranchi, Fonti per la Storia di Venezia, sez. 2: Archivi Ecclesiastici (Venice: Alfieri Editore, 1947), pp. 97–106.

Peter Pascalis on oath said that as far as he can remember he knows the disputed water is St Lorenzo's. Asked how he knows, he responds that as a boy he saw this when they made fish-traps; he went there just as boys were accustomed to do, and he saw that those who made the fish-traps had to give a fifth of the fish they trapped to the Church of St Lorenzo. Asked if he knew who the people were who made fish-traps and had to donate a fifth of their fish, he replied: 'My stepmother and her children.'

CHAPTER 4

WIDOWS

Introduction

As noted above in the introduction to Chapter 3, widowhood as a life stage for women has attracted considerable attention from historians, especially those keen to find women acting independently in medieval society.[1] Just as marriage is a highly visible life stage for women, so its ending, and the untangling of the property and family ties that it brought with it, was also the subject of record, meaning that the subject is still rich for research, despite the work which has already been done. We have in fact met numerous widows throughout the preceding sections, because they are so well documented, even if we did not highlight their marital status there.

Yet one reason for this high visibility is that widows occupied a uniquely dichotomous position in medieval society: in all cultures and religions, from the earliest times, they had epitomized what it was to be vulnerable, requiring protection, and their fatherless children were often described as 'orphans'; yet at the same time they were objects of suspicion – the uncontrolled or 'merry' widow representing a disruptive force within the family, potentially dissipating the patrimony, if her actions were not kept in check (text 99, however, shows how checks could be maintained even in the direst situations).[2]

Such vulnerability could take various forms. Widows from poorer backgrounds might find that their livelihood disappeared with the death of their husbands: for example, if they were unable to renegotiate tenancy agreements of lands which had been held by their husband (text 100). Others might be forced to liquidate property in order to live (texts 101–2). Some sought security and avoided the perils of being made homeless by entering service with others (text 103). Widows might take out loans – though these were not always a signal of poverty – and other widows might assist them as lenders (texts 104–6). In short, 'widows, orphans and the poor' became the shorthand for those whom the wealthy and powerful, especially rulers and religious leaders, were bound to protect and help.[3] And how those in power treated these groups became a measure by which they were judged at their death.

In the case of wealthy widows, however, their vulnerability derived from, and was increased by, the pressure they often came under from their own family, or that of their late husband, to remarry. In a highly centralized kingdom such as England, we find royal involvement in marriage and remarriage cases from the early eleventh century onwards. During the two (admittedly exceptional) periods of conquests by Danes and Normans, kings Cnut and William the Conqueror were particularly concerned with the vulnerability of widows in times of war, even though their concern did not prevent them marrying suitable wealthy widows off to their followers.[4] Under Henry II (d. 1189) the English crown even had a register of eligible widows drawn up, the wardship of whom (or of whose children) could be profitably farmed out.[5] Remarriage was not uncommon, especially at aristocratic level, although serial remarriage lower down the social scale was not encouraged.[6] Clearly a wife's age in relation to her first husband was a decisive factor in how probable it was that she would be widowed, and for young widows not yet past their childbearing years there may well have been family pressure to contract another marriage. Even if they were older, widows might decide to remarry to pool economic resources, rather than to start a new family – such appears to be the motivation behind some high-profile Jewish widows' second and third unions in thirteenth-century England.[7] High-profile widows might also find themselves under threat during times of war, although the straits in which the two Norman widows found themselves in text 107 might be exceptional.

Widowhood was a time of uncertainty, and even if a significant proportion of marriages did not originate in ties of affection, the loss of a husband could still be a devastating emotional, as well as economic, blow. Documents relating to property transactions can hardly be expected to show up this personal side to the loss of a husband, but creative or literary texts, such as poems and letters, at the very least point up the kind of behaviour a widow might be expected to display (texts 108 and 109).

A widow's position in relation to her own or her husband's family (as we indicated above in our discussion of birth), might depend heavily on whether she had borne children. If so, she maintained some control over economic resources on their behalf, and might therefore be able to enjoy some security until her death. Husbands often appointed their wives as executors of their wills, and even if they did not, would leave instructions as to what their wife might take from the estate. This provision, however, might be revoked if she remarried – documents (and the laws from which they derive, text 110) speak of 'keeping the bed chaste' as a condition of continued support. The fear here was clearly that of a second husband – and possibly a second set of offspring – usurping the rights and property of the children of the first marriage. Whether or not she acted as head of the household, a widow might have to fight for her rights, for example, to retain her dowry (which was hers to dispose of regardless of whether she had children), and litigation cases provide a rich seam of evidence for the trials she could face (texts 111–12).

There is no doubt, however, that the sources teem with active, independent widows, caring for their children whilst also engaging in business transactions and sponsoring charitable causes (texts 113–17). Some of these clearly 'worked the system', perhaps playing on the image of the vulnerable widow to gain some advantage (this may be one reading of text 112).[8] They have therefore presented an attractive subject for women's historians who sought to challenge the notion that medieval women were always dominated by men, and in fact are a group whose voices can genuinely be heard through the filter of the male scribe's transcription. But even if the careers of certain wealthy widows stand out (such as the female crusader in text

118), we cannot generalize from this that widowhood was at all a pleasant time of life. A widow's comfort and self-determination rested largely on a set of contingent conditions – and as her children grew up she might need to make agreements with them to ensure their continuing support for her into her old age (see next section, text 121), if she did not remarry.[9] She might also continue to work for their welfare, as in the highly visible case of the Empress Matilda (text 119). It is no coincidence that many widows instead sought the support of the Church, sometimes removing themselves to convents as lay sisters, and often giving gifts of property to ecclesiastical houses in return for specific benefits.[10]

99. A Widow Makes Alternative Arrangements to Sell her Land, Salerno, 882

This document attests to the strength of legal custom in southern Italy, even in the face of the most difficult circumstances, especially the continuous threats of attacks from Saracens.

Newly translated from: *Codex diplomaticus Cavensis*, Vol. 1, ed. M. Morcaldi et al. (Naples: Hoepli, 1873), no. 86, pp. 109–11.

In the name of the Lord, in the sixth year of the principate of Lord Waimari, Prince, in the month of February in the fifteenth indiction. I, Rodelenda, daughter of Rodelaupi, widow of Polcarus, son of Lupus, declare that the aforementioned Polcarus, my husband, on the day of our marriage and copulation handed over to me the *morgengab* according to the rite and custom of our Lombard people, that is, a quarter-part of all of his property; now I wish to sell this quarter to make use of it, but I have heard – through learned and most wise men – that a woman, when she wishes to sell her things, cannot conceal it, but should notify two or three of her relatives, and equally must go before respectable men and declare everything to them so that the sale may take place with their permission and so that whatever of her property should be given in this way to whomever should through this way remain firm [contractually binding]. And since I heard and knew this from the most learned and wise men and want to observe this custom, just as the law has it, so I told Lupicisi, son of Lupus, and Liodorisi, son of Poricus, who are my nearest relatives, and together we went into the presence of Nandipert the gastald [i.e. a local official in charge of royal land] and told him everything, so that through his permission I might be allowed to sell my quarter for my own uses; but he asked me, the above-mentioned woman, whether I had other closer relatives who were my *mundoalds*, so that I could make this sale according to the law. I told him that I do have two sons, one was taken by the Saracens, and the other is not here because he lives in Nocera, and I cannot have him as my *mundoald* to make this sale with me because he cannot come here on account of this barbarous race of the Saracens, by whom we are surrounded here in Salerno. So the aforementioned Nandipert the gastald, when he saw and heard our declaration, through the fear of all-powerful God and the mercy of our Lord and for the good of his soul gave permission to my relatives to act as my *mundoalds* and to make this sale with me, so that I might live. Thus he asked me, the above woman, if it was my will to sell, and whether I had suffered any violence from any man; and I swore in his presence and that of my relatives that I was not forced [to do this] by violence from any man and was acting through my own free will and according to the law, with my relatives consenting, and through the permission of the gastald. Therefore, I, the above-named Rodelenda, of my own free will and with my relatives, sell to you, Radelghisus, son of Radipertus, all my quarter, which I take by law from the property of Polcarus, my husband, in the place called Mitiliano at Priatu, with my quarter of the house and olive press – but I reserve my moveable goods. And of the above-mentioned quarter which I take from the property of my husband, neither I, Rodelenda, the vendor, nor anyone shall keep any portion of it, but I sell all of it with its boundaries and roads and its use of water to you, Radelghisus, to possess and to do with as you please. And in confirmation of my above sale just as is written above, I receive now from you, Radelghisus, the purchaser, a final price of ten *solidi*-worth of new-figured [newly minted with a different design] Salernitan *denarii* at a rate of twelve *denarii* per *solidus*; and the sale is made so that now and for ever you, Radelghisus, and your heirs, may have and possess what is written above. And I, Rodelenda, promise and obligate myself and my heirs to you, Radelghisus, and your heirs, to maintain and defend this sale, and if anyone does not wish to do so, we promise to pay you double the sale price; and moreover whatever may be remitted to you in any part we shall repay to you at a just price and we swear this according to the laws and this charter as above. And I asked Inghelprandus, Notary, to write it. Done at Salerno in the month and indiction above.

*

+ the above seller, who asked me [Inghelprandus the notary]
to write it.

+ I, Nandipertus, signed it.

+ I, Bestehiso, Notary, am witness.

+ I, Maurus, witness.

+ I, Maurus, signed as witness.

+ I, John, son of Ursus

+ I, Walpertus, witness.

+ I, Rodegari, witness.

+ I, Wiselgardus, witness, signed.

+ I, Ragemprandus, son of Polcarus, am a witness.

+ I, Ursus, son of Alerisus, signed as witness.

+ I, Wiselmari, signed as witness.

+ I, Cusselgari.

+ I, Ursus, signed as witness.

+ I, Ercepertus, signed as witness.

+ I, Radelgis.

100. A Widow Taking Over her Husband's Tenancy, Barcelona, 31 January 975

We should note here that the transfer of the land appears to be carried
out as a result of an earlier request (or perhaps bequest) of Aurundina's deceased husband. The 'tenth' referred to in this and the following
text indicates a portion of property which was transferred to a wife to
support her in widowhood, going to her children on her death. Hence
in this document Aurundina receives half her husband's vineyards outright, plus her tenth to live on out of the property going to her children.

Newly translated from: Àngel Fabreca i Grau, ed., *Diplomatari de
la Catedral de Barcelona Documents dels anys 844–1260, Volum 1:
Documents dels anys 844–1000* (Barcelona: Capitol Catedral de Barcelona, 1995), no. 113.

In the name of the Lord. I, Mirone, also called Lubeto, to you,
Aurundina, and your sons, Unigillus and Venrellos and Guist-
rimirus and Mascharellus.

It is shown that I gave to you, Aurundina, and to your deceased husband Guifredi, father of these sons, two pieces of land to plant vines *per precaria* [under a particular type of lease], which I have in the county of Barcelona, in Maretima, in the village of Primiliano, and, between them, a boundary; and you were to plant them with vines, which you did. And I made to you a legal charter about the half you were to receive for your work and planting, just as I am doing now; and I transfer to your possession, for the planting and work you did there, which you fulfilled as agreed, half of the vineyards; and this is shown. [List of four vineyards with boundaries follows.] And of all that lies within these boundaries and by this charter, I give you these vineyards, to you, Aurundina, woman, half and a tenth, and to your children the other half, by the request of their father. And I transfer them to your possession, on the understanding that you are not allowed to sell them, nor exchange them, nor alienate them, neither you, nor your heirs, unless it is to me or my heirs. And if I or my heirs do not wish to buy them at a just price set by good men, then you are allowed to sell them (with their entry and exit), or do freely with them what you wish; in God's name, you will have that power. But if I, the donor, or any of my heirs or anyone else comes against this donation to divide or break it, it is not worth revenge, but may they or I pay to you double the price of these vineyards; and may this donation remain permanent for all time.

This donation and division was made on the second Kalends of February, in the twenty-first year of the reign of King Lothar, son of Louis.

+ Mirone, who made this donation and asked for it to be confirmed.

+ Suniefredus.

+ Tidela.

+ Suniarus, Subdeacon.

+ Mirone, Priest, who wrote this donation on the day and year above.

101. A Widow and Children Selling Land, Barcelona, 29 December 942

Like many legal documents, the circumstances behind this sale are not stated. It is, however, unlikely that Bonamoca and her children were destitute, since they asked for the price of the property in kind, rather than hard cash.

Newly translated from: Àngel Fabreca i Grau, ed., *Diplomatari de la Catedral de Barcelona Documents dels anys 844–1260, Volum 1: Documents dels anys 844–1000* (Barcelona: Capitol Catedral de Barcelona, 1995), no. 27.

In the name of the Lord. Bonamoca, and my children, who are named: Eigofredus, Sesenanda, Salla, Ennego, Tructeiria, Lupus, Golteredus and Ermovigia are sellers to you, Heno, woman and Senderedo, buyers.

By this charter of sale we sell to you a house with a courtyard and a garden and two pieces of land, which came to me, Bonamoca, through my tenth, and to us children from our father, Sesebaldus, deceased. It lies in the county of Osona, in the territory of the castle of Orsali, in the place called Villa de Montabri. The house, garden and courtyard are bordered to the east, by the house and garden of Uvitiza; to the south, the road; to the west, the garden of Behari; to the north, the road which goes to the house belonging to St Stephen's. And the boundaries of the land are: to the east and south, woodland; to the west, a stream; to the north, the land of Leopardo and his heirs. And the boundaries of the other piece of land are: to the east, the vineyard of Dato; to the south, the vineyard of Bradila; to the west and north, the land of Uviteiro. We sell all of the house, courtyard, garden and two pieces of land within these boundaries, completely, with entrance and exit, for the price of ten *solidi*-worth of goods, and nothing remains to be paid of this price, as is shown. And if we, the sellers, or any man comes to break this sale, may this not be worth revenge, but may we or he pay double the price as reparation; and may this sale be firm for all time.

*

This document of sale was made on the fourth of the Kalends of January, in the seventh year of the reign of Louis, son of Charles.

+ Bonamoca
+ Eigofredus
+ Sesenanda
+ Salla
+ Ennego
+ Tructeirus [sic]
+ Lupus
+ Golteredus
+ Ermovigia, who all made this sale and asked the witnesses to confirm it.
+ Reinardus
+ Argila
+ Dato, above-mentioned.

Eudo, Priest, wrote this charter of sale on the above day and year.

102. A Sale between Women, Palermo, Sicily, 1164

The interest in this document is the fact that it illustrates the multicultural nature of medieval Sicilian society. The vendor and purchaser may both have been of Muslim origin, to judge by their names ('Sitt' in Arabic means 'Lady'), and the sale is made without any male intervention, except that of the vendor's son, suggesting that she was a widow.

Newly translated from: Francesco Trinchera, ed., *Syllabus Graecarum membranarum* (Naples: Joseph Cattaneo, 1865), 66, pp. 218–19.

+ Sitelciul, daughter of Caitseut.
+ Nicolas, her son.

I, Sitelciul, and my son, Nicolas, who have placed the sign of the venerable and living cross on this document above, declare through our own counsel and voluntary choice, without grief or fraud or ill-doing, or any other evil reason or force, but in wholeness of mind and judgement and of our free will, that we sell to you, Sitelciul, daughter of Cala, daughter of John Romaios, and to your daughter, Sitenna, equally, our vineyard with its land and fruit trees, which we obtained with its appurtenances by paternal inheritance from Nicolas Zicri, son of Langobardi, of the same surname, sited in the suburb of Palermo, in the field of Maria, for a price of three hundred and fifty *tari*, each one minus one grain [i.e. these coins were lightweight]. And we have received these whole and legitimate three hundred and fifty *tari* from you, and we have handed over to you the vineyard, and control over it, and we have conceded it to you, Sitelciul, above, and your daughter, Sitenna, by the force of this sale, so that you can possess it for your use, with the power to do with it whatever you want, by sale, or gift, or as a dowry, and to do anything with it which the rule of law allows, just as you have received the right and permission from us to do.

The boundaries of the property are these: to the east is the road and gate, where it has its entrance and exit; to the west is the vineyard of Tziphnis; to the south is the vineyard of the Jew, Thepet; and to the north is the vineyard of Basil Rapti, and there the boundary ends. [A penalty clause follows with a fine of thirty-six *nomismata* if the vendors fail to adhere to the terms of the sale.]

And thus let the present document remain firm, which has been written under the reign of our holy and powerful lord, William the Great King, in the presence of the judges below, by the hand of Kalokyros, Scribe, in the month of October, thirteenth indiction, in the year 6673, in the presence of witnesses:

+ Christodoulos, son of Phillip, with his own hand.
+ Theodoros, unworthy priest of the holy martyr, Pantaleo.
+ Nicolas, son of Leo.
+ Consta, son of Stephen Romaios.
+ Philip, Curator.
+ Christodoulos, Judge.

103. A Widow Entering Service,
Marseilles, 15 April 1248

We have already come across notarial documents recording the entry of children into service. Here, a widow makes similar arrangements for herself for two years, at a relatively high pay rate.

Newly translated from: J. H. Pryor, ed., *Business Contracts of Medieval Provence: Selected Notulae from the Cartulary of Giraud Amalric of Marseilles, 1248* (Toronto: Pontifical Institute of Medieval Studies, 1981), no. 68, pp. 189–90.

I, Isabel, widow of Peter Olivani, in good faith and without any grief, place and give myself and my work to you, Niello Mora and Asbeline, husband and wife, to make a lodging with you and to do every service for you from the first of May coming up for two continuous and complete years, for the price of fifty *solidi* in mixed money current in Marseilles, that is, for twenty-five *solidi* per annum. And I promise and confirm to you that I have received and had this money (renouncing and not counting any money already handed over to me). If it happens that I should die within the above time, I will to you all my present and future goods as the repayment of any service which I do not complete for you.

Witnesses: Marcellus Ponderator, Peter Pinelli and Robert de Dia.

104. A Widow Taking a Loan, Marseilles,
14 April 1248

This loan was not due to poverty, but part of the active business life which women appear to have led in medieval Marseilles, investing in commercial voyages and, in this case, in the ships that made them. Interestingly, the last sentence shows that the widow's note detailing what she owed to Guillelmo de Cadeneto was cancelled; we do not know why. But whether Berengaria de Argileris had fully paid him or not, he was satisfied.

Newly translated from: J. H. Pryor, ed., *Business Contracts of Medieval Provence: Selected Notulae from the Cartulary of Giraud Amalric of Marseilles, 1248* (Toronto: Pontifical Institute of Medieval Studies, 1981), no. 24, p. 134.

On the same day, in the same place.

I, Berengaria de Argileris, widow of Peter de Argileris, confirm and recognize to you, Guillelmo de Cadeneto, citizen of Marseilles, that I owe to you one hundred and thirty-three pounds, six shillings and seven pence of Tours as the price of a half of one-sixth of the ship which is vulgarly called *St Blasius*. Which ship, John de Acco, citizen of Marseilles, bought at Pisa. And I promise and stipulate that I shall give and pay to you the above one hundred and thirty-three pounds, six shillings and seven pence when the above-mentioned ship comes to Marseilles, along with my share of the expenses for the above one-sixth of the above ship which you and I share. You can count against payment of the above sum twenty-five pounds in mixed money current in Marseilles which you had from me, as is recorded in this instrument today, written by the hand of Giraud Amalric, Notary.

By the order of the above Guillelmo de Cadeneto, this note was cancelled.

Witnesses: Guillelmus de Venella, Ponsius de Rogerio, Vincent Sabaterius.

105. Widows in a Loan Agreement, Crete, 1301

By contrast to text 104, this extract does suggest real need on the part of the debtor, to the extent that the document records this as an interest-free loan. See the introduction to text 31, Chapter 2, for more information about these sorts of transactions and the way that they were written down.

Newly translated from: *Benvenuto de Brixano, Notaio in Candia, 1301–1302*, ed. Raimondo Morozzo della Rocca, Fonti per la Storia di Venezia, sez. 3: Archivi Notarili (Venice: Alfieri Editore, 1950), p. 69.

Entry 185: 16 June 1301

I, Pereria, widow of Marco Barastro, inhabitant of Candia, with my heirs, received from you, Tilla, widow of Fini de Parlaso, ten *perpera*, which you lent me out of love from now until the month of September, and for your greater security I give you as pledge my feather-bed, which I have in my power etc. And I must give it to you within four days of you asking for it. This agreement etc.

Witnesses: N. Pizolo, Gibertus and P. Fuscari.

To be completed and dated.

106. The Business Circle of the Jewish Widow, Helea, Crete, 1310

The records here derive from the Venetian domination of Crete. The record of Helea's goods, required by the treasurer on account of her [unstated] crime (possibly her unexpected flight), gives an insight into her business circle.

Newly translated from: *Duca di Candia: Bandi*, ed. Paola Ratti Vidulich, Fonti per la Storia di Venezia, sez. 1: Archivi Pubblici (Venice: Il Comitato Editore, 1965), pp. 24–9.

16 October 1310

A public clamour was made by John de Xeno, stating that when Helea the Jewess, widow of Sambathini Cumani the Jew, disappeared, and it appeared that she had fled, the lord duke ordered that if there was any person keeping her in their house, or who knew where she was, and did not hand her over to the lord within the space of a day, they would suffer a penalty of three hundred *hyperpera* at the lord's will.

And the lord duke ordered that if there was any person who had any goods of the above Helea, Jewess, whether in pawn or for safekeeping, and did not present them to the lord within the space of a day, then they should suffer the above penalty of three hundred *hyperpera*. And if anyone should accuse another of having such goods of Helea in their house and does not present them as stated, let those accused have a fifth of the [false] accuser's goods and they will be believed.

Also if anyone should show or tell where Helea the Jewess is, and that through their accusation the said Helea the Jewess is found, let them have twenty-five *hyperpera* and be held as trustworthy.

Maria, the wife of John de Portu, presented a pair of gilded silver forks and one fork of gold with pearls, an old silver belt, three silver rings, *tabarum blavi clari* [light blue cloths] with vermilion silk, all worth forty *hyperpera*.

Leonard Quirino presented himself, saying that his father-in-law, Marchisinus Barbo, has an old cloak of thick velvet, with plumes and buttons, worth forty *hyperpera*. Also, a ribbon of pearls worth ten *hyperpera*, which he gave in pledge to Anice Languvardo for the above-mentioned ten *hyperpera*.

Sambathi the Jew presented a silk veil, which he holds in pledge for two *hyperpera*.

Iacobus Cortesi presented himself, saying that he had in pledge for twenty *hyperpera* two silver belts from the above Helea.

Maria, once the slave of Maria Pasqualigo, presented herself with a gold fork, which she had as a pledge for three *hyperpera* from the above Helea, and for another twelve *hyperpera*, certain documents of freedom and rents.

Pechiolda, wife of Leonard de Fano, presented a quilt which she had in pledge for four *hyperpera* from the said Helea.

Kali Pelesuno presented herself, saying that she had one pair of silver bracelets from the above Helea by signed pledge.

Lichiacus the Jew, son of Plunarii, presented himself, saying that he had an old cloak of vermilion silk, a Greek shirt, two *auriliares* [probably hairnets] worked in silk and two purses worked in gold as pledges from the said Helea.

Peter Rubeus the mason presented himself, saying that he

had in pledge for fifty *hyperpera* three silver belts, two gold forks and a gold ring with a bar from the above Helea.

Gisla, the wife of Cerculini, had it declared that she had in pledge for fifty-seven *hyperpera* and two *grossi*: one ribbon of pearls, and a silver belt, and seven gold buttons, and a cloak of Tripoli, and a gold ring, and a gold fork.

Potha the Jew, wife of Moses the Jew, had it declared that she has in pledge for six *hyperpera* a feather pillow from the above Helea and for a piece of silk (which she herself sold), and two *auriliares*, and a linen cloth, and a tablecloth.

Agnes, once the nurse of Lord Angelus Quirinus, says that she has in pledge for nine *hyperpera* a fork weighing four ounces and four carats from the said Helea the Jewess.

Alamana the Jewess says that she has in pledge for twenty-four *hyperpera* five buttons, and a belt of silver, and a silver apple from the said Helea.

Marcus Cordano said that he has in pledge for forty-three *hyperpera* a silver belt, and seven gold rings, and two earrings from the above Helea.

John Avonale said that he has in pledge for fifty-eight *hyperpera* a silk mantle with spotted skins, and five gold rings, and a silver inkpot with chains from the above Helea the Jewess.

Sophia of Lesena said that she had as a pledge for five *hyperpera* a silk shirt from the above Helea.

Erini, wife of Pantaleo Spiga, said that she had in pledge for twelve *hyperpera* and five *grossi* a kerchief from the above Helea the Jewess.

Donusdeus Calica had it declared that he had in pledge for twenty-six *hyperpera* two silver belts.

Herina Catelanisa said that she had in pledge for twenty *hyperpera* a pair of silver bracelets, and a silver chain, and a gold ring weighing one ounce from the above Helea the Jewess.

Scolarena, the wife of Cusani the Jew, had it declared that she had in pledge for seven *hyperpera* an old silver belt and a silver bracelet from the above Helea the Jew.

Thomas Cristiano said that he had in pledge [from Helea] two Greek smooth shirts and a silk bonnet (the latter was his daughter's), and he had these things just as is said above [to the value of] six *hyperpera*, and that debt was owed to him for silk which he had sold to Helea the Jewess.

26 February 1315

A public announcement was made by Peter Vido that the lord duke makes it known to all who should receive [reparation] from Helea the Jewess, who is in prison, should come to the Church of St Mark next Monday after nones, to make a list of the creditors of the said Helea, for the bettering of their business.

107. Widows and Political Upheaval, Normandy, 1219

Two charters from 1219 reveal how widows of men who had possessed land in England and Normandy deal with King Philip Augustus of France (1180–1223) in the aftermath of the king's acquisition of Normandy in 1204. Note that Isabella, Countess of Pembroke (d. 1220), widow of William Marshall (d. May 1219), can keep her land in Normandy for free, whereas Alice, Countess of Eu (d. after 1222), not only has to pay a substantial fine for the same privilege, but also has to give certain lands back, and, in other cases, state that she won't try to reclaim any of the land that the king has 'in seisin' (for an explanation of land being held in this way, see the introduction to text 47, Chapter 2), and even has to negotiate with the king to remain unmarried. For a commentary, see D. Power, 'The French interests of the marshal earls of Striguil and Pembroke, 1189–1234', *Anglo-Norman Studies* 25 (2002), 199–225, at 210.

Newly translated from: *Cartulaire Normand*, ed. Léopold Delisle (Caen: Léopold Delisle, 1882), no. 1120, p. 304 (Isabelle of Pembroke) and pp. 304–5 (Alice of Eu).

I, Isabelle, Countess of Pembroke, one-time wife of Lord William Marshall, announce to all present to scrutinize these writings, namely that I have an agreement with the lord king. The lord king has given to me and to my sons our land in Normandy, which my lord William Marshall had been seised with on the day he died, save for his rights and services. Let it be known too that the lord king has given permission to my sons, William and Richard, to enter and leave France, as they wish, with five knights and their followers in such manner that they as well as their knights swear to the lord king that they will not harm him or his kingdom through themselves or through others, and that if they know of anyone who would, they will let the lord king know as soon as possible. Also they who guard my fortresses at Longeville and elsewhere in Normandy should swear to the lord king that they themselves – or by their order – will return them to him by great or small force. I pledge my land in Normandy to my lord the king as surety for firmly keeping these agreements. In order that this may be a firm and stable agreement I confirm the present letters with the authority of my seal. Enacted near Pont de l'Arche, in the month of July, in the year 1219.

I, Alice, Countess of Eu, make it known to all, present and future, that I shall pay a fine to my most beloved Lord Philip, by God's grace, illustrious King of the French, for the county of Eu in this way, that the lord king returns to me the county of Eu, except for the pleas of the sword and his Jews and except for the other justices and services and rights which the county of Eu owes to the Lord of Normandy [i.e. the King of France], as my father and his ancestors did to Henry and Richard, former kings of England, and their ancestors, in such a way that in Driencourt and its appurtenances, in fief and in demesne [land held under certain conditions], I do not reclaim anything nor shall my heirs; nor shall I or my heirs reclaim anything at Mortemer or its appurtenances, neither in hay or in wood nor in fief or demesne, or in any other things that pertain to Mortemer which the lord king is seised with and holds there, nor in Arques, nor anywhere that belongs to Arques.

Moreover, the lord king gives back to me what the Count of Eu, my late husband, held at Roumare when he went to John, King of the English, except for the forest of Roumare, and Neufmarché, where I claim nothing from the Lord King of the

French and except for the pleas of the sword and other justices and services and rights as are owed to the Lord King of the French as Lord of Normandy, and except for any other rights.

And let it be known that the lord king keeps for himself the fief of Bulli, which Robert de Melville holds on his behalf via the bailli [administrative office] of Neufchateau at Driencourt. I also give the lord king my assurance, through me and through my men, that I shall not marry unless by his wish, and that the lord king shall not force me to marry. I and my heirs confirm that we shall not reinforce or weaken any fortress beyond their present condition, unless by the wish of the lord king, and concerning this I give him my assurance through myself and through my men. In order that this may be agreed, I promise to give the lord king 15,000 silver marks of Tours (to the standard weight): 5,000 marks on the feast of the Virgin's Assumption, 5,000 marks on All Saints' Day, 2,500 at Easter and 2,500 on the feast of St Rémi, and by giving these goods to the lord king I have his assurance.

And let it be known that Geoffrey de Capella, on behalf of the king, and Robert de Melville, on my behalf, receive all returns and provisions from the county of Eu that belong to me, in such a way that they shall count towards the payment of my aforesaid debts. Enacted at Melun, in the month of August, in the year 1219.

108. Emma, Widow of King Lothar, Writes to her Mother, Empress Adelaide, France, Late Tenth Century

The following letters were written during the final dramatic moments of the rule of the Carolingian dynasty that had begun with Charlemagne (d. 814). In 987, after the deaths, in rapid succession, of Queen Emma's husband, King Lothar I (d. 986) and her son, King Louis V (d. 987), a member of a rival dynasty was elected King of France: Hugh Capet. In the Middle Ages, letters were more public than private documents and were often preserved in the collections of a famous person's correspondence: in this case, the correspondence of Archbishop Gerbert of Reims, later Pope Sylvester II (d. 1003), who might well have acted as the queen's secretary. This does not necessarily mean that he wrote down letters dictated by her, but that he kept copies of these letters as part of his archive. Similarly, Bishop Adalbero of Laon (977–1031), another player in the dynastic game, kept an archive of correspondence between important people, and some duplicate copies of these letters were also kept by him.

The following three letters have survived amongst the correspondence of Archbishop Gerbert (c.940/50–1003), and all were written in the name of Emma (d. after 988), widow of King Lothar of France (954–86), to her mother, Queen Adelaide (d. 999), herself the widow of King Otto I of the Holy Roman Empire (936–73), her second husband. Adelaide's son, Emperor Otto II (d. 983) was married to Empress Theophanu (d. 997); their son was Emperor Otto III (d. 1002). The correspondence illustrates how aristocratic kinswomen living in different parts of Europe tried to keep in touch with each other and on occasion would ask for (military) support for themselves or their husbands or their sons. The situation of danger in which they often found themselves was as much to do with private quarrels in their immediate family as it was to do with more public politics. The last letter reveals that Queen Emma was kept in captivity by Charles of Lotharingia (d. 991), the youngest brother of her late husband, probably in order to have her at hand as a hostage in negotiations with the new king, Hugh Capet. But Charles was unable to renegotiate his own claim to the throne, and the fate of Queen Emma after this point is unknown.

Newly translated from: *Die Briefsammlung Gerberts von Reims*, ed. F. Weigle, MGH, Die deutschen Geschichtsquellen des Mittelalters 500–1500. Die Briefe der deutschen Kaiserzeit, 2 (Berlin, Zurich and Dublin: Weidmannsche Verlagsbuchhandlung, 1966), no. 74, pp. 104–5; no. 97, pp. 126–7; no. 128, pp. 155–6.

Letter 74 [March 986]

Emma, once queen, now deprived of the light of France, to the Lady Adelaide, forever august empress.

Gone are the days of my delight, gone is the time of my joy, my lady, oh my dear mother, for he in whose flower of life I flourished, in whose reign I ruled until now as wife, he has left me as widow in perpetuity. Oh, bitter day, the second of March, which took away my husband and precipitated me into such misery. May a dear mother listen to the grief and anxiety of her daughter, full of sorrow. I do not wish more than that God has left my mother as a consolation. Oh, when shall I see her, when shall I speak with her? My men wish that I and my son [Louis V] meet with Your Majesty and King Conrad in the vicinity of Remiremont on the borders of the realms on the eighteenth of May. But for me this [is] delay of a thousand years. You know that the princes of Francia have sworn an oath of fealty to both me and my son. In this matter, as in all others, we will follow your judgement as to what to do and what to avoid, so that you shall be known not only as the mother of Queen Emma, but also as the mother of all kingdoms. Moreover, remember your words, that you loved my husband for my sake. May these affectionate feelings benefit your mind, and what you are unable to show in this world, you may recompense through the holy fathers [present gifts to monasteries where the monks would pray for the royal family's wellbeing], that is, the bishops, abbots and monks, the most religious of all God's servants.

Letter 97 [Reims, October 986–February 987]

My grief has increased, oh my lady, oh my sweet name of Mother. When I lost my husband I put my faith in my son. He has now turned into my enemy. My once dearest friends have turned away from me. To my shame, and to that of my whole family, they have put together a most criminal charge against the Bishop of Laon. They have persecuted him and intend to deprive him of his own honour [i.e. his bishopric] in order to injure me with everlasting blame, as if it is the most just case that they take away my honour [i.e. her queenship]. Support, dear Mother, your daughter, filled with grief. My enemies boast that I have left no brother, kinsman or friend to give me support. Dear lady, listen to this: allow your daughter-in-law [Empress Theophanu] back into your grace; may she through you be willing to help me and allow me to love her son [Emperor Otto III], because mine has turned into my enemy. Bind the princes of your realm to me; my alliance will be of benefit to them. The very powerful counts, Otto and Heribert, together with me, will share your counsel. If it is possible, free yourself from business so that we can engage in discussion or, alternatively, collect together your wise and age-old thoughts. Prepare attacks against the Franks from unexpected angles so that their ferocious aggression against us be blunted. And, meanwhile, tell us by letter or by a trustworthy envoy what we should do.

Letter 128 [August /September 988]

With what anxieties my lady Emma is afflicted and to what extent she is troubled is witnessed by her letter sent a long time ago to Lady Empress Theophanu. We have sent a copy of the letter to you so that you know what has happened – although nothing has happened to her benefit – and in order that you investigate the cause of deception, if indeed it is deception. Previously, it has been clear that you have been the most famous lady and mother of the kingdoms, whom we believed to be willing to come to the support of her daughter, once loved, in all our dangers, wherever they occurred. Whether your authority has been taken away, or whether it does not exist, it does not help your grieving daughter. We beg you to enquire by ambassadors from Charles whether he wishes to deliver her to you or whether to deliver her to somebody else's trust. It seems that he is obstinately determined to keep her with him so that he does not seem to have taken her for no reason.

109. A Fictional Widow's Lament on the Loss of her Husband, Austria, 1194

This lyrical text composed by Reinmar of Hagenau on the death of Leopold V of Austria in 1194 is a classic piece of male ventriloquism: it tells us very little about the actual grief of Leopold's widow, but does offer a glimpse into the ideal of female behaviour in these circumstances.

Newly translated from: Karl Simrock, *Lieder der Minnesinger*
(Eberfeld: R. Friderichs, 1857), pp. 123–4.

They say that summer now is here, and delight has
        come, and I too should be glad as I was before,
But rather I guess and say that death has dazed me,
What I would like to get over, I never will.
What do I need, for spring to triumph?
Leopold, man of all my joy, lies there in the grave,
Whom my eye never saw to mourn,
In him I have lost the world,
A loss so pitiful as happened to no man.

To me, poor woman, it was too comfortable,
When I remembered him,
How my welfare lay in his life.
Now I shall have this no more,
So all the time passes in misery that I should still live.
The mirror of my happiness is lost,
Whom I alone in all the world chose to be my
        consolation,
And whom I must now be without.
When they told me he was dead, straightaway I lost
        the heart's blood of my soul.

The death of my dear lord has forbidden joys to me,
So that I should instead do without them.
But there must not come anger from it,
Thus I must struggle with my need,
And my plaintive heart is full of misery.
The one who cries for him all the time, this is I,
Many-blessed man, it pleased me only to live
        with you,
Now he is there: what should I do here?
Be merciful to him, Lord God!
For this virtuous guest never came to your servants.

110. Customs on Widows' Property, Amalfi, Thirteenth Century

For an introduction to this source, see above, text 59, Chapter 3.

Newly translated from: *Consuetudines Civitatis Amalfie*, ed. A. de Leone and A. Piccirillo (Cava de Tirreni: Di Mauro Editore, 1970), pp. 44–52.

That a Woman after the Death of her Husband Might Be Lady and Mistress

A married woman after the death of her husband is lady and mistress of the property of her husband, to hold and control and manage these goods on behalf of her children and her husband's heirs for as long as she keeps the bed of her husband [remains chaste]. That is, if she does not marry nor go to a second marriage and whilst she keeps the bed of her husband, then she must be clothed and given shoes out of the property of her husband, but she must not sell or give away even one pennyworth of her husband's property. If her children and the heirs of her husband do not wish to give her a living, as set out, and do not buy these things, then the aforementioned woman will be allowed to keep her husband's bed, and by decree of the local officials, to sell as much of her husband's property as is sufficient for her living and subsistence, and, if she has such, to have male and female servants. After her death, everything which remains of her husband's property and hers will belong to her children and the heirs of her husband after expenses for her funeral have been extracted in order to give her an honourable obituary, just as she would have seen fit. Nor is it possible to leave or give more property to one child than another, unless it is the wish of the woman, and the other children, and her husband's heirs; otherwise the property should be divided equally between them just as in the custom of Amalfi, and also this woman, their mother, can give away or sell the portion which comes to her to whomever she wishes, or do with it what she wishes. If, however, she has underage children and keeps her husband's bed, then she is the legal guardian of these children and can alienate (with the decree of the bailiff and judges) as much of her husband's property as is necessary for her life and subsistence and that of her children, and for the debts left by her husband, without a requisition being made to her underage children. And all the goods of her husband must come to her and be in her power for her to keep on behalf of her children and the heirs of her husband, notwithstanding if her husband had appointed another legal guardian for her children; but the mother must give a trustworthy guarantor to faithfully govern and keep safe the property of the children.

11. When a Woman [Widow] May Have a Dowry and Quarter and When Not

But if after the death of her husband [a woman] does not wish to keep the bed of her husband, if she was a virgin at their marriage and was deflowered by him, leaving two sons or daughters, or one male and one female by him from constant marriage, or they had more than two of each sex, then, when her dowry is restored, she may also have a quarter of her husband's property. But if she was not a virgin when she married her husband, whether married before or simply cohabiting with another man, then when her dowry is restored she may not request the aforementioned quarter, nor have it, except from the man who deflowered her. If indeed more than two sons or daughters remain from her and her husband, whether she was married as a virgin or not, the wife may have, as well as her dowry, a portion of the property according to the number of people, including her and her children, that are dividing it; so if there are three children, then she gets a quarter; if five children, then she gets a fifth [sic]; and so on even if there are twenty children or more. And her children may not provoke or compel her to make her divide the property, but she can make them do so if she wishes to keep her husband's bed. If the man dies, having left children by a first wife, the second wife who has no children cannot remain the mistress of her husband's property. If, however, the second wife has children, once the dowries and rights of the first and second wives are settled, whatever remains must be divided between the children of each marriage, and the second wife can be the mistress of the property of her children. If the wife predeceases her husband she will not have a quarter of his property. Also, only male heirs or brothers may succeed to their brothers and all male and female relatives in the father's line, and sisters and all women are excluded [i.e. the customs were restricting inheritance to an exclusively male line, a phenomenon visible in most of Italy at this time].

111. A Widow in Conflict with her Brother, Barcelona, 8 May 1000

Like earlier documents from Barcelona featured above (texts 100 and 101), this one deals with the aftermath of war, and, quite unusually, shows a woman sitting in judgement, Lady Hermisindis (the wife of Count Raimundus, Count of Barcelona).

Newly translated from: Àngel Fabreca i Grau, ed., *Diplomatari de la Catedral de Barcelona Documents dels anys 844–1260, Volum 1: Documents dels anys 844–1000* (Barcelona: Capitol Catedral de Barcelona, 1995), no. 345.

At the court of the Lady Hermisindis and her judges, who are Guifredus, Aurutius and Bonushomo, in the palace of the count in the city of Barcelona, and in the presence of Hudalardi, Viscount, and all the palace officials, and with the noble and powerful men attending, there came into their presence a certain little captive woman called Matrona —, tearfully pursuing a quarrel about her inheritance and paternal property, which her brother, Bonushomo, had been dissipating and embezzling all the time that Matrona had been kept in the chains of captivity in the city of Cordoba. Bonushomo had been left with the above-mentioned patrimony when Barcelona was captured by the Saracen people; and he usurped the inheritance and patrimony of this his sister, Matrona, together with that of her deceased husband, Ennego, with whom she had had a daughter, who had remained with her in the above-mentioned captivity after his [Ennego's] death; and by sales and exchanges and various charters he had by deceit transformed and transferred all the property to himself, desiring it to be taken away from the above-mentioned Matrona.

When the appointed judges checked this, their insistent discussion and this story was related to the ears of the above-mentioned countess: that the above-mentioned Bonushomo appeared guilty of the related things and contrary to the truth. Then the countess sent the aforementioned judges and Viscount Hudelardus, and they held a meeting with other respected men about this inheritance, which this Bonushomo had transformed by the deceitful use of many charters to his own hands, and they found much had been traded for a little, and usurped by this evil deceit, and in a contrary manner, so that the aforementioned inheritance now remained sold or given away from Matrona's possession, and so that afterwards no repetition of it could be started or occur; and since the aforementioned men recognized this, they gave a small portion in place of the large inheritance to the aforementioned Matrona, which consisted of: 5 *modiatas* of vines, called De Goma, the boundaries of which are [the boundaries are described]; and small lands in the place called Mogoria [boundaries described]; and other land [boundaries described].

And to fulfil the use and right of justice, and to avoid future lawsuits and disagreements, Bonushomo handed over these aforementioned vineyards and lands and gave them and transferred them from his property and into the hands and possession of Matrona entirely at the court of the countess in the presence of the viscount and judges, in order to repay the debt of the inheritance and properties which he had fraudulently dissipated.

And on account of this, in the name of God, and out of respect for my lord and master, Count Raimundus, I

Hermesindis, by God's grace, Countess, along with my judges, ordered this, our judgement, to be confirmed and corroborated, so that no one should ever dare in any way to tamper or change it, because it is not permitted that our statutes, drawn up and corroborated with our judges, should in any way be infringed or challenged, but we decided that they should remain always stable, and remain forever firm and established by the vigour of law. Thus we consign and transfer the vineyards and lands above irrevocably into the hands and dominion of the above Matrona, into her property, with their entrances and exits, so that she can do with them whatever she wants. And whoever presumes to challenge this, may he not profit by his audacious temerity, but may he pay a penalty of a pound of gold as his punishment; and from now on may these vineyards and lands, written by pen on this page and corroborated, remain and be in the possession of the aforementioned Matrona perennially.

This document of consignment was made on the eighth of the ides of May, in the fourth year of the reign of Robert the King, son of Hugh.

    + Bonucius, Priest.

    + Hermesindis, by the grace of God, Countess, who ordered this consignment and made it perpetually valid by the addition of my seal.

    + Uvifredus, Judge.

    + Vuilara, Priest.

    + Gelmirus.

    + Audegarius, Priest.

    + Giscafredus, called Bonutius Glaromontensis.

    + Silvus, Deacon.

    + Borrellus, brother of Ugo.

    + Suniefridus Garricensis.

    ✳ Aurucio, Judge. [The Chi Ro symbol is an anagram of the first two letters of Christ in Greek and some officials, such as Judge Auricio, used it as their mark.]

    + Ato, Priest, healer of children.

    + Bonushomo, Deacon, wrote it on the day and year above.

112. A Widow Disputing the Status of Land, Normandy, c.1206

Basilia de Glisolles (d. c.1207), known as Basilia de Formeville on her seal, found herself in dispute with the monks of the Abbey of La Noe (Normandy) c.1206. This document gives the impression that Basilia initially had falsely claimed to hold land under a mortgage, but there was in fact other evidence that she held it as dowry land. At the time of this charter, Normandy had very recently been annexed by Philip Augustus, King of France, and the land was no longer held there by a duke on his behalf: so all former ducal income now flowed directly into the king's coffers. As a result all landowners in Normandy, and especially the churches and monasteries, wanted to make sure that the lands they held could not be taken away from them by the king, or burdened with extra taxation. Thus, the monks of La Noe wished to be sure that the lands Basilia had once given them in Glisolles (an area of land under her jurisdiction) were not under the burden of a mortgage (which meant that they could be recalled by the person who provided the mortgage), but dowry land (which came with no strings attached).The charter reveals that Basilia had her own seal, which meant that she could make legal transactions on her own behalf, without needing representation by a male guardian.

Newly translated from: *Cartulaire Normand*, ed. Léopold Delisle (Caen: Léopold Delisle, 1852), no. 145, p. 25.

May all, who are present and to whom this writing is addressed, know that I, Basilia de Glisolles, confess before God and man that against God and the salvation of my soul, at the instigation of some people, deceitfully and with ill-intention, I have said and I even had recorded in writing, that everything I held in Glisolles in fief [land held under certain obligations] I held in pledge and mortgage, which I now reject; as is well known and true, I hold and have it, according to my lawful dowry and my just inheritance.

And so in order that as a result of the wicked and untrue written record my gifts shall not be reduced, nor that the men who by my gift hold [land] from me in fief may be harmed or lose out or suffer, I humbly plead with the Lord King of the

French and all his baillifs and our venerable Father L[uke, 1203–20], Bishop of Evreux, to whom I [have] humbly and pleadingly confessed my most serious sin, namely that the written record contains a manifest, scandalous and wicked lie that ought not to bring harm to anyone.

Moreover, may everyone know for certain that all records of the monks of La Noe concerning their grange at Jumelles to which my seal is attached are now completely correct and lawful; that I, and anyone who after me will hold my inheritance, shall always be bound to uphold and protect them. All these things, in order that forever and in perpetuity they be ratified and stable, I corroborate them with the witness of my seal and confirm them lawfully in the presence of witnesses: Luke, Bishop of Évreux; R., Dean; H., Precentor; Master William of Pacy, Archdeacon; Gilo of Évreux, Archdeacon; William the priest, brother of Henry the Chanter; and many others who have heard this, I confess the truth of this case, and I acknowledge the truth of my dowry in God's truth. Amen.

113. A Widow Making a Gift, Barcelona, Late Tenth Century

We are assuming that Dadil's statement that no one would redeem her from captivity is an indication that her husband, Guilara, was either dead or that Dadil was not in contact with him.

Newly translated from: Àngel Fabreca i Grau, ed., *Diplomatari de la Catedral de Barcelona Documents dels anys 844–1260, Volum 1: Documents dels anys 844–1000* (Barcelona: Capitol Catedral de Barcelona, 1995), no. 349.

Scattered by the capture of Barcelona, Dadil, woman, wife of Guilara, mother of Malanego.

I, miserable captive, when I was in captivity my son died in Barcelona, and he was buried in St Michael's Church; and when I was in captivity there was never any man or woman who could redeem me. I have in Uercio, near the tower of Foreto, houses and courtyards, lands and vineyards and uncultivated land, and on account of God and for the sake of my soul I give half of them to God, the Holy Cross and St Eulalia; let Bonefilius Gelitensis have all of the other half. And if there is anyone who wishes to take it, let him share in the fate of Judas the traitor. Let all Christians know that I sent this charter by my friend Vito, and I had it written in the city of Osca.

+ Dadil, woman, who ordered this to be written and confirmed.
+Aderico.
+Peter.
+Guilelmo.
+ Mirus, Priest.

114. A Widow Renting Out Property, Marseilles, 30 April 1248

Gostiana, like other Marseilles widows featured in this section, appears to have been a wealthy businesswoman, able to dispose of more than one property and demand a significant rental income.

Newly translated from: J. H. Pryor, ed., *Business Contracts of Medieval Provence: Selected Notulae from the Cartulary of Giraud Amalric of Marseilles, 1248* (Toronto: Pontifical Institute of Medieval Studies, 1981), no. 71, pp. 191–2.

I, Gostiana, widow of Berengari de Oliveria, in good faith and without any grief, rent to you, Peter Regi, son of Regina Barberia, a shop and house of mine which border on one side with the house of Guiraudi Fabro, and on the other side with the house of Hugh Boquerii, and on the other with the house of Jacob Ruffi. I rent to you all the above from the next feast of St Michael for ten years at a price of fifty *solidi*-worth of current money at the time of payment, and this will be twenty-five pounds for the next ten years.

Witnesses: Guillelmus Caminalis, Ricardus Caminalis, John de Pairaco and Guillelmus de Cusello.

*115. Account of Expenses Made by Richard of
Anstey in his Case against Mabel de Francheville,
England, 1158–63*

Although the Jewish women in this text are referred to as doing business with Richard of Anstey on their own account, they may not necessarily be widows.

Newly translated from: *English Lawsuits from William I to Richard I*, Vol. 2: *Henry II to Richard I (nos. 347–665)*, ed. R. C. van Caenegem (London: Seldon Society, 1991), no. 408, E, excerpts at pp. 402–4.

In the first year of my plea [1158–9], when I sent John, my brother, overseas for the king's writ, I borrowed the forty shillings (which I spent) from Vives, the Jew of Cambridge, upon usury, a groat a week per pound; I kept the moneys during the fourteen months and I rendered for hire of the same, thirty-seven shillings and four pence; and this was on the third day after mid-Lent. And after Easter following, the said Vives lent me again sixty shillings, at a groat a week per pound; which I kept six months, and for the hire thereof I rendered twenty-four shillings. And when I myself crossed the sea for the king's writ for pleading, then Comitissa of Cambridge lent me four pounds and ten shillings at a groat a week per pound, which I spent on the journey; which moneys I kept nine months and for which I rendered for usury, fifty-four shillings. [. . .] And when my uncle's land was decreed to me at Woodstock [probably in 1162–3], then Mirabella, the Jewess of Newport, lent me four pounds and ten shillings, at a groat a week per pound, which I kept a year; for which I rendered for usury, seventy-eight shillings. And when I rendered to Ralph the physician his moneys, at the first term Hakelot the Jew lent me seven pounds, at three pence a week per pound, which I kept a year and a half; and for which I rendered for usury, six pounds and sixteen shillings and six pence. And at the next term of payment, Comitissa of Cambridge lent me one hundred shillings, which I kept for two months, at three pence per week per pound, and for which I rendered for usury, ten shillings.

116. Will of Regina, Jewess of Puigcerda, Pyrenees, 23 October 1306

See the introduction to text 96, Chapter 3, for an explanation of the presentation of this type of document. The will's last line is oddly cryptic; but as Astruch Iuceff is mentioned as the executor of the will, it is probable that he wished to have it recorded that he owed the sum of five *solidi* to Regina, the author of the will, as it would have made up part of the assets of her estate.

Newly translated from: Robert I. Burns, *Jews in the Notarial Culture: Latinate Wills in Mediterranean Spain, 1250–1350* (Berkeley: University of California Press, 1996), pp. 177–8. This will is discussed at pp.101–4.

Regina, widow of Bondia Coras the Jew, whilst I am unwell etc., make and draw up my will of my goods, ordering etc. First I order my body to be buried. And I order to be given to Iuceff Choen, one hundred *solidi*, which I leave to him. Also I leave to Isaac de Soall, thirty *solidi*. Also to the heirs of the late Iuceff de Soall, Jew, thirty *solidi*. And twenty *solidi* to Momete the Jew. And I leave to Mancosa, widow of Abrahe de la Rotxela, Jew, a hundred *solidi*. And I leave to Aster, sister of the said Mancosa, fifty *solidi*. And I order that charity be done for my soul on the day of my death, for which deed, I assign and leave one hundred *solidi*. And I leave to Aster, my daughter, wife of Fagim Benet the Jew, for the part of her inheritance belonging and owing to her from my goods a hundred Barcelonan *solidi*; in these things, and in the dowry which she had at the time of her marriage to her husband, I constitute her my heir, and unless anything else etc. Also I leave in alms to the Jews of Puigcerda, out of love of God and for my soul, my bed with all its sheets and coverings, and let it be situated in the *scola* [school] of the aforementioned Jews. And I constitute as my representative and executor of this will of mine, Astruch Iuceff the Jew, to whom I give licence etc. [. . .]

I name as heirs to the remaining goods in my property,

wherever and whatever they might be, Bondia and Iuceff, my grandsons, sons of the late Astruch Bondia, Jew. This will etc.

Witnesses: Matheus de Oliana, Arnaldus Payleres, Raimundus Rahedor, Astruch de Besalu, Iacob Abrahe Choen, Bernard Duran, Iuceffe Abrahe, and Vitalis, son of Astruch Crexent.

Astruch Iuceff owes five *solidi*.

117. A Widow in Business as a Miller, Crete, 1301

Mills were traditionally high-value properties, but milling work itself was a laborious task, and millers were often the focus of mistrust in medieval society. For a woman to take on the rental of a mill was somewhat unusual, and the document also suggests that Moscana and her son would be doing the actual milling.

This document is written from the point of view of Michael Gradonico, who was renting the mill to Moscana and her son; there would also have been another document, which would have registered the agreement of Moscana and her son to the arrangement. It was usual for there to be two documents, written from the point of view of each party.

Newly translated from: *Benvenuto de Brixano, Notaio in Candia, 1301–1302*, ed. Raimondo Morozzo della Rocca (Venice: Alfieri Editore, 1950), p. 20.

Entry 44: 19 April 1301

I, Michael Gradonico, inhabitant of Candia, and my heirs, make clear to you, Moscana, widow of Rayneri Consilio, called Cacaliare, and to Michael Consilio, son of the same Rayneri, inhabitants of the village of Macrendichi, and your heirs, that I give, concede and rent to you my mill in Placha in the district of Scalari, with its land, ready and prepared for milling, with all its necessary equipment for milling, stones and wheels, from now until the fourteenth of July coming, and thereafter for two years, with full virtue and power etc. You will be held to pay all necessary expenses, and keep it in good condition, except that the weir of the mill still requires work to be done to it, with [the addition of] a wall, and you will help with your persons in this work. For rent you must pay to me four *perpera* for each complete month, and you must mill for me 4 *saumas* [measures] of grain each month, free of charge, under a penalty [for default] of double the above rent, for whatever period [I specify], and double the above milling work. And at the end of the rental period, you must return the mill to me complete, and I shall hold it and give to whomever I wish. This under a penalty of twenty-five *perpera*. A firm and lasting charter.

Witnesses: Comes and Terca.

To be completed and dated.

118. A Frustrated Female Crusader, France, 1098

We are assuming this is a widow, since no reference is made to her husband – we could be wrong. Giles Constable, 'Medieval charters as a source for the history of the crusades', reprinted in Thomas Madden, ed., *The Crusades* (Oxford: Blackwell, 2002), states that Emerias is the only woman known to have taken the cross herself. See also E. Magnou-Nortier, *La société laïque et l'église dans la province ecclésiastique de Narbonne de la fin du VIIIe à la fin du XIe siècle* (Toulouse: Publications de l'Université de Toulouse-Le Mirail, 1974), A20, pp. 562–3.

Newly translated from: C. Devic and J. Vaissete, *Histoire générale du Languedoc*, Vol. 5, 2nd edn (Toulouse: É. Privat, 1872–5), no. 401, pp. 756–8.

Let it be known that Isarnus, the just and good Bishop of Toulouse, went to see how the churches of the diocese of Toulouse were faring, and when he came to St John's, the exceedingly honest man, Fortius of St John, prepared a great meal, and the knights of the whole province came to see the bishop and to have a meal with him. It happened that Emerias de Alteias, who had lifted the cross on to her right shoulder in order to go to Jerusalem, came to the meeting and entered to see the bishop and receive his blessing. Having given her a blessing, the bishop said to her that it would be better for her to build a house in God's honour where the poor of Christ might be received. Having heard this, she agreed to his advice; and on the same day Ebs and Ademarius de Scalvernia and Bernard de Mormum came before the bishop, and all with one voice said that if he wished it, they would donate their Church of St Orient, which for a long time had remained destroyed among thorn bushes, and, by his advice, also the ecclesiastical first fruits and tithes – for the love of God and the remission of their sins and those of their family – to the woman named Emerias, so that she might restore the church in God's service, and that they and their family might receive every benefit from it, both dead and alive. Indeed, the bishop, having heard these words, had the Lady Emerias called before him and spoke thus to her: 'Already, daughter, a place has been prepared by the Lord in your province, and I in the name of the Lord order that this place not be neglected by you.' She, moved by the mercy of God, replied to him that by his advice she would accept the place. Ebs and Ademarius de Scalvernia and Bernard-Raymond de Mormum got up, and all together placed in the hand of Isarnus, the Bishop of Toulouse, the church, and the revenues which belonged to it, whatever they might be, first fruits and tithes in the whole parish, entry and exit ways, and the produce of the whole land, both cultivated and uncultivated, and he freely gave them to Emerias and all those living there after her, to serve God there; and this having been agreed, if any of them or their family in this country or during this time should die, the inhabitants of the house and his friends should take him there as soon as they can, no one there prohibiting it, and should bury him fittingly, and he should have the benefits of commemoration in the house as if he had lived there.

The witnesses to this matter were: Ayraldus, sacrist de Podio, and Fortius of St John, and Gifredus the chaplain, and Feraldus de Osas. This charter was made on the nones of April on a Tuesday in the year of the Lord, 1098, at the Church of St John. Galfred wrote it.

119. An Eyewitness Account of Empress Matilda Acting as an Intermediary in the Case of Thomas Becket, Normandy, 1164

This is a letter written by Prior Nicholas of Mont-aux-Malades in Rouen to Thomas Becket, Archbishop of Canterbury, while in exile in France. Prior Nicholas acted as a secretary to Empress Matilda in her mediating role between her son Henry II (1154–89) and Thomas Becket, Archbishop of Canterbury (1162–70). Composed around Christmas 1164, the letter constitutes exceptional testimony to Empress Matilda's reception of letters, her listening to them being read aloud to her, and her command of languages (French and Latin). The so-called Constitutions of Clarendon, mentioned in the letter, were a series of royal demands issued there by King Henry II, which the king wished his bishops (and nobles) to accept. They redefined the jurisdiction of the king and that of the archbishop over a number of issues pertaining to the relationship of the Crown and the Church: for example, the problem of clerks (senior clergy figures such as deacons, priests and bishops, who were not monks) who committed crimes. Henry II stipulated that such clerks convicted of a capital offence in an ecclesiastical court ought then to be taken to the royal court to receive punishment. Thomas Becket refused to accept this royal demand as he felt that this particular measure meant that in effect these clerks would be punished twice. Part of the problem with the Constitutions of Clarendon was that for the first time these particular royal demands were presented to his court in writing, whereas up to that time they had been formulated orally. Any oral legislation was much more flexible than recorded statements of the law, and would have allowed the bishops and nobles more legal leeway. The matter was extremely sensitive and Empress Matilda knew exactly why it was so.

As is often the case in medieval letters of this sort, politically sensitive subjects are alluded to rather than spelled out in detail. It was common for the bearer of any letter to deliver an oral exposition rather than the document itself, in order to avoid embarrassment if the letter fell into the wrong hands. Master H., referred to at the end of the letter, has not been identified, but the document he had lost was probably a version of the Constitutions of Clarendon. Richard of

Ilchester, whom Empress Matilda is recorded as having conversed with, was at the time Archdeacon and Treasurer of Poitiers Cathedral and later became Bishop of Winchester (1173–83).

Newly translated from: *The Correspondence of Thomas Becket, Archbishop of Canterbury*, 2 vols., Vol. 1, ed. and trans. A. Duggan, Oxford Medieval Texts (Oxford: Clarendon, 2000), pp. 159–69, no. 41 (excerpts).

To the venerable lord, Father Thomas, by God's grace Archbishop of Canterbury, Brother Nicholas sends greetings with all his devotion.

On his return from the [papal] court, John of Oxford [. . .] came to the court (which had been convened by the lady empress), in order that he might provoke her against you, as he and others had already done before, and he instilled malice into her as much as he could. [. . .] For in England the crime of offenders accused before bishops is punished not by the imposition of penance, but by the gift of money. They also claimed that God was not present in your actions, and that she ought to know that from the start of your appointment as archbishop you have gathered around you, not monks, but educated noblemen, whom they called by a shameful name which I consider better to suppress. They also said that you have conferred ecclesiastical benefices, not with God in mind, but for your own service. They also asserted that you went away, not on account of royal customs, but because of a financial reason. It is fitting that you should not be unaware of the malice told against you, both for your own sake and in order for you to understand the reason of the lady's [Empress Matilda] exasperation.

On the third day after their departure we came to the empress; for a short while she was unwilling to receive your letter, saying sharply to us that we had gone to see you, even though we knew that you were in the [papal] court; she did not believe that you would have reached the court so quickly; we did not, however, give up, but told her on one occasion and then on another all the good things we could think of, despite her unwillingness. On the third occasion, after a few words, she kindly took your letter, albeit secretly (wishing to hide it from her clerks), and ordered us to read it to her. After she had listened to it, she apologized first that she had spoken sharply about you to me, and to others, in private and in public, and even for having sent word to the lord king. For she claimed that her son had hidden from her all that he wished to do in ecclesiastical affairs because he knew that she favoured ecclesiastical freedom more than royal will. Now, however, she had sent her letter to her son by one of her clerks, requesting him to tell her everything he had in mind about the state of the Church and you in a letter to her. 'And then,' she said, 'when I know what he wishes, if I consider that my labour can be fruitful, I shall endeavour as much as I can for ecclesiastical peace and his.'

[. . .] On our return to the lady empress, we again set out in order what you had instructed; we relayed orally the king's customs [i.e. the Constitutions of Clarendon] because Master H. had lost the document; we added to it that some of the customs were against the faith of Jesus Christ, and nearly all were against the liberty of the Church; and that for these reasons she and her son ought to fear for their eternal salvation and also for their temporal one. But then she ordered us to send you a copy of those customs. By God's will, that same day the copy was found, and on the next day, having sent everyone out of her chamber, she ordered us to read them in Latin and then explain them in French. The woman belongs to a race of tyrants, and she approved some of them; such as the clause about not excommunicating the king's justices and servants without his agreement. I, however, did not wish to explain any others without first discussing this one and quoting the gospel's precept – when Peter is told: 'Tell the Church,' and so on, not 'Tell the king' – and many other things. She disapproved of many clauses and what really annoyed her, above all, was that they had been recorded in writing and that the bishops had been forced to promise to uphold them, for this had not previously been the case. After a very long talk with her, when I pressed her strongly as to what would be the first moment of peace, we put this [suggestion] to her and she agreed: that if it were at all possible, the lord king should follow the counsel of his mother and that of other reasonable people, who would negotiate the matter in such a way that without promise or written record the ancient customs of the kingdom would be observed, and that they would be upheld, with the addition that the secular justices would not take away the liberty of the Church, nor that the bishops would abuse it. Know that the lady empress was shrewd in the defence of her son, excusing him on account of his zeal for justice, and of the malice of the bishops, and she herself shrewd in understanding rationally and sensibly the origins of the Church's trouble. We praised and supported her opinion of some of the things she said [. . .] The lady empress has talked about this on occasion with Richard of Ilchester [. . .] Thus, if you love the liberty of the Church on account of God, show in word and deed that what has been said here displeases you; and, if you send a letter to the lady empress, underline the same from whatever angle. In the name of truth we say to you that we have written the above out of love for righteousness and for the salvation of your soul. If it has been said unwisely, forgive us, and may what we have said be hidden. We were unable to send a messenger to you more quickly, since we prepared the letter to be sent to you with all haste at the time that we sent the customs to the lady empress. Now we ask you especially that you send us a letter about your situation and what your plans are. We shall faithfully do what you ask us to do. Again we ask your forgiveness both for the length [of the letter] and the audacity [of writing it].

CHAPTER 5

OLDER WOMEN AND DEATH

Introduction

'Who were old in the Middle Ages?' asked Shulamith Shahar in a famous article.[1] Shahar's rather surprising answer was that, contrary to most belief, 'old age' did not begin at forty, an age cited in some ages-of-man schemata, but was more likely to correspond with reaching sixty or even seventy years; but rather than concentrate on numerical age, it was more important to focus in on a person's continued usefulness and function within his or her society to reach any conclusion about being 'old'.[2] Shahar makes a valid point, but to equate 'old' with 'no longer useful' risks accepting the negative images portrayed in fictional texts (some of which are translated below). It has also been suggested that old age was de-gendered, with men and women treated equally (and poorly) because they no longer fulfilled recognizably gendered roles within their society.[3] Both approaches take as their starting-point a value judgement, rather than searching for the elderly and then exploring the reasons why they appear in our sources.

Whether or not the age of forty or sixty should be taken as the demarcation line between middle and old age, we must remember that life could, of course, be brutally short – we have only to read accounts of battles, of outbreaks of disease or famine, even of accounts in coroners' rolls in later medieval England of accidental deaths – to realize that the potential for mortality before achieving a great age was greatly increased.[4] And as Joel Rosenthal has pointed out, age at death is rarely recorded, even in medieval England.[5] To find older women in the records, then, we need to dig more deeply.[6]

One route to finding them is to focus on family records in

which more than two generations are visible. Our texts include several where grandmothers are visible, often helping their grandchildren (text 120 below, and see text 116 above). Such activities might win them respect, and it may not have been unusual for an older relative such as a grandmother to remain in the family home with her adult children (an older, unmarried female relative might also find a home with her relatives in this way, presumably in return for some contribution to the family's income or work).

Older women inhabited a difficult space in medieval society, however, particularly if they had little or no family support of this type.[7] Marital patterns might mean a preponderance of elderly widows over widowers; property-holding did not necessarily cushion older women against vulnerability, and as the Middle Ages progressed there was increasing wariness of older women's knowledge and insight, leading in extreme cases to accusations of witchcraft.[8] Older people of both sexes sometimes found themselves in the position of making arrangements so that they continued to be supported when they could no longer work productively (text 121). In the secular world, to summarize, old age could be – and often was – the occasion for satire or derision rather than sympathy (see texts 122 and 123 below). This is in stark contrast to the religious world, where old age was seen as a blessing, and older members of the community were respected for the accumulation of knowledge and experience they had built up.[9] However, this dichotomy was not universal, particularly not at times when new religious forms of living and cohabiting developed. In the late twelfth and early thirteenth centuries the earliest Beguines, (young and old single women (many of whom had been widowed)), began to live in communities – with the support of their immediate families, but in the face of derision from many clergy.[10]

So was there anything positive to be said about old people in the Middle Ages? Only in the context of witness testimonies, used to back up evidence in court cases, was old age more valued in secular life. The memory of an older person – preferably, but not exclusively male – could be crucial in convincing a judge to decide in favour of one party over the other (text 124).

Collect together a group of old people corroborating each other and the testimony became an even more potent weapon.[11] But even in these most legalistic of records it is rare to find a person who really knew her actual age, and approximations were often well wide of the mark. In this context, witnesses – or at least those who called them – had an almost vested interest in inflating their age, and whilst male witnesses were for the most part viewed as more reliable than females, older women nevertheless do appear in such records.[12] How far their actual voices are recorded is of course open to conjecture. We touched on this issue in the general introduction. The whole purpose of calling witnesses in medieval court cases was to establish a body of credible accounts that largely agreed with each other. The ensuing record, therefore, might only note the key parts of each statement that corroborated, and might also 'tidy up' the oral statement into something more coherent. Nevertheless, the witness's voice is not completely erased in this process, and this type of source provides some of the liveliest and most direct testimony of women's lives.

What then of death? To what extent might a woman expect to be commemorated after she had died? This was of course dependent on her status when she lived – we have no shortage of epitaphs of high-born or prominent women who had achieved some visibility within their communities (texts 125–7 and 138). We even have the description of some deathbed scenes: both these and epitaphs were designed to magnify the virtues of their subject (texts 128 to 131). It must be remembered that such evidence had a public function, projecting an image of the person which they (or perhaps more accurately their relatives) wished to portray. (A similar point can be made about the furnishing of graves with grave goods – rather than providing an intimate insight into the possessions of the deceased, such deposits were instead invested with meaning for the community left behind.) Ecclesiastical houses, also, often kept careful records of dead benefactors in books of memory, which can provide a barometer of female charitable activity in relation to the house (text 132).

Rather harder to gauge is the impact that the death of a

woman had on the practical, day-to-day life of her family.
Unlike the death of a father, the death of a mother did not
mean that her children were orphans. And widowers are by far
the most elusive group to find in medieval sources. Even when
we find them, for example, Einhard, the biographer of Charlemagne, the consolatory letter which he received on the death of
his wife, Imma, hardly addresses his emotional loss, and does
not even name his wife (text 134 below)! Unlike widows, who
might often find their actions circumscribed by the contents
of their husbands' wills, widowers rarely had to deal with the
distribution of their late wives' goods (with the exception of
women who were heiresses to significant estates), and it is possible that husbands were rather slower to commemorate
deceased wives, than the other way round.[13] One of the earliest
examples of a wife being commemorated in north-western Europe, at royal level, is the order from Henry I to his chamberlain
and sheriffs of London for the commemoration of the late
Queen Edith/Matilda that half a shilling a day from the farm of
London be paid to Westminster Abbey Church for a light to
burn in her memory (cf. text 133).[14] We should note, however,
that he did not attend her funeral. Nevertheless, we do find
some examples of women's wills being contested (texts 135
and 136) or being executed without apparent dispute (text
137). It has been suggested that women's wills were in fact
a great deal more 'autobiographical' than men's, precisely
because they rarely had much say in the patrimony and so con-
centrated instead on giving more personal gifts to friends and
family.[15] This aspect of women's testamentary behaviour has
proven a rich seam to mine throughout the present book (see
also text 139), and again there is further work to be done on
this issue.

We have reached the end of women's journey through life.
The multiplicity of experiences documented in the texts we
have translated cannot begin to be summarized or distilled into
a 'typical' life pattern, but perhaps some themes have emerged
which would reward further investigation.

Chief amongst these is the issue of whose voice we hear in
the sources. If there was no such thing as an 'author' in the

Middle Ages, if all written texts were dictated not by the realities of the situation but by a set of societal rules – laws, received practice, demands of genre – can we really determine female voices and female intentions coming through the male or clerical filter? Obviously some of our texts are observations *about* women, rather than revealing their own outlook, but even these should not be dismissed, since they often reveal ideals against which real women might be judged. And those texts which purport to transmit a woman's voice – in a petition, or a witness statement, or a property transaction – should not be dismissed, even if they too adhered to conventions about what should and should not be recorded. For all that the scribe adhered to models about *how* to write up the documents, *what* he wrote up must have mirrored the wishes of his female client.

Another feature which stands out in this collection of texts is the occurrence of violence against women. Some work has begun to be done on this issue as a feature of medieval life, and certainly we are not short of literary and documentary texts recounting violence against girls and women.[16] As yet, however, there has not been a substantial study of the subject in the Middle Ages, a somewhat surprising omission given the importance of the topic to feminist historians of the early modern and modern periods.[17]

Finally, this collection reveals just how the pattern of recording women's lives largely reflects the concern of the writers with property of one kind or another; when women did not own, or were not considered as, property, they attracted less attention. Their visibility certainly diminishes when they become older and no longer able to bear children (itself relevant to the issue of property and its division within the family), and a study of the lives of older women in medieval Europe is sorely needed. The richness and diversity of the records presented in this volume suggests that the project of writing the history of medieval secular women still has a considerable way to run.[18]

120. A Grandmother Invests for her Grandchildren, Crete, 1301

See text 117, Chapter 4 for an explanation as to why two documents would have been created to record a single business transaction.

Newly translated from: *Benvenuto de Brixano, Notaio in Candia, 1301–1302*, ed. Raimondo Morozzo della Rocca, Fonti per la Storia di Venezia, sez. 3: Archivi Notarili (Venice: Alfieri Editore, 1950), entries 204 and 205 (pp. 75–6).

Entry 204: 29 June 1301

I, Maria, widow of Bartolini de Perino, make clear that I received from you, Margarita, my daughter, and your successors, one hundred *perpera*, which P. de Vigonzia must give to you from the Kalends of next January until one or both of your children, Tantalisa and Leonardelo, should come of age. From this time until then I must do business with the money in Candia, just as it seems best to me, and then I must give it to them [her grandchildren], along with any profit which God may have given me (except for any expenses incurred). And it should be known that these *perpera* are intended for marrying your above-mentioned daughter, unless, by chance, she should have been married by promises [i.e. if the daughter had contracted her own marriage, independent of her parents' wishes]. If this should happen and these arrangements should be overtaken by these promises, then your son shall have the money. And if I do not observe this agreement, let me pay double [the one hundred *perpera*] to the children or their representative etc.

Witnesses: Francischinus Zapano and Nicoletus de Cavalero.

To be completed and given into the care of the Franciscans [i.e. the document is lodged with them for safekeeping, although the reason for keeping it with the friars is unclear].

Entry 205: same day

The above Margarita commissions the above Maria to manage

the hundred *perpera* which she will receive by charter from Peter de Vigonza [sic].

Witnesses: As above.

To be completed and dated.

121. Will of Florita, Making Provision for her Old Age, Ravello, 1199

We know that Florita was at least sixty-five when making this document, as we have her marriage agreement, made earlier on. Newly translated from: Vincenzo Criscuolo, ed., *Pergamene dell'Archivio Vescovile di Minori* (Amalfi: Centro di Cultura e Storia Amalfitana, 1987), no. 88, p. 89.

On the fourth day of the month of February, second indiction, Ravello, 1199, and the first year of the reign of our Lord Frederick. Florita, daughter of the late Sergii Galli and widow of Manso Riczuli, whilst seriously ill, makes her will and makes clear that her daughter, Floreria, wife of Sergius, who was son of the late Mauro Regilli, should take care of her in her old age and infirmity, and thus she wishes that all of her goods should come into the hands of her aforesaid daughter, with this condition: if Sergius and Urso, [Florita's] sons and brothers of the said Floreria, will give within the space of four months two ounces of Sicilian *tari* to the same Floreria for the [funeral] expenses of the said testatrix, then each of them shall have a third portion [of the inheritance]. She leaves two *solidi* to the Church of St Maria Rotunda, where her body will be buried.

Sergius, witness, son of Mauri Carissimi.

Mauro, son of Master Sergio Rufulo.

Leo, Priest and Scribe, son of Constantine Mutilionis the judge, wrote it.

122. Old Women, According to the Poem 'Ruodlieb', Germany, c.1050

On descriptions such as these see Richard J. Shrader, *God's Handiwork: Images of Women in Early Germanic Literature* (Westport: Greenwood Press, 1983).

Newly translated from: *Waltarius and Ruodlieb*, Vol. 3, ed. and trans. D. M. Kratz, Garland Library of Medieval Literature, series A (New York and London: Garland, 1984), pp. 182–3.

> Woman, who is equal to the moon in the flower
>   of youth,
> Is equal to a little old ape after the onset of old age,
> Brow furrowed with wrinkles, which was before
>   smooth,
> And her eyes, once dove-white, now are gloomy.

123. Epigram on an Old Woman by Ulger, Angers, France, c.1111

Ulger, a teacher, was a student of Marbod of Rennes, whom we met above, text 46, Chapter 2. His satirical writing does not appear to have prevented his later elevation to the bishopric of Angers!

Newly translated from: F. J. E. Raby, *A History of Secular Latin Poetry in the Middle Ages*, Vol. 2, 2nd edn (Oxford: Clarendon Press, 1957), p. 42.

> Poor Delia had four teeth left,
> She lost two when she coughed,
> But it's known the poor wretch has none now –
> Her third cough saw them off!

124. Old Women as Reliable Witnesses, Venice, 1196

The case revolves around rights to water claimed by St Lorenzo: older witnesses were valued for their long memories, proving that such rights were long established.

Newly translated from: *S. Lorenzo di Ammiana*, ed. Luigi Lanfranchi, Fonti per la Storia di Venezia, sez. 2: Archivi Ecclesiastici (Venice: Alfieri Editore, 1947), pp. 97–106.

Merada Sadullo said on oath that she is at least fifty years old and has always lived in Amianus, and as far as she can remember, she remembers that the waters at issue have always been fished on behalf of St Lorenzo. And she says that Marcus Dedo is a fisherman and fishes the water for St Lorenzo whenever the time is right to fish. And she sees Aurius Vitalis the priest taking away the traps and weirs of those who fish here without permission, and she sees him do this often and he always does it publicly. On the other questions she knows nothing . . .

Maria Sadullo spoke on oath. She says she is more than sixty years old and was born and has always lived in Amianus. And she says that she remembers that fifty years ago she knew that the water was always St Lorenzo's and had always been held and possessed peacefully by St Lorenzo without any controversy. And she says that her father, Martin Sadullo, and her husband, Marcus da Puzo, and her sons today, that is Matthew, Andrew and Martin and Marinus, are all fishermen in St Lorenzo's waters and says that they give fish to the priest of St Lorenzo as rent. [. . .]

Rosa says on oath that she remembers that for forty years the lamp fishermen of Dorso Duro have come to illuminate the waters at issue, which John Mastro Leon de Constantiaco fished for St Lorenzo. And that John, when he heard of these lamplighters, persecuted them and captured them under the

house [i.e. church] of St Lorenzo de Litore Albo, and prohibited their paths with his band of men, and they broke their
boats, and afterwards, when in the morning they were in Amianus before good men, the above lamp fishermen swore that
from now on they should not fish in that water nor light it
without the permission of the priest of St Lorenzo, and that
afterwards their paths and boats were restored to them. Asked
how she knows this, she responds reliably, because all of this
was done publicly in Amianus and she saw them taking the
oath. And she says that her nurse, who was a hundred and fifty
[sic!] years old when she died, used to say publicly that the
water at issue was St Lorenzo's, and that the priest of St Lorenzo
did a bad thing when he permitted the Abbot of St Felix a mill
there, because this would cause trouble. Asked when the mill
was there, she says she does not remember.

125. Epitaph of the Jewess Scarlatta, Aquileia, Italy, 1140

This text is unusual in that it suggests its subject met a violent death,
although there is very little documentary evidence of the Jewish community in this city at this time. The twelfth century was a time of
renewed (and more violent) Christian fervour following the First Crusade. The ellipses below indicate where the inscription is incomplete
(due to erosion on the stone).

Newly translated from: V. Colorni, 'Gli ebrei nei territori italiani a
nord di Roma dal 568 agli inizi del secolo XIII' in *Gli ebrei nell'alto
medioevo: Settimane di Studio del Centro Italiano di Studi sull'Alto
Medioevo*, Vol. 26 (Spoleto: CISAM, 1980), p. 303.

Let this stone. . . At the head of S. C. R. L. T. V. . . daughter of
Abraham. She was killed on the first of Shevat in the year 4900.
And may her death be her atonement and her rest. And may
she receive justice forever [Ps. 110: 3]. And she will flower like
the grass [Ps. 71: 16].

126. Epitaph of Urania of Worms, Leader of Female Synagogue, Germany, Thirteenth Century

Jewish women, particularly those who, like Urania, were the daughters of rabbis, were sometimes able to rise to positions of prominence within their communities. They were not, however, permitted in Jewish law to act as religious leaders in their own right.

Reproduced from: Israel Abrahams, *Jewish Life in the Middle Ages* (London: Macmillan, 1896 and reprints), p. 26.

This headstone commemorates the eminent and excellent Lady Urania, the daughter of Rabbi Abraham, who was the chief of the synagogue singers. His prayer for his people rose up unto glory. And as to her, she too, with sweet tunefulness, officiated before the female worshippers, to whom she sang the hymnal portions. In devout service her memory shall be preserved.

127. Epitaphs of Sicardis, Languedoc, 1199

The warning verse in both of these was a common trope of epitaphs. The first of these texts is written in rhyming verse, the second is less flowery: both may have been literary exercises rather than actual epitaphs.

Newly translated from: C. Devic and J. Vaissete, *Histoire générale de Languedoc*, Vol. 5, 2nd edn (Toulouse: É. Privat, 1872–5), nos. 76–7, p. 22.

In the year of our Lord, 1199, on the second ides of October; here lies decorated with the crown of virtues, Sicardis, the mother of Martin the scribe –

> who looks at me
> what you are I was
> what I am you will be
> say an Our Father.

In the year of our Lord, 1199, on the ides of October; the mother of Martin the scribe, called Sicardis, lies here, in this tomb her body rests –

> who looks at me
> what you are I was
> what I am you will be
> say an Our Father.

128. The Death of Empress Adelaide, Orbe, Switzerland, 999

Adelaide, daughter of King Rudolf of Burgundy, was married first to King Lothar of Italy and second to Emperor Otto I of the Holy Roman Empire (whom she outlived by twenty-six years). Their son was Emperor Otto II (d. 983). (See text 108, Chapter 4, for letters to Empress Adelaide from her daughter, Emma.) Not only is this a vivid eyewitness account of the death of Empress Adelaide at Orbe (in canton Vaude in Switzerland) in 999, as recorded by Odilo, Abbot of Cluny (994–1048), but the text also sheds an interesting light on the role of medieval queens: first of all, Empress Adelaide is shown in a mediating role in her country of birth, helping her nephew in his negotiations with the aristocracy, then in her role as benefactor of churches and monasteries, and finally she is shown as giving instructions to Odilo, the author of the piece, that part of her son's imperial mantle is to be donated to the Monastery of St Martin in Tours, following the example of St Martin's famous gift of half of his mantle to a pauper (i.e. Christ).

Newly translated from: Odilo of Cluny's *Epithaphium Adalheidae imperatricis*, ed. H. Paulhart, *Die Lebensbeschreibung der Kaiserin Adelheid von Abt Odilo von Cluny*, Vol. 20.2, Mitteilungen des Instituts für Österreichische Geschichtsforschung (Graz and Cologne: 1962), c. 12, 16–18.

Then, in the last year of her life, when, as I believe, she must have realized that her departure from this life could not be

longer avoided, this constant friend of peace came to her paternal land for the cause of peace and charity in order to bind
together the followers of her nephew, King Rodulf [III, 993–
1032], and she brought peace to the people amongst whom she
could establish it, and she committed, as she was wont to, the
people to whom she could not bring peace to God. Otherwise
there is no need to spell out that with application and great
devotion she strove to visit the shrines of saints. On the same
occasion, she went to the Monastery of Payerne, which she herself had nobly founded with her own and her mother's
possessions, in honour of the Virgin Mary, for the salvation of
the soul of her mother who was buried there.

[. . .]

Then she went to the city of Geneva, where she wished to visit
the church of the most victorious martyr, Victor. From there, she
travelled to Lausanne, where she prayed most devoutly to the
memory of the Virgin Mary. Thereafter, having been honourably welcomed in all these places by the king and the bishops, his
nephews, she continued to the village of Orbe. She spent some
time there providing the poor and the miserable she encountered
with their needs as much as she could; with the king of the land
she held discussions about matters of peace and honour, and she
also arranged various gifts to churches. Which church or monastery, linked to her by affinity or closeness, did not deserve her
gifts or riches? Let me just say a little about many things. At that
time, when she had only a few days left to live, she bestowed
upon the most holy Father Benedict gifts from her own
resources – however meagre they were; and in particular she
loved Father Maiolus of holy memory, already crowned with
the glory of heaven, whom while still alive she supported above
all other mortals of the [Benedictine] order. Nor did she forget
Cluny, the monastery she knew very well.

As for the restoration of the Monastery of the most holy confessor of Christ, St Martin [at Tours], which not long before
had gone up in flames, she arranged for it to be sent a large sum
of silver and also to honour its altar with a piece of the cloak

which had belonged to her only son, Emperor Otto. And so may we remember her sweetest words to him, for whose service they were given, she said, amongst other things: 'I beg you, my dearest one, I beg you to address the holy priest thus: "Receive, Priest of God, as a sign of my veneration, these small presents sent to you by Adelaide, servant of God's servants, who herself is a sinner and by God's grace an empress. Receive a piece of the mantle of Emperor Otto, my only son, and pray for him to Christ, He whom you dressed in a mantle divided in two when in the person of a poor man [He appeared to you]."'

That very day, and that very hour, when she had planned to leave the town [Orbe], she died in the presence of us sinners, a perfect example of humility; without arrogance and with humility she revealed that she possessed the spirit of prophecy. There was present a monk [i.e. Odilo], who, although unworthy, was called Abbot, and for whom she had a certain respect. When she turned her eyes towards him, and he looked at her, they both shed copious tears. I may say that in this she did more than if she had cured many sick people. Humbly, she took the rough cloth which he was wearing, and with kisses pressed it on her holy eyes and her serene face, and broke the silence with these words: 'Remember me, my son, in your thoughts and know that never again I will see you with these eyes. Once I abandon all things mortal, I confide my soul to the prayers of the brothers.' Then the next journey she took brought her to the place where, by divine guidance, she decided that a tomb should be prepared for herself.

129. The Death of Queen Matilda I of Germany, 968

The *Life of Matilda* contains a description of Queen Matilda I's death-bed, upon which occasion she hands over to her granddaughter, the thirteen-year-old Matilda (d. 999), Abbess of Quedlinburg, a roll with the names of deceased nobles to be commemorated upon it.

The thirteen-year-old Matilda, born around 954/5, was in fact the daughter of Empress Adelaide, whom we encountered in the previous text (128). In the Holy Roman Empire (i.e. Germany), it was common for royal princesses to be appointed as abbesses of the royal nunneries. This had three advantages, firstly, princesses appointed as abbesses would remain unmarried and not require a dowry; secondly, they would not produce children who needed provision in cash or land; and thirdly, their position as abbesses provided them with an opportunity to put the nunnery directly at the disposal of their royal/imperial fathers or brothers or nephews as a sort of palace for the royal family to stay in, a garrison for the army, an administrative centre for tax collection, a judicial court and, at times, a prison. Nunneries also were places of education and learning and as such acted as a sort of finishing school for aristocratic women who would not necessarily become nuns. Therefore, nunneries were extremely important centres which represented wealth in land and cash, so that royal princesses would be put in charge of them at the earliest possible opportunity in order to keep these assets within the royal/imperial family.

Newly translated from: *Vita Mahthildis reginae antiquor*, ed. R. Koepke (Hanover: Hahn, 1852), MGH, SS 10, p. 581.

Then one Saturday, on which day she [Queen Matilda] had always loved performing charitable deeds, when [the time] for her final deeds had arrived, she called her granddaughter [Matilda], daughter of the Emperor [Otto I] and Abbess of the Nunnery [of Quedlinburg] and greeted her with warnings and advice that she should be devout and humble, prudent and careful. She also admonished her that she should look after the flock committed to her care and that she should rarely leave the monastery, that she should indulge her mind in sacred scripture, and that she should teach what she had read, and in everything in which she might give advice to others she herself should first set an example, and then leave it to others to follow her in doing good work. She [Queen Matilda] placed in her [Matilda's] hands a list with the names of the nobles who had died on it, and she commended to her care the soul of Henry [I], she also commended her own soul to her care and those souls of all the faithful, [details of] whose memory she had collected.

130. Queen Margaret of Scotland's Deathbed, Scotland, 1093

Described by her biographer T., who might be Turgot, Prior of Durham (1094–1107/9); he later became Bishop of St Andrews (1107/9–15). This account is based on an eyewitness report of one of the queen's priests. Margaret died shortly after the deaths of her husband, King Malcolm III of Scotland (1058–93), and her eldest son, Edward, during their expedition in Northumbria in November 1093. Malcolm died on 13 November and Edward three days later. For the recent state of research on the authorship of the text, see L. Huneycutt, *Matilda of Scotland. A Study in Medieval Queenship* (Woodbridge: Boydell, 2003), pp. 161–2.

Newly translated from: *Vita s. Margaretae Scotorum reginae auctore ut quibusdam videtur Turgoto monacho Dunelmensi*, ed. H. Hinde, in *Symeonis Dunelmensis opera et Collectanea*, Vol. 1 (Durham: Surtees Society, 1868), pp. 234–54, at 251–4.

For a little more than half a year, he [the priest] said, she had not been able to sit on a horse, and seldom got up from her bed. On the fourth day before her death, while the king was on a military expedition at a long distance of land away, so she could not have known from any messenger, however swift, what was happening to him that day, she suddenly became very sad and said to us who were attending to her: 'Today such a great evil has happened to the realm of the Scots as has not happened for many times past.' When we heard this we paid little attention to her words, but, after a few days, a messenger arrived, from whom we heard that the king had been killed on the very day that the queen had spoken. And as if foreknowing what the future held in store, she had earlier strongly forbidden the king going out with his army anywhere, but I do not know for what reason he did not obey her foreboding. On the fourth day after the king had been murdered, feeling a little better, she went to her chapel to hear Mass. There, knowing that death was imminent, she took great care to prepare for her death by taking the holy sacrament of the Lord's body and blood. Having been [briefly] refreshed by their salutary taste, her previous pains returned, and, lying prostrate in bed, her illness got worse and was pushing her strongly towards her end. But, what might I have done? What might I have done to procure a delay? Almost as if I could postpone my lady's death and prolong her life, now I fear I am approaching [the subject of] her end. But all flesh is like grass and all its glory is like the flowers of the grass; once grass has dried out the flowers have fallen. Her face had already become deathly pale when she requested me, and the other ministers of the holy altar with me, to stand by her and to commend her soul to Christ by singing psalms. She also ordered us to bring her cross, which she used to call the Black Cross, and which she had always held in great veneration. And when it took some time for the container in which it was kept to be opened, the queen sighed heavily and said: 'O, we miserable people, O, we sinners. We shall not now be granted a last glimpse of the Black Cross.' When, however, it was taken out of its case and brought to her, she took it with reverence, embraced and kissed it, while she strove to make crosses with it across her face and eyes. Now her whole body cooled down, although there was still some warmth in it; nevertheless, she kept praying, singing the fiftieth psalm right through and holding the cross herself before her eyes with both hands.

Meanwhile her son [King Edgar, 1097–1107], who at present still governs the realm after his father [Malcolm], returned from the expedition and entered the queen's chamber. What distress was waiting for him! How crushed his heart was! He stood there surrounded by misery on all sides and knew not where to turn. He had come to announce to his mother that his father and brother [Edward] had been killed; and here he found his mother, whom he had loved especially, on her deathbed. He did not know whom to mourn first. But the departure of his dearest mother, whom he saw laying on the point of death in front of him, pierced his heart with sharp pains. Moreover, anxiety for the state of the realm was pressing upon him, because he knew for certain that it would be troubled because of his father's death. Enveloped in grief, thoroughly miserable, pain besieged him from all sides. The queen, lying in agony and thought by those present to have passed away, suddenly regained her strength and spoke to her son. She asked about his father and brother; but he refrained from telling her the truth in case by hearing the news of their death she would die at once; instead he answered that they were well. But she gave a deep sigh and said: 'I know, my son, I know. By this holy cross and by the closeness of our blood, I beseech that you speak out and tell the truth so that it be known.' And because he was forced by her, he told her what had happened. What do you think she might have done? Who would have believed that amongst such adversity she would not have murmured against God? At the same time she had lost her husband, she had lost a son, she was crushed to death by disease, but in all this she had not once sinned with her lips [Job 2: 10], nor did she say anything foolish against God. Instead, she raised her eyes and her hands to heaven, praising and giving thanks, and said: 'I render praise and thanks to You, Almighty God, whose will it was that towards my end I endure such anguish, by which I hope you may wish to cleanse me from some of the stain of sin.'

Realizing that death was near, she soon began to say the prayer which is usually said by the priest after the taking of the Lord's body and blood: 'Lord Jesus Christ, who, by the will of the Father and with the help of the Holy Spirit, have by your death given life to the world, deliver me.' While she was saying 'deliver me' her soul was released from the chains of the body and departed to Christ, the creator of true liberty, whom she had always loved. In this way she shared the felicity of those whose examples of virtue she had followed [in life]. Her death occurred in so much calm, with such complete tranquillity, that there is no doubt that her soul departed to the region of eternal rest and peace. Moreover, amazingly, her face, which had become so pale in death, as is common in the dying, became so flushed with red and white after her death that she might be believed to be asleep instead of dead. And so her body was shrouded with the honour befitting a queen and was carried to the Church of Holy Trinity [in Dunfermline] which she had herself built. There we buried her as she had commanded, opposite the high altar and the venerable sign of the holy cross which she had erected. Therefore her body now rests in the very place where she used to kneel, shedding tears, while offering vigils and prayers.

131. Death in Childbirth of Countess Christina of Guînes, Flanders, 2 July 1177

As recounted by Lambert of Ardres, chaplain of Arnold V, Count of Ardres (c.1178–1220) and II of Guînes (1206–20), c.1200. (It was in fact through the marriage of this Christina with Baldwin II of Guînes that the two families had merged. For an account of the chronicler Lambert and the family relationships, see texts 53 and 55 above.)

Newly translated from: *Lamberti Ardensis historia comitum Ghisnensium*, ed. J. Heller, MGH, SS 24 (Hanover: Hahn, 1879), pp. 550–642, at 600–601.

How Countess Christina Died and Was Buried at Ardres

One year after the deaths of the Lord of Ardres, Arnold of Colvida [Arnold IV, c.1147–76], and of his noble wife, Adelina (after she had given birth to her last child), Countess Christina of Guînes was on her sickbed, as is common for women in childbirth, and while her husband was in England for business reasons. Having received messengers and heard from them the news that his wife was very seriously ill, to the point of death, the count just reached her, lying ill at Ardres, whereupon his doctors and masters, namely Herman and Geoffrey, in despair about her life, left her in the count's care and comfort, ready to be soon mourned and lamented. 'Chalisticis' medicines did not do her any good, but rather provoked her death, O! The most Christian Countess Christina of Guînes died on the second of July. Because she was born and then died at Ardres, with the agreement and consent of the monks of the Church of Ardres, she was honourably buried at the feet of her mother, the venerable Adeline of Ardres, near the brickwork of the church, opposite her ancestors, in the presence of the venerable Abbot Godschalk of Saint-Bertin, Alger of St Mary of the Chapel,

Peter of Ardres, Robert of Licques and other priests, clergy and innumerable lay people, celebrating the funeral Mass in tears. Grief, distress and laments were omnipresent there.

> Here the count, here her sons and daughters,
>   the kinsmen knights
> Were lamenting her; the ether rang with cries
> Where hand stretched out to hand, mouths
>   were bleeding,
> They cried out for their lady. The people of Ardres
> Filled with grief, stood by with miserable laments;
> Each person's grief increased the lamentations,
> Their faces wet with tears;
> For the more the fire of love burned within,
> The more and greater grief for she who had
>   nourished them
> Bore upon the miserable people.

When the noble matron Countess Christina of Guînes had been buried and honourably covered with the marble tombstone, we inscribed the marble with these verses as her epitaph:

> Here lies the countess, sprung from flourishing stock,
> Christina by name, on a par with and equal to
>   her husband,
> May all take note of the sixth nones of July,
> May her day of dying be known for a long time,
> One thousand years, one hundred, seventy-seven,
> Stand full between Christ's birth and her funeral.

132. Benefactors of the Hôtel-Dieu, Listed for Commemoration, Beauvais, 1292

Many religious institutions kept records of the deceased benefactors they were required to pray for, including members of their own community if a monastic house. Some benefactors specifically asked to have their names written into these records when making wills. Such lists rarely give details of dates of death, but do offer a valuable source of information regarding the social composition of ecclesiastical communities (and, as the text below seems to indicate, these communities often included lay sisters who worked alongside the nuns). This list is edited to show solely female benefactors.

Newly translated from: M. Le Docteur Leblond, 'Obituaire de l'Hôtel-Dieu de Beauvais (1292)', *Bulletin Philologique et Historique*, 1917 (Paris, Imprimerie Nationale, 1919), pp. 343–441, at 352 ff.

Death of Lady Marie de Becfort, who gave us the tithe at Soutrene. This Marie's body rests in our church.

Death of Ermentrudis, mother of the poor and sister of this house.

Death of Sgaus, servant of the poor.

Death of Albree, wife of Hugo de Villari, on whose behalf we received twelve *denarii* of the tax.

Death of Ermeline the needlewoman, Sister.

Death of Ricaudis, wife of Hugh the squire, from whom we had twenty *solidi* to buy roof beams.

Death of Havydis, Dispenser [the person in charge of wine and/or medicines], our sister.

Death of Odeline, wife of Dragonis le Cornier, from whom we had forty *solidi* and her bed.

Death of Havydis, wife of Peter de Hodinc, Sister.

Death of Havydis, sister of Erembert the priest, who gave us sixty *solidi*, less eight *denarii* in tax, plus a kitchen.

Death of Ermeline, widow of Ade Babouin, who gave us three and a half *solidi* for the kitchen, for the day of her anniversary [i.e. for the nuns to commemorate the anniversary of her death].

Death of Florie, recluse, of St Omer en Chaussée.

Death of the wife of Philip Balduin.

Death of Omeline, daughter of Odeline, who gave us seven *solidi*.

Death of Petronilla, daughter of Guilbert Sachet, from whom we had a bed and ten *solidi*.

Death of Reginalde, mother of William, priest of this house; she died in 1196 AD.

Death of Maria, Cloth-maker, Sister.

133. 'Competitive' Commemoration after the Death of Queen Matilda II, England, 1118

The Warenne Chronicle was probably written c.1157 and used near-contemporary documentation as its source for the story of the 'sale' of commemorative prayers for Queen Matilda II (who died in 1118). It is the first such account to survive for a member of the English royal family. The anonymous author, who may have been the clerk Master Eustace of Boulogne, chancellor to William IV, Earl of Warenne, interestingly underlines the religiosity of the secular clergy at Queen Matilda's court, perhaps in response to criticism that the clergy at the queen's court were too worldly.

Newly translated from: *The Warenne Chronicle*, ed. and trans E. van Houts and R. Love (Oxford: Oxford University Press, forthcoming).

In the year of the Lord's incarnation, 1118, when King Henry [I, 1100–35] was in Normandy, the venerable Queen of the Norman-English, the Lady Matilda, the faith of faithful hopes, was swept up to heaven on the thirtieth of April in the seventeenth year of her rule, and in the fifty-third year after the coming of the Norman-English to England. She was a truly incomparable woman, in whose lifetime England flourished and at whose death, England's flower was cut off, and all its beauty was taken away by her. For if she had lived in the times of St Jerome, certainly, he would have extolled her with infinite praises, with his well-ordered eloquence. For she, above all women, was filled with twofold love to such an extent that it was her entire intention to please God everywhere and to be a stumbling-block to no man. And so she rendered service to the Lord every day at the established hours, so devotedly, so joyously, that you would think that her chapel was not an assembly of court clerics, but a most fervent one of religious monks. Indeed the bishops and her most noble clerics were eager to be of service to her, and, as they themselves admitted, they could not hear enough of her discourses. So then, almost all of England's bishops, nobility, abbots, priors, and indeed the innumerable common masses assembled for her crowded funeral, and with many tears they attended her burial. At the urging of Roger, Bishop of Salisbury [1102/3–39], all offered for her soul with utmost devotion an infinite multitude of masses, prayers, alms and other benefits. That same bishop had the gifts of each written down in the presence of a large congregation, and although no man can rightly grasp the gifts of alms performed for her, yet here in brief is a summary of those gifts collected within eight days: money for 47,000 masses to be said; for 9,000 psalters [books containing the text of the Psalms] to be bought, for 80 trentals [books containing thirty days of prayers for the dead]; and the poor who were sustained for a day, 67,820; those sustained for a year, 108, and those for life, 128. It is related that at least as much was done in her name in Normandy, and thirteen monks were made [given grants to support and maintain them for life] on her behalf. She was buried in the Church of St Peter the Apostle at Westminster, by order of King Henry, next to the altar on the east side, daughter of the east. On her tomb these verses are seen inscribed:

Here lies the distinguished Queen Matilda the Second,
Who surpassed both young and old in her time.
Pattern of morals, and beauty of life,
She was for all.

I can sum up her praise in this brief declaration that from the time when England was first subject to kings, of all queens none was found like her, nor will a similar queen be found in coming ages, she whose memory will be held in praise and whose name will be blessed for centuries. So great was the sorrow at her absence and so great a devotion filled everyone that several of her noblest clerics, whom she had much esteemed in life, stayed at her tomb for thirty days in vigils, prayers and fasting, and they kept mournful and devoted watch. Also until the present day her memory is kept as new. Moreover, in order that it might be shown that England was made strong by her merits and that King Henry reigned by her prayers, within eight days of her burial, a new and apparently inextinguishable conflict arose against him.

134. Letter to Einhard Commiserating on the Death of his Wife, Imma, 836

We have already met Einhard's wife, Imma (above, Chapter 3, text 50): it is tempting to speculate that Lupus was moved to write this bracing letter as a response to Einhard's perhaps too-demonstrative grief at her loss.

Newly translated from: *Lupi abbatis Ferrariensis epistolae*, ed. Ernest Dümmler, MGH, *Epp Karol Aevi*, 6 (Berlin: Weidmann, 1925), pp. 1–126, at 9.

To his most desirable preceptor, Einhard, from Lupus:

Disturbed by the most horrible news of the death of your venerable wife, I would choose now more than ever to be with you, so that I could raise you up with my compassion, or, having understood your feelings, console you with the divine words of the sermon. Truly, whilst God makes it possible, I suggest that you contemplate the human condition, which we have deserved on account of our sins, and that you bear modestly and wisely the sadness that has happened. Nor must you give in to this unfortunate grief, you who have always strongly defeated the blandishments of good fortune. But invoking God, now go out and bring forth those powers of tolerance, which you would probably call upon a most dear person seized by similar circumstances [to show]. I desire that you should fare well.

135. Guisanda's Will Disputed, Bari, 1021

It is unclear what lay at the root of this dispute, and there are internal contradictions within the document, which suggest that the scribe was not sure of the outcome either. The 'will' itself, assuming it even existed in written form, has not survived.

Newly translated from: *Codice Diplomatico Barese, IV: Periodo Greco*, ed. F. Nitti di Vito (Bari: Commissione provinciale per la storia patria, 1900), no. 10, pp. 17–19.

In the name of our Lord, Jesus Christ. In the sixty-second year of the rule of lords Basil and Constantine, in the month of May, fourth indiction.

I, John, son of Maiorano of Noa, whilst in the city of Bari, declare before the good men signing as witnesses below, that when my wife, Guisanda, daughter of Angelus who lives here in Bari, died in earlier days, she took account of her soul and made a disposition of all her moveable goods, and made Dumnellus, son of Pufani the priest, and Ursus, son of Ermengardus, both of Noa, her executors.

And she commissioned them to sell a quilt, a silk cloth, a blouse, a cape, a small old broken bed, a cauldron and small poles [probably a tripod or spit], a pair of flax combs and a wool comb, and to give the price to the priests and the poor for the benefit of her soul.

And my above-mentioned wife left a blanket, a mattress and a fulled [beaten so that the fibres were softened] cloth to Sandulus, our small son; and she left a pair of scales to Juliana the nun, and according to her orders, which she committed into the hands of her executors, this was all carried out.

But now I have made a complaint about the above-mentioned Angelus, my father-in-law, in the court of Lord Romuald, *protospatharius* [i.e. Byzantine official], in the presence of Alefantus the judge, that he has taken all the goods of Sandulus, his small grandson, after the death of his mother – the goods that my wife had – and is keeping them with him.

When my father-in-law was asked about this he replied to

the judge that he did not have these things, but that when his daughter died she disposed of everything into the hands of her executors just as is set out above.

So Alefantus the judge called the above-mentioned executors into his presence, and asked them whether this will was true, and they responded that it was, and that she had placed it in their hands, as can be read above.

The judge decided that he should summon two witnesses who were there when my wife made her will, who would witness that they saw and heard all that she had asked as above, and that he should confirm their testimonies on the gospels. And he made them guarantee that they should come and swear their testimony to me, but before this happened I came to a final and amicable agreement with them, and gave them an oath by document, and received *launegild* [a symbolic settlement payment] from them.

And, through this agreement, they gave me from the moveable goods my wife had disposed of for the benefit of her soul, the cauldron, the poles and the flax combs, and the wool comb, and the bed, which I have at my house. I received them and will keep and guard them safely until my young son reaches legitimate age, and, when he is of age, I will give these things I have received to him.

Now I, John, of my own free will, in the presence of the above witnesses, give a guarantee to you, Ursus and Dumnellus, the above executors of my wife's will, and place myself as guarantor, that at no time in the future will I or my heirs seek to challenge you or your heirs, either personally or through a representative about anything which my above-mentioned wife placed into your hands for the benefit of her soul, just as is written above, but I and my heirs shall remain content always with that which I have now received as written above, through my agreement with you as written above. [Further promises to this effect follow.] And if we do not do this just as we have contractually obliged ourselves to do, and instead try to summon and question you, or if we do not keep the things which I received safely for my son, just as is written above, I promise that I or my heirs will pay a penalty to you or your heirs of twenty Constantinian *solidi*, and twenty to the treasurer, and we will remain silent towards you and complete everything for you just as is written above through the guarantee that I have made to you and your heirs, and you will have the right to take the goods from me or my heirs wherever you may find them if we do not comply as is written above.

And may this charter of agreement remain firm for all time. I asked you, Urso, Deacon and Notary, to write it down in the above city of Bari, where I was.

Peter, witness; John, witness.

136. The Will of Eva Peche Disputed, Cambridge, 1286

Eva, wife of Hamo Peche (d. 1242), died in 1286. She had made a will with a bequest in it of ten pounds to the prior and canons of Barnwell Priory in Cambridge. However, according to the canons, her sons tried to hide their mother's will. In the Middle Ages, it was not unusual for sons to be in contention with their mothers' bequests to religious institutions, as these gifts often meant that the total amount of land or income given to their heirs was reduced. And this was the case here, despite the fact that one of Eva's sons, Gilbert of Peche (d. 1291), mentioned here, was a patron of Barnwell Priory.

Newly translated from: *Liber Memorandorum ecclesie de Bernewelle*, ed. J. W. Clark (Cambridge: Cambridge University Press, 1907), Book 3, c. 108, p. 176.

Plea for [request to execute] the Will of Eva Peche

The mother of Lord Gilbert Peche (our patron), Eva Peche, a noble and good woman, died on the third day after Epiphany [i.e. 6 January 1286], but her body remained unburied until Palm Sunday [7 April 1286]. Then her three sons, knights, and a fourth person, a clergyman, Dom Hamo, came, and they buried her body with all honour next to her husband in the Chapel of the Virgin Mary, and the total amount of [candle] wax [burned at her funeral and subsequent anniversaries of her death] came to about two hundred pounds [in weight], plus [there were] three cloths of gold thread and two horses carried the coffin. After all rites had been performed, her above-mentioned sons left, without mentioning their mother's will. But because the prior had heard from others that the lady had bequeathed, along with her body, many goods to the church where she had chosen to be buried, he called in Dom Hamo, her principal executor, in the presence of an official of the Bishop of Norwich in order to ask one hundred marks from him in the name of a bequest. The bishop's proctor [ecclesiastical practitioner of law] denied the case for almost two years until the return of his lord from overseas. When finally his lord came, he willy-nilly confessed that ten pounds had been bequeathed; having shown the will in the presence of the judge, he was ordered to pay the ten pounds, as well as at least fifty shillings for the costs [of the case].

137. Beneficiary of a Will, Crete, 1301

This document is a receipt, proving that the executors of Ailise's will had done their work, and ensuring that there would be no further claim from Rosana on the estate. See the introduction to text 31, Chapter 2, for more information about these sorts of legal documents and the way that they were written down.

Newly translated from: *Benvenuto de Brixano, Notaio in Candia, 1301–1302*, ed. Raimondo Morozzo della Rocca, Fonti per la Storia di Venezia, sez. 3: Archivi Notarili (Venice, Alfieri Editore, 1950), p. 70.

Entry 190: 21 June 1301

I, Rosana, servant of Jacob Dandulo, inhabitant of Candia, with my successors, make a full and irrevocable security to you, the executors of Ailise, widow of Peter Villelmo, about all the bequests which she left me at her death. Now this etc.

Witnesses: Pispolo and Paduanus.

To be completed and dated.

138. Commemoration Stone Erected by Helmgöt for his Deceased Wife, Odendis, Sweden, Tenth to Eleventh Centuries

Only a very small percentage of memorial stones in Scandinavia were erected by husbands for wives. The elaborately decorated memorial stone (Vs 24, Hassmyra) can still be seen in Hassmyra (Västmanland in Sweden). Although it is undated, it can be assigned to the Viking Age, i.e. tenth to eleventh centuries.

Newly translated from B. Sawyer, *The Viking-Age Rune-Stones: Custom and Commemoration in Early Medieval Scandinavia* (Oxford: Oxford University Press, 2000), p. 60 and plate 13.

The good landowner Holmgöt had [this stone] raised in the memory of Odendis, his wife. To Hassmyra, a better housewife administering the farm, will never come. Rödballe cut these runes. Odendis was a good sister of Sigmund.

139. The Will of Æthelgifu, England, Tenth Century

This document 'of exceptional importance for the social and economic history of tenth-century England' [J. Crick], in Old English, was drawn up by a noble woman called Æthelgifu. In the second half of the tenth century, she held land in Bedfordshire, Hertfordshire and Northamptonshire, and some property in London. It has not been established with complete certainty whom Æthelgifu was married to, but it is thought that her husband (referred to here as 'her lord') had been a man named Æthelric. It is generally believed that Æthelgifu was a widow who had vowed to live the rest of her life in a spirit of religious devotion.

As was standard practice, Æthelgifu used her will to pay her 'heriot', that is to say, to buy (via substantial gifts: gold, horses and hounds) the support of the king and queen to safeguard her bequests, and to ensure the salvation of her soul by generous donations to the Monastery of St Albans, and also to religious houses at Hitchin, Braughing and Welwyn.

However, such bequests were complex. The will includes some 'reversionary gifts': one complicated aspect of giving land to monasteries in medieval England was that land could be given to family members for life, or for up to three lifetimes, and after that it reverted to the monastery. Another technical aspect of such arrangements is that of 'food-rent', also mentioned here. This was rent in the form of food, which was payable from specified estates to the monastery in anticipation of the monks receiving the land outright in due course.

The will is informative about Æthelgifu's kin, many of whom are mentioned by name. But little is known about Æthelgifu's husband; only one of his relatives is named, namely Ælfgifu, probably his daughter (i.e. Æthelgifu's stepdaughter). However, it *is* clear from this document (see section 6) that at one stage Æthelgifu was forced to defend the terms of her deceased husband's will against his avaricious kinsmen. Moreover, the will contains fascinating information about Æthelgifu's moveable possessions, which she distributed to her kinsmen and household women, as well as about the manumission of slaves. In particular, it testifies to three female slaves: Ælfwaru, Leofruna and Æthelflæd, who, once freed, were expected to pray for her soul.

Translated by Julia Crick from *Charters of St Albans*, Vol. 12, ed. Julia Crick, Anglo-Saxon Charters (Oxford and London: Oxford University Press for the British Academy, 2007), pp. 148–51, with commentary and analysis on pp. 91–100.

We are extremely grateful to Julia Crick for allowing us to use her translation and also for her help with the commentary on this text.

1. Æthelgifu declares her will to her royal lord [King Æthelred, 978–1016] and to her lady [the queen] and to her friends, what she wishes to render to God, what to her lord, what to her friends.

2. That is, to her lord, thirty *mancuses* [coins worth thirty pennies] of gold and two stallions, which must be offered to him, and her deer-hounds; and to her lady, thirty *mancuses* of gold.

3. And the land at Westwick, as stocked, and the land at Gaddesden, to St Albans, on condition that the monks ever have the use of it in common [i.e. not individually, but as a whole community]; and thirty *mancuses* of gold and thirty oxen,

twenty from Gaddesden and ten from Oakhurst, and twenty cows, ten from Gaddesden and ten from Oakhurst – and that is to be carried out in return for [the burial of] her body – and one hundred and fifty sheep from Langford, fifty ewes with their lambs and fifty sheep which yield no milk; and a herd of swine [is to be given] from Oakhurst, and the swineherd with it. And from the estate, Ymma and Ealdhelm and Wulfhelm and his children and Siwynn's younger son are to be freed, and all the others [to be given] to St Albans; and two silver cups, and two [drinking] horns, and one book, and the best wall-hanging, and the best seat-cover, for the benefit of her and her lord's soul. At Gaddesden, Edmund and his son and Heahulf and Eadwig are to be freed; Æthelwine and his wife are to be given to Æthelstan, and their children are to be freed; Wynstan and Heremod and Cuthmund's daughter and Osmund and his wife [are to be given] to St Albans.

And the land at Langford [is to be given] to Ælfnoth for his lifetime, and five men; and Mangod and Mantat are to be freed. And Ælfnoth is to have Wine the miller and [or: Mangod, Mantat and Wine the miller are to be freed. And Ælfnoth is to have] the swineherd's son and wife, and the younger shepherd, and two hundred sheep, one hundred ewes and one hundred sheep which yield no milk, and the herd of swine, and one plough-team of oxen and four oxen, on condition that he pay every three-days-food-rent to Hitchin. And, after his lifetime, the land at Langford [is to be given] to Hitchin. And to Leofwine, my sister's son, the land at Clifton, and Eadric and his wife; and their children are to be freed. And fifty ewes with their lambs [are to be given] from Langford to Hitchin, and fifty sheep to Bedford, and thirty to Flitton, and twenty to Ashwell, and ten to Henlow, unless she have money. And, with the surplus, one is to think about the vigils [prayers for the dead] and [give it] to the priests. And the half-hide which Wineman possessed [is to be given] to the church, and Edwin the priest is to be freed, and he is to have the church for his lifetime on condition that he keep it in repair, and he is to be given a man. Ufic and the fuller are to be freed, Bryhstan's sister [is to be given as a nun] to Stondon for Edwin [presumably to pray for his soul],

on condition that she and her lord have every year three masses
a week [said for them], and that he ever raise intercession for
them. And Tiddulf and Boga and Domic and his wife, and Siric
and his stepdaughter are to be freed. And Edwin, [when] free,
is to have Ælfswyth and her children and the miller's wife and
her children. If there be any surplus [i.e. any of her moveable
possessions left over after the bequests have been made], let it
be divided among her household.

And Ælfwold is to have the land at Munden for his lifetime,
on condition that he pay every Lent six measures of malt, and
meal and fish in addition, to Braughing, and as much to Welwyn; and to each minster [i.e. church] four swine at Martinmas.
And he is to have two plough-teams of oxen and four men,
Oswig and his wife, and Cinesige and his wife – and their children are to be freed – and Brihtwine, and Godere and his herd.
Four oxen are to be given to Hertingfordbury and four to Welwyn from the estate, and ten cows to Ælfwold. If there be any
surplus, two are to be given to Mann. And Boga and all his family are to be freed, and Wynsige and his wife, and Mann and his
wife, and Dufe the Old and Æthelthryth. And after Ælfwold's
lifetime half the land at Munden is to be given to Braughing and
half to Welwyn, and they are to sing thirty masses every year.
And the land at Standon [is to be given] to Leofsige; and four
oxen and two cows are to be given from it to Braughing. And
Eadstan the swineherd is to be freed, and his son is to have
charge of the herd, and the family otherwise is to be freed, and
Grim and his wife, and Eadgith, and Eadflæd, and Byrnferth,
and Wulfrun, and Brynstan the swineherd. And Leofsige is to
have the younger swineherd and the herd which Eadstan has
charge of. And Wulfric the huntsman is to be given two oxen
and two cows from the estate. And Leofsige is to have everything else for his lifetime; and after his lifetime it is to be given
to Ælfwold; and after their lifetimes to St Albans. And they are
to sing for her and for her lord's soul thirty masses and thirty
psalters [books containing the text of the Psalms] every year,
and the monks are always to have the use of it [the estate] in
common. The land at Offley, and all that the charter directs, is
to be given to Leofsige, and the land at Tewin as swine-pasture

for him, on condition that he provide from those two estates for the community of St Albans three-days-food-rent each year, or sixteen measures of malt and three of meal and one *sester* of honey from Offley with the rent, and eight castrated rams and six lambs, and one bullock for slaughter and thirty cheeses; and, from Standon, one measure of wine and twenty cheeses and six swine and one bullock. And this same amount is to be taken from each estate for the thirtieth day [i.e. every month], both from Gaddesden and from all others which there are in [her] land. And, at Offley, Cyneleofu, and Martin and his wife, and Dearmod and his wife, and Bryhtwaru, and Theodild, and Wulfstan of Cockernhoe, and his two sons and his stepdaughter are to be freed. And Leofsige is to have the land at Weedon, on condition that he deliver every year one barrel full of ale for the benefit of her [Æthelgifu's] father's soul and her mother's and her brother's and for herself and for her lord, and all that belong to that place. If he have a child, he is to give it to that child; if he have not, he is to give it to his lawful kindred. And Leofric is to be freed at Weedon, and Ælfric, and Bryrhtelm and his sister. And he [Leofsige] is to give the land at Offley to his child. If he have no child in wedlock, he is to give it to St Albans, except the land which Tatulf and Æthelferth and Æthelswith occupy; that is to be given to her lord's daughter, Ælfgifu, if she is still alive; if she is not alive, it is to be given to St Albans. And every year thirty masses and thirty psalters are to be sung for her and for her lord's soul. And she prays her lady [the queen] of her charity that she watch over him, and that he be allowed to serve the Ætheling [the king's son], and [that she] does not consent that any man rob him of his lands, and that she orders him to be supplied with clothing from the land.

And half the messuage [houses or plots of land] in London [is to be given] to Ælfwold, and half to Ælfheah. And a herd of swine at Gaddesden is to be given to Ælfgifu, and the younger swineherd and two men in addition. And the herd which Briht-elm was in charge of, and his younger son and Wulfstan and his wife, are to be given to Leofwine, my sister's son.

And the land at Watford is to be given to my kinswoman, Leofrun, and two men and eight oxen at Weedon, and her saddle-gear and her cups and her [drinking] horns, unless she should have given it to her before; and after her lifetime the land at Watford is to be given to her daughter, Godwif.

And the land at Thrupp she is to give after her lifetime within her own kindred, on condition that she gives her a pledge and lays aside all anger, and [that] she does not ask for anything more. If she is not willing, it is to be divided among her children.

4. And to my kinswoman, Wulfwynn, [is to be given] a dish, and a brooch, and a wall-hanging, and a seat-cover, and all the best bedsteads she has available, and her brightest kirtle; and to her kinsman, Wulfmær, the smaller silver cup. And five *mancuses* are to be cut from her headband for Witsige, unless she should have done it before, and five for Leofwine, Wulmær's son, and five for Wulmær, my sister's son, and five for Godwif and five for Ælfgifu, my sister's daughter. And her blue kirtle, which is untrimmed at the bottom, and her best head-dresses are to be given to Beornwynn. And her three purple kirtles are to be given to Lufetat and Ælfgifu and Godwif. And Wulfgifu is to be given some of her other, dun-coloured kirtles. And afterwards her household women are to divide what is left between them. And three wall-hangings, the better of such as are then there, and two seat-covers and two bedsteads are to be given to Leofsige. And Godwif and Ælfgifu are to divide the others between them; and each of them [is to have] two chests. And Leofsige is to have her carriage, and is to bequeath afterwards the homestead to all, and occupy it.

5. And Mann, her goldsmith, is to be freed, and his eldest son, and the youngest, and his wife, and the wife of Wulfric the huntsman and their children, and Ælfwaru, their daughter, on condition that she sing four psalters every week, within thirty days, and a psalter every week, within twelve months, and Leofrun is to be freed on the same conditions, and Æthelflæd. And Liofing of Henlow is to be freed and he is to have land on condition that every year he remembers her and her lord. And Mann's boy is to be freed.

And she begs for the love of God that from the residue of

men from Munden and at Gaddesden and from Langford two
men be given to Wulfric and his wife, and two to Mann and his
wife, and that the son of Dufe at Munden be given to George
the priest. The shepherd is to be freed and Ælfwold is to have
the dairymaid. And her godson, Æthelric, is to be remembered
with some man, and the under-shepherd is to be given to Æthel-
weard the priest, and Ælfnoth is to have Godere in exchange
for that. And the lame boy is to be given to Gundburth,
Æthelferth's son. And for Boga, her priest, a young man is to
be found from the remainder, if there be one; if there [be] not,
a cow from Offley is to be given to him. And Leofsige is to have
Æthelwyn and Sidemon and his wife and Æthelwine and his
wife, and their children are to be freed, and Dudewine,
Cynewynn's daughter [is to be given] to Ælfgifu, her kinswoman; and to Godwif, Eadwynn; and Byrnflæd – unless she
herself free her and give her another.

6. All the manumission and all the almsgiving which is stated
here she wishes to be her alms because they were her lord's
acquisitions. And she begs her royal lord of his charity, for his
royal dignity, for the love of God and St Mary, that you two [i.e.
this included the queen] allow no man, for money, to change
her will. Sire, her lord bequeathed it for her to give to whom she
wished, which her lord's kinsmen did not allow her. Then she
produced an oath at Hitchin, twenty-hundred oaths; there were
included [present] Ælfhere and Ælfsige *cild* [Young Ælfsige]
and Byrnric, who was then reeve [local officer], and all the chief
men belonging to Bedford and Hertford, and their wives. In
spite of the will and [text illegible].

Eadelm, the son of her lord's sister, dispossessed her of her land
at Standon. Then I appealed to the king and gave him twenty
pounds; then he [Eadelm] gave me back my land against his will.

She does not expect it of her lord or her lady [the king and
queen]; but if anyone ask that this will may not be allowed to
stand, may he be cast on the left hand when the Saviour pro-
nounces his judgement, and may he be as hateful to God as was
Judas, who hanged himself; unless she herself change it hereafter,
and those be not alive to whom these things are now bequeathed.

Notes

CHAPTER 1: BIRTH AND INFANCY

1. Peter of Eboli, *De Rebus Siculis Carmen*, ed. E. Rota, Rerum Italicarum Scriptores 31 (Città di Castello: S. Lapi, 1904), table 10; *Self and Society in Medieval France: The Memoirs of Abbot Guibert of Nogent*, ed. J. F. Benton (New York: Harper Torch-books, 1970), p. 42.

2. *Chroniques des comtes d'Anjou et des seigneurs d'Amboise*, ed. Louis Halphen and René Poupardin (Paris: A. Picard et fils, 1913).

3. Janet L. Nelson, 'Queens as Jezebels: The careers of Brunhild and Bathild in Merovingian history', in *Medieval Women*, ed. Derek Baker (Oxford: Blackwell, 1978), pp. 31–77.

4. Dudley Wilson, *Signs and Portents: Monstrous Births from the Middle Ages to the Enlightenment* (London: Routledge, 1993); Irina Metzler, *Disability in Medieval Europe: Thinking about Physical Impairment in the High Middle Ages* (London: Routledge, 2006), pp. 86–8, 94. See also this volume, text 94, below.

5. Sally Crawford, *Childhood in Anglo-Saxon England* (Stroud: Sutton, 1999).

6. Amy Eichorn-Mulligan, 'Contextualizing Old Norse-Icelandic bodies', paper read at the thirteenth International Saga Conference, Durham/York, 6–12 August 2006, and published at http://www.dur.ac.uk/medieval.www/sagaconf/eichorn.htm (accessed 9/09/2008).

7. See Becky R. Lee, 'A company of women and men: men's recollections of childbirth in medieval England', *Journal of Family History*, 27 (2002), 92–100, where the dynastic concerns of men caused them to remember and record births.

8. Jennifer C. Ward, *Women in Medieval Europe, 1200–1500* (London: Longman, 2002), p. 55.

9. Helen Rodnite Lemay, 'Anthonius Guainerius and medieval gynaecology', in *Women of the Medieval World*, ed. Julius Kirshner and Suzanne Wemple (Oxford: Blackwell, 1985), pp. 317–36; Monica H. Green, *Making Women's Medicine Masculine: The Rise of Male Authority in Pre-modern Gynaecology* (Oxford: Oxford University Press, 2008).

10. Renate Blumenfeld-Kosinski, *Not of Woman Born: Representations of Caesarean Birth in Medieval and Renaissance Culture* (Ithaca: Cornell University Press, 1990). A very early example of Caesarean section, but on a woman who had died in late pregnancy from TB and was found in a twelfth-century burial at Wharram Percy in North Yorkshire: brief note on 'Medieval Caesarean', *History Today*, November 2005.

11. J. M. Riddle, *Contraception and Abortion from the Ancient World to the Renaissance* (Cambridge, MA: Harvard University Press, 1992).

12. Suzanne Bartlet, *Licoricia of Winchester: Marriage, Motherhood and Murder in the Medieval Anglo-Jewish Community*, ed. Patricia Skinner (London: Vallentine Mitchell, 2009). The record of the case is translated below, text 81.

13. See Carol Neel, *Medieval Families: Perspectives on Marriage, Household and Children* (Toronto: University of Toronto Press, 2004), pp. 86–7 and Tommaso di Carpegna Falconieri, *The Man Who Believed He was King of France*, trans. William McCuaig (Toronto and Chicago: University of Chicago Press, 2008).

14. Becky R. Lee, 'The purification of women after childbirth: A window onto medieval perceptions of women', *Florilegium*, 14 (1995–6), 43–55. A similar separation from the religious community accompanied childbirth for Jewish women: Elisheva Baumgarten, *Mothers and Children: Jewish Family Life in Medieval Europe* (Princeton: Princeton University Press, 2004).

15. See below, text 13, and Baumgarten, *Mothers and Children*.

16. In some cases she was not even free to choose to wet-nurse: Rebecca Lynn Winer, 'Conscripting the breast: Lactation, slavery and salvation in the realms of Aragon and kingdom of Majorca, c.1250–1300', *Journal of Medieval History*, 34 (2008), 164–84. There is more information from the Muslim world: Avner Giladi, *Infants, Parents and Wet-nurses: Medieval Islamic Views on Breastfeeding and their Social Implications* (Leiden: Brill, 1999).

17. Emily Coleman, 'Infanticide in the early Middle Ages', in *Women*

in *Medieval Society*, ed. Susan Mosher Stuard (Philadelphia: University of Pennsylvania Press, 1976), pp. 47–70. Shulamith Shahar, *Childhood in the Middle Ages* (London: Routledge, 1992), p. 129.

18. D. Lett, *L'enfant des miracles. Enfance et société au Moyen Âge (XIIe-XIIIe siècle)* (Paris: Aubier, 1997), pp. 93-8.

19. Brenda Bolton, '"Received in His name": Rome's busy baby box', *Studies in Church History*, 31 (1994), 153–67.

20. See *The Child in Christian Thought*, ed. Marcia J. Bunge (Grand Rapids: William B. Eerdmans, 2001), esp. pp. 1–133.

21. John Boswell, *The Kindness of Strangers: The Abandonment of Children in Western Europe from Late Antiquity to the Renaissance* (New York: Pantheon Books, 1988). See also Sharon Farmer, *Surviving Poverty in Medieval Paris* (Ithaca: Cornell University Press, 2005). Work of this type has been done very effectively for a slightly later period: Philip Gavitt, *Charity and Children in Renaissance Florence: The Ospedale degli Innocenti, 1410–1536* (Ann Arbor: University of Michigan Press, 1990).

CHAPTER 2: GIRLS AND YOUNG WOMEN

1. That is not to say girls were not given to the Church, only less commonly: see Mayke de Jong, *In Samuel's Image: Child Oblation in the Early Medieval West* (Leiden: Brill, 1995). See also John Boswell, '*Expositio* and *oblatio*: The abandonment of children and the ancient and medieval family', *American Historical Review*, 89 (1984), 10–33.

2. E.g. *How the Good Wife Taught her Daughter*, ed. T. Mustanoja (Helsinki: Suomalaisen Kirjallisuuden Scuran, 1948), a mid-fourteenth-century English text; the slightly later French *Book of the Knight of La Tour Landry*, ed. D. B. Wyndham Lewis and G. S. Taylor (Kila: Kessinger Publishing, 2003), and *The Good Wife's Guide (Le Menagier de Paris): A Medieval Household Book,* trans. Gina L. Greco and Christine M. Rose (Ithaca: Cornell University Press, 2009) – the latter written for the *menagier*'s very young wife, rather than a daughter.

3. S. Mosher Stuard, 'Ancillary evidence for the decline of medieval slavery', *Past and Present*, 149 (1995), 3–28.

4. P. J. P. Goldberg, 'Girls growing up in later medieval England', *History Today*, 45 (June, 1995), 25–32.

5. Georges Duby, 'Youth in aristocratic society: northwestern France in the twelfth century', in *id., The Chivalrous Society*,

trans. Cynthia Postan (Berkeley: University of California Press, 1980); *Becoming Male in the Middle Ages*, ed. Jeffrey Jerome Cohen and Bonnie Wheeler (New York: Garland Publishing, 2000); Ruth Mazo Karras, *From Boys to Men: Formations of Masculinity in Late Medieval Europe* (Philadelphia: University of Pennsylvania Press, 2003).

6. William F. MacLehose, *A Tender Age: Cultural Anxieties over the Child in the Twelfth and Thirteenth Centuries* (New York: Columbia University Press, 2008), pp. 175–211.

7. Kim Phillips, Katherine Lewis and Noel James Menuge, eds., *Young Medieval Women* (London: Sutton, 1999). See also Fiona Harris Stoertz, 'Young Women in France and England, 1050–1300', *Journal of Women's History*, 12 (2001), 22–46.

8. Deborah Youngs, *The Life Cycle in Western Europe, c.1300–1500* (Manchester: Manchester University Press, 2006), p. 120.

9. Elisabeth Bos, 'The literature of spiritual formation for women in France and England, 1080 to 1180', in *Listen, Daughter: The Speculum Virginum and the Formation of Religious Women in the Middle Ages*, ed. Constant J. Mews (New York: Palgrave, 2001), pp. 201–20, at 204–7 (Peter of Blois to Anselma, and Arnulf of Lisieux to a woman called G, who had been betrothed since the age of seven to his brother).

10. The competition between saints and doctors was not simply a product of the hagiographic imagination: see Patricia Skinner, 'A cure for a sinner: Sickness and health care in medieval southern Italy', in *The Community, the Family and the Saint: Patterns of Power in Medieval Europe*, ed. Joyce Hill and Mary Swann (Turnhout: Brepols, 1998).

11. *The Trotula: An English Translation of a Medieval Compendium of Women's Medicine*, ed. Monica H. Green (Philadelphia: University of Pennsylvania Press, 2002), p. 66.

12. Darryl W. Amundsen and Carol Jean Diers, 'The age at menarche in medieval Europe', *Human Biology*, 45 (1973), 363–9; Joan Cadden, *The Meanings of Sex Difference in the Middle Ages*, p. 145; Clarissa Atkinson, *The Oldest Vocation: Christian Motherhood in the Middle Ages* (Ithaca: University of Cornell Press, 1991), p. 39 note.

13. Judith Bennett, *History Matters: Patriarchy and the Challenge of Feminism* (Philadelphia: University of Pennsylvania Press, 2006), Chapter 6: 'The L-word in women's history'. See also Cordelia Beattie's useful discussion 'A room of one's own? The legal evidence for the residential arrangements for women without

husbands in late fourteenth- and early fifteenth-century York', in
Medieval Women and the Law, ed. Noel James Menuge (Woodbridge: Boydell, 2000), pp. 41–56. The study of medieval single
women is gathering momentum: see *Singlewomen in the European Past, 1250–1800*, ed. Judith M. Bennett and Amy M. Froide
(Philadelphia: University of Pennsylvania Press, 1999).

CHAPTER 3: MARRIED WOMEN
AND MOTHERS

1. Among works on the subject, David D'Avray, *Medieval Mar-
riage: Symbolism and Society* (Oxford: Oxford University Press,
2005); Frances and Joseph Gies, *Marriage and Family in the
Middle Ages* (New York: Harper and Row, 1989); C. N. L.
Brooke, *The Medieval Idea of Marriage* (Oxford: Oxford Uni-
versity Press, 1991); Philip Lyndon Reynolds, *Marriage in the
Western Church: The Christianization of Marriage during the
Patristic and Early Medieval Periods* (Leiden: Brill, 1994); Sue
Sheridan Walker, ed., *Wife and Widow in Medieval England*
(Ann Arbor: University of Michigan Press, 1994).

2. A protracted court case dealing with a clandestine marriage in
Italy is studied by Gene Brucker, *Giovanni and Lusanna: Love
and Marriage in Renaissance Florence* (Berkeley: University of
California Press, 1988).

3. Diane Owen Hughes, 'From brideprice to dowry in Mediterranean Europe', *Journal of Family History*, 3 (1978), 262–96.

4. Rothari law 183: 'If anyone purchases the *mundium* of a free
woman and she is handed over to him as wife . . . ', in *The Lombard Laws*, ed. Katherine Fischer Drew (Philadelphia: University
of Pennsylvania Press, 1973), pp. 85–6; on *mundium*, see
pp. 115–16.

5. Julius Kirshner, 'Wives' claims against insolvent husbands in
late medieval Italy', in *Women of the Medieval World*, ed. Julius
Kirshner and Suzanne Wemple (Oxford: Blackwell, 1985),
pp. 256–303.

6. We should not make too hard-and-fast geographical distinc-
tions, however: Jennifer Smith, 'Unfamiliar territory: Women,
land and law in Occitania, 1150–1250', in *Medieval Women and
the Law*, ed. Noel James Menuge (Woodbridge: Boydell, 2000),
pp. 19–40, provides an important corrective to the image of

Occitan women as having more freedom than their northern
French sisters.

7. See the useful essays by Corinne Saunders, 'A matter of consent:
Middle English romance and the law of *raptus*', and Kim Phillips, 'Written on the body: Reading rape from the twelfth to
fifteenth centuries', both in Menuge, ed., *Medieval Women and
the Law*, pp. 105–24 and 125–44 respectively.

8. Alwyn A. Ruddock, *Italian Merchants and Shipping in Southampton, 1270–1600*, Vol. 1, Southampton Records Series
(Southampton, University College, 1951), pp. 177–8.

9. The classic statement on this problem is Richard M. Smith,
'Geographical diversity in the resort to marriage in later medieval Europe', in *Woman is a Worthy Wight: Women in English
Society, 1200–1500*, ed. P. J. P. Goldberg (Stroud: Tempus, 1992),
pp. 16–59. See also Diane Owen Hughes, 'Urban growth and
family structure in medieval Genoa', Past and Present, 66 (1975),
3-28.

10. James Brundage, *Law, Sex and Christian Society in Medieval
Europe* (Chicago: Chicago University Press, 1987) – see especially the flowchart on p. 162.

11. See also Dyan Elliott, *Spiritual Marriage: Sexual Abstinence in
Medieval Wedlock* (Princeton: Princeton University Press, 1995).

12. Although when Norman couple Germundus and his wife Ber-
senta made a pilgrimage to Rome to seek help for their
childlessness in 1063, the charter of gift they made to the Abbey
of St Trinity, Mont de Rouen, specifically states that they were
infertile (*eo quod steriles errant*): *Cartulaire de l'Abbaye de la
Sainte-Trinité du mont de Rouen*, ed. A. Deville, published as an
appendix within *Cartulaire de l'Abbaye de St Bertin*, ed. M.
Guérard, Collection de Documents inédits sur l'Histoire de
France, Cartulaires, Vol. 3 (Paris: Imprimerie royale, 1841), no.
68, p. 452.

13. Tensions discussed by Janet L. Nelson, 'Monks, secular men and
masculinity' in *Masculinity in Medieval Europe*, ed. D. M. Hadley (London: Longman, 1998).

CHAPTER 4: WIDOWS

1. E.g. numerous essay collections: *Upon My Husband's Death:
Widows in the Literature and Histories of Medieval Europe*, ed.
Louise Mirrer (Ann Arbor: University of Michigan Press, 1992);

Widowhood in Medieval and Early Modern Europe, ed. Sandra Cavallo and Lyndan Warner (London: Longman, 1999); *Wife and Widow in Medieval England*, ed. Sue Sheridan Walker (Ann Arbor: University of Michigan Press, 1993); *Veuves et veuvage dans le haut moyen âge*, ed. M. Parisse (Paris: Picard, 1993); *Medieval London Widows, 1300–1500*, ed. Caroline Barron and Anne Sutton (London: Hambledon, 1994). Specific studies include: Janet Nelson, 'The wary widow', in *Property and Power in the Early Middle Ages*, ed. Wendy Davies and Paul Fouracre (Cambridge: Cambridge University Press, 1995), pp. 82–113; Albrecht Classen, 'Widows: their social and moral functions according to medieval German literature, with special emphasis on Erhart Gross's *Witwenbuch*' (1446), *Fifteenth Century Studies*, 28 (2003), 65–79; Emmanuelle Santinelli, *Des femmes éplorées? Les veuves dans la société aristocratique du haut moyen âge* (Lille: Presses universitaires du Septentrion, 2003).

2. Cavallo and Warner in *Widowhood*, 'Introduction', p. 6, identify three types - the vulnerable, the merry and the good and chaste.

3. Patricia Skinner, 'Gender and poverty in the medieval community', in *Medieval Women in their Communities*, ed. Diane Watt (Cardiff: University of Wales Press, 1997), pp. 203–21, and *ead.*, 'Gender and the sign languages of poverty', in *The Sign Languages of Poverty: International Round Table Discussion, Krems-an-der-Donau, October 10 and 11 2005*, ed. Gerhard Jaritz (Vienna: Verlag der Österreichischen Akademie der Wissenschaften, 2007), pp. 59–74, discuss this issue in more detail.

4. Pauline Stafford, 'Women and the Norman Conquest', *Transactions of the Royal Historical Society* (Sixth Series), 4 (1994), 221–49.

5. The *Rotuli de dominabus et pueri et puellis de XII comitatibus* of 1185, discussed in Susan Johns, *Noblewomen, Aristocracy and Power in the Twelfth-Century Anglo-Norman Realm* (Manchester: Manchester University Press, 2003), pp. 165–94.

6. Barbara Hanawalt, 'Remarriage as an option for urban and rural widows in late medieval England', in *Wife and Widow in Medieval England*, pp. 141–64.

7. Suzanne Bartlet, 'Three Jewish businesswomen in thirteenth-century Winchester', *Jewish Culture and History*, 3 (2000), 31–54.

8. See specific examples discussed in Skinner, 'Gender and poverty'.

9. Susan B. Steuer, 'Family strategies in medieval London: Financial

planning and the urban widow', *Essays in Medieval Studies, 12: Children and Family in the Middle Ages*, ed. Nicole Clifton (Morgantown: West Virginia University Press, 1995), online edition at http://www.illinoismedieval.org/ems/VOL12/steuer.html (accessed 22/09/2009).

10. Pat Cullum, 'Vowesses and veiled widows: Medieval female piety in the province of York', *Northern History*, 32 (1996), 21–41.

CHAPTER 5: OLDER WOMEN AND DEATH

1. Shulamith Shahar, 'Who were old in the Middle Ages?' *Social History of Medicine*, 6 (1993), 313–41. See also *ead.*, *Growing Old in the Middle Ages: 'Winter Clothes us in Shadow and Pain'* (New York: Routledge, 1997).

2. On this issue see also Michael Goodich, 'The virtues and vices of old people in the late Middle Ages', *International Journal of Aging and Human Development*, 30 (1990), 119–27.

3. Such, at least, is suggested for Old Norse society by Carol J. Clover, 'Regardless of sex: Men, women and power in early northern Europe', *Speculum*, 68 (1993), 363–87.

4. The classic study of coroners' rolls is R. F. Hunisett, *The Medieval Coroner* (Cambridge: Cambridge University Press, 1961, repr. 2008). On their use for social history, see Barbara A. Hanawalt, *'Of Good and Ill Repute': Gender and Social Control in Medieval England* (New York and Oxford: Oxford University Press, 1998).

5. J. T. Rosenthal, *Old Age in Late Medieval England* (Philadelphia: University of Pennsylvania Press, 1996), *passim*.

6. Much of the research done so far focuses on the later Middle Ages: notable exceptions are Valerie L. Garber, 'Old age and women in the Carolingian world', in *Old Age in the Middle Ages and the Renaissance: Interdisciplinary Approaches*, ed. Albrecht Classen (Berlin: Walter de Gruyter, 2007), pp. 121–70 and T. Evergates on the ages of members of the Champagne aristocracy, see his *The Aristocracy in the County of Champagne 1100–1300* (Philadelphia: University of Pennsylvania Press, 2007), pp. 140–66. But see also Gretchen Mieszkowski, 'Old age and medieval misogyny: The old woman', in *Old Age in the Middle Ages*, pp. 299–320.

7. See, for example, the ambivalent attitudes towards the Marseil-

leise widow, Margarida, in Susan McDonough, 'Impoverished mothers and poor widows: Negotiating images of poverty in Marseille's courts', *Journal of Medieval History*, 34 (2008), 64–78.

8. The classic study of medieval witchcraft is Jeffrey Burton Russell, *Witchcraft in the Middle Ages* (Ithaca: Cornell University Press, 1984), although its conclusions are not particularly influenced by gender studies. See also Richard Kieckhefer, *Magic in the Middle Ages* (Cambridge: Cambridge University Press, 1990); and, for a moment when older women might be especially susceptible to suspicion, Thomas R. Forbes, *The Midwife and the Witch* (New Haven: Yale University Press, 1966). An extensive bibliography on medieval witchcraft is at http://www. the-orb.net/bibliographies/magic.html (accessed 11/09/2009).

9. Jane Tibbetts Schulenburg, *Forgetful of their Sex: Female Sanctity and Society, ca. 500–1100* (Chicago: University of Chicago Press, 1998), pp. 365–77, discusses the longevity of male and female saints in comparison to laymen and women, and finds a distinct disparity in favour of the former.

10. W. Simons, *Cities of Ladies: Beguine Communities in the Medieval Low Countries, 1200–1565* (Philadelphia: University of Pennsylvania Press, 2001), Chapter 5, pp. 118–37, and R. Blumenfeld-Kosinski, 'Satirical views of the Beguines in northern French literature', in Juliette Dor, Lesley Johnson and Jocelyn Wogan-Browne, eds., *New Trends in Feminine Spirituality: The Holy Women of Liège and their Impact* (Turnhout: Brepols, 1999), 237–50.

11. Both editors of this volume have addressed the issue of memory and testimony: E. van Houts, 'Gender and oral witnesses in Europe (800–1300)', *Transactions of the Royal Historical Society*, sixth series, 9 (1999), 201–20; *Medieval Memories. Men, Women and the Past, 700–1300*, ed. E. van Houts, especially the contributions by Patricia Skinner, pp. 36–52, Judith Everard, pp. 72–91 and Renee Nip, pp. 113–31.

12. Patricia Skinner, 'Disputes and disparity: Women at court in medieval southern Italy', *Reading Medieval Studies*, 22 (1996), addresses the issue of women's access to courts and their credibility once there.

13. This observation finds support from the statistical analysis of gendered commemoration on burial stones in Scandinavia, where only a minute fraction concerns widowers: see B. Sawyer, *The Viking-Age Rune-Stones: Custom and Commemoration in*

Early Medieval Scandinavia (Oxford: Oxford University Press, 2000), p. 40; cf. text 138.

14. J. Green, *Henry I: King of England and Duke of Normandy* (Cambridge: Cambridge University Press, 2006), p. 140.

15. Victoria Thompson, 'Women, power and protection in tenth- and eleventh-century England', and Katherine J. Lewis, 'Women, testamentary discourse and life-writing in later medieval England', both in Menuge, ed., *Medieval Women and the Law*; Julia Crick, 'Women, wills and moveable wealth in pre-Conquest England', in *Gender and Material Culture in Historical Perspective*, ed. M. Donald and L. Hurcombe (London: Macmillan, 2000), pp. 17–37; Patricia Skinner, 'Women, wills and wealth in medieval southern Italy', *Early Medieval Europe*, 3 (1993), 133–52; Nathaniel L. Taylor, 'Women and wills: Sterility and testacy in Catalonia in the eleventh and twelfth centuries', *Medieval Encounters*, 12 (2006), 87–96.

16. *Violence against Women in Medieval Texts*, ed. Anna Roberts (Gainsville: University Press of Florida, 1998). See also the first chapter of Albrecht Classen, *The Power of a Woman's Voice in Medieval and Early Modern Literatures* (Berlin: Walter de Gruyter, 2007). All too often texts present women as victims: for views on women as *perpetrators* see Ross Balzaretti, '"These are things men do, not women": The social regulation of female violence in Langobard Italy', in *Violence and Society in the Early Medieval West*, ed. Guy Halsall (Woodbridge: Boydell, 1998), pp. 175–92. Dianne Hall, ed., *'A Great Effusion of Blood': Interpreting Medieval Violence* (Toronto: University of Toronto Press, 2004).

17. E.g. for the early modern period, *Violence, Politics and Gender in Early Modern England*, ed. J. P. Ward (London: Palgrave Macmillan, 2008); J. D. Gammon, *Narratives of Sexual Violence in England, 1640–1820* (Manchester: Manchester University Press, 2004); *Representing Rape in Medieval and Early Modern Literature*, ed. Elizabeth A. Robinson and Christine A. Rose (London: Palgrave Macmillan, 2001). The literature on violence against women in the modern era is too vast to list: a useful starting point is the bibliography at http://www.europrofem.org/material/books/09.book.htm (accessed 7/12/2009).

18. The publication of *Women and Gender in Medieval Europe: An Encyclopaedia*, ed. Margaret Schaus (London: Routledge, 2006) offers a myriad of ideas for further research.

Bibliography

(N.B. This bibliography contains references to some primary sources (those mentioned in the Introduction and introductory sections to chapters) as well as modern secondary sources. However, full references to the source texts included in this volume are given next to the texts themselves.)

Karen Adler, Ross Balzaretti and Michele Mitchell, 'Practising gender history', *Gender and History*, 20 (2008), 1–7.

Darryl W. Amundsen and Carol Jean Diers, 'The age at menarche in medieval Europe', *Human Biology*, 45 (1973), 363–9.

Darryl W. Amundsen and Carol Jean Diers, 'The age of menopause in medieval Europe', *Human Biology*, 45 (1973), 605–12.

Anna Komnena, *The Alexiad*, trans. E. R. A. Sewter (London: Penguin Books, 2004; originally published 1969).

The Archaeology of Infancy and Childhood: Proceedings of the conference held at the University of Kent, 2005), ed. M. Lally (Oxford: Archaeopress, 2009).

Clarissa W. Atkinson, *The Oldest Vocation: Christian Motherhood in the Middle Ages* (Ithaca: Cornell University Press, 1991).

Suzanne Bartlet, *Licoricia of Winchester: Marriage, Motherhood and Murder in the Medieval Anglo-Jewish Community*, ed. Patricia Skinner (London: Vallentine Mitchell, 2009).

Suzanne Bartlet, 'Three Jewish businesswomen in thirteenth-century Winchester', *Jewish Culture and History*, 3 (2000), 31–54.

Robert Bartlett, 'Symbolic meanings of hair in the middle ages', *Transactions of the Royal Historical Society*, Sixth series, 4 (1994), 43–60.

Elisheva Baumgarten, *Mothers and Children: Jewish Family Life in Medieval Europe* (Princeton: Princeton University Press, 2004).

Cordelia Beattie, 'A room of one's own? The legal evidence for the residential arrangements for women in late fourteenth- and early fifteenth-century York', in Menuge, ed., *Medieval Women and the Law*.

Cordelia Beattie, *Medieval Single Women: The Politics of Social Clarification in Later Medieval England* (Oxford: Oxford University Press, 2007).

Becoming Male in the Middle Ages, ed. Jeffrey Jerome Cohen and Bonnie Wheeler (New York: Garland Publishing, 2000).

Judith Bennett, *Ale, Beer and Brewsters: Women's Work in a Changing World* (Oxford: Oxford University Press, 1996).

Judith Bennett, *History Matters: Patriarchy and the Challenge of Feminism* (Philadelphia: University of Pennsylvania Press, 2006).

Judith Bennett, *Women in the Medieval English Countryside: Gender and Household in Brigstock before the Plague* (Oxford: Oxford University Press, 1987).

Renate Blumenfeld-Kosinski, *Not of Woman Born: Representations of Caesarean Birth in Medieval and Renaissance Culture* (Ithaca: Cornell University Press, 1990).

Katrinette Bodarwé, *Sanctimoniales litteratae. Schriftlichkeit und Bildung in den ottonischen Frauenkommunitäten Gandersheim, Essen und Quedlinburg* (Münster: Aschendorff, 2004).

Brenda Bolton, '"Received in his Name": Rome's busy baby box', *Studies in Church History*, 31 (1994), 153–67.

Book of the Knight of La Tour Landry, ed. D. B. Wyndham Lewis and G. S. Taylor (Kila: Kessinger Publishing, 2003).

Elisabeth Bos, 'The literature of spiritual formation for women in France and England, 1080 to 1180', in *Listen, Daughter: The Speculum Virginum and the Formation of Religious Women in the Middle Ages*, ed. Constant J. Mews (New York: Palgrave, 2001), pp. 201–20.

John Boswell, '*Expositio* and *oblatio*: The abandonment of children and the ancient and medieval family', *American Historical Review*, 89 (1984), 10–33.

John Boswell, *The Kindness of Strangers: The Abandonment of Children in Western Europe from Late Antiquity to the Renaissance* (New York: Pantheon Books, 1988).

C. N. L. Brooke, *The Medieval Idea of Marriage* (Oxford: Oxford University Press, 1991)

Gene Brucker, *Giovanni and Lusanna: Love and Marriage in Renaissance Florence* (Berkeley: University of California Press, 1988).

James Brundage, *Law, Sex and Christian Society in Medieval Europe* (Chicago: Chicago University Press, 1987).

J. A. Burrow, *Ages of Man: Studies in Medieval Writing and Thought* (Oxford: Clarendon Press, 1986).

Jeffrey Burton Russell, *Witchcraft in the Middle Ages* (Ithaca: Cornell University Press, 1984).

Joan Cadden, *The Meanings of Sex Difference in the Middle Ages* (Cambridge: Cambridge University Press, 1993).

Chris Callow, 'Transitions to adulthood in early Icelandic society', in Crawford and Shepherd, eds., *Children, Childhood and Society*, pp. 45–55.

The Cambridge Companion to Medieval Women's Writing, ed. Carolyn Dinshaw and David Wallace (Cambridge: Cambridge University Press, 2003).

Cartulaire de l'Abbaye de la Sainte-Trinité du mont de Rouen, ed. A. Deville, published as an appendix within *Cartulaire de l'Abbaye de St Bertin*, ed. M. Guérard, Collection de Documents inédits pour l'Histoire de France, Cartulaires, Vol. 3 (Paris: Imprimerie royale, 1841).

The Child in Christian Thought, ed. Marcia J. Bunge (Grand Rapids: William B. Eerdmans, 2001).

Children, Childhood and Society, Vol. 1, Institute for Archaeology and Antiquity Interdisciplinary Studies, ed. S. E. E. Crawford and G. B. Shepherd (Oxford: Archaeopress, 2007).

Chroniques des comtes d'Anjou et des seigneurs d'Amboise, ed. Louis Halphen and René Poupardin (Paris: A. Picard et fils, 1913).

Albrecht Classen, *The Power of a Woman's Voice in Medieval and Early Modern Literatures* (Berlin: Walter de Gruyter, 2007).

Albrecht Classen, 'Widows: Their social and moral functions according to medieval German literature, with special emphasis on Erhart Gross's *Witwenbuch* (1446)', *Fifteenth Century Studies*, 28 (2003), 65–79.

Carol J. Clover, 'Regardless of sex: Men, women and power in early northern Europe', *Speculum*, 68 (1993), 119–27.

Emily Coleman, 'Infanticide in the early Middle Ages', in *Women in Medieval Society*, ed. Susan Mosher Stuard (Philadelphia: University of Pennsylvania Press, 1976), pp. 47–70.

Consent and Coercion to Sex and Marriage in Ancient and Medieval Societies, ed. Angeliki E. Laiou (Washington: Dumbarton Oaks, 1998).

Lynda L. Coon, 'Somatic styles of the early Middle Ages', *Gender and History*, 20 (2008), 463–86.

Sally Crawford, *Childhood in Anglo-Saxon England* (Stroud: Sutton, 1999).

Sally Crawford, 'Companions, coincidences or chattels? Children in the early Anglo-Saxon multiple burial ritual', in Crawford and Shepherd, eds., *Children, Childhood and Society*, pp. 83–92.

Julia Crick, 'Women, wills and moveable wealth in pre-Conquest England', in *Gender and Material Culture in Historical Perspective*, ed. M. Donald and L. Hurcombe (London: Macmillan, 2000), pp. 17–37.

Pat Cullum, 'Vowesses and veiled widows: Medieval female piety in the province of York', *Northern History*, 32 (1996), 21–41.

David D'Avray, *Medieval Marriage: Symbolism and Society* (Oxford: Oxford University Press, 2005).

Mayke de Jong, *In Samuel's Image: Child Oblation in the Early Medieval West* (Leiden: Brill, 1995).

C. Donahue, *Law, Marriage and Society in the later Middle Ages* (Cambridge: Cambridge University Press, 2007).

Peter Dronke, *Women Writers of the Middle Ages: A Critical Study of Texts from Perpetua to Margaret Porete* (Cambridge: Cambridge University Press, 1984).

Georges Duby, 'Youth in aristocratic society: North-western France in the twelfth century', in *id.*, *The Chivalrous Society*, trans. Cynthia Postan (Berkeley: University of California Press, 1980).

Amy Eichorn-Mulligan, 'Contextualizing Old Norse-Icelandic bodies', paper read at the thirteenth International Saga Conference, Durham/York, 6–12 August 2006, and published at http://www.dur.ac.uk/medieval.www/sagaconf/eichorn.htm (accessed 9/09/2008).

Dyan Elliott, *Spiritual Marriage: Sexual Abstinence in Medieval Wedlock* (Princeton: Princeton University Press, 1995).

English Historical Documents, Vol. 1, ed. D. Whitelock, 2nd edn (London: Eyre Methuen, 1979).

T. Evergates, *The Aristocracy in the County of Champagne 1100–1300* (Philadelphia: University of Pennsylvania Press, 2007).

Tommaso di Carpegna Falconieri, *The Man Who Believed He was King of France*, trans. William McCuaig (Chicago: University of Chicago Press, 2008).

Fama: The Politics of Talk and Reputation in Medieval Europe, ed. Thelma Fenster and Daniel Lord Smail (Ithaca: Cornell University Press, 2003).

Sharon Farmer, *Surviving Poverty in Medieval Paris* (Ithaca: Cornell University Press, 2005).

Kirsten A. Fenton, *Gender, Nation and Conquest in the Works of William of Malmesbury* (Woodbridge: Boydell Press, 2008).

Thomas R. Forbes, *The Midwife and the Witch* (New Haven: Yale University Press, 1966).

Framing Medieval Bodies, ed. Sarah Kay and Miri Rubin (Manchester: Manchester University Press, 1994).

Allen Frantzen, 'Where the boys are: Children and sex in the Anglo-Saxon penitentials', in Cohen and Wheeler, eds., *Becoming Male in the Middle Ages*, pp. 43–66.

J. D. Gammon, *Narratives of Sexual Violence in England, 1640–1820* (Manchester: Manchester University Press, 2004).

Philip Gavitt, *Charity and Children in Renaissance Florence: The Ospedale degli Innocenti, 1410–1536* (Grand Rapids: University of Michigan Press, 1990).

Patrick Geary, *Living with the Dead in the Middle Ages* (Ithaca: Cornell University Press, 1994).

Gender and Material Culture in Historical Perspective, ed. M. Donald and L. Hurcombe (London: Macmillan, 2000).

Gendering the Master Narrative: Women and Power in the Middle Ages, ed. Mary C. Erler and Maryanne Kowaleski (Ithaca: Cornell University Press, 2003).

Frances and Joseph Gies, *Marriage and Family in the Middle Ages* (New York: Harper and Row, 1989).

Avner Giladi, *Infants, Parents and Wet Nurses: Medieval Islamic Views on Breastfeeding and their Social Implications* (Leiden: Brill, 1999).

'*A Great Effusion of Blood': Interpreting Medieval Violence*, ed. Dianne Hall (Toronto: University of Toronto Press, 2004).

P. J. P. Goldberg, 'Girls growing up in later medieval England', *History Today*, 45 (June 1995), 25–32.

P. J. P. Goldberg, *Women in England, 1275–1525* (Manchester: Manchester University Press, 1995).

The Good Wife's Guide (Le Menagier de Paris): A Medieval Household Book, trans. Gina L. Greco and Christine M. Rose (Ithaca: Cornell University Press, 2009).

Michael Goodich, 'The virtues and vices of old people in the late middle ages', *International Journal of Ageing and Human Development*, 30 (1990), 119–27.

Dennis Howard Green, *Women Readers in the Middle Ages* (Cambridge: Cambridge University Press, 2008).

Monica H. Green, *Making Women's Medicine Masculine: The Rise of Male Authority in Pre-modern Gynaecology* (Oxford: Oxford University Press, 2008).

F. J. Griffiths, *The Garden of Delights: Reform and Renaissance for Women in the Twelfth Century* (Philadelphia: University of Pennsylvania Press, 2007).

Guidance for Women in Twelfth-Century Convents, trans. V. Morton, with an interpretative essay by J. Wogan-Browne (Cambridge: D.S. Brewer, 2003).

Barbara Hanawalt, 'Of Good and Ill Repute': Gender and Social Control in Medieval England (Oxford: Oxford University Press, 1998).

Barbara Hanawalt, 'Remarriage as an option for urban and rural widows in late medieval England', in Wife and Widow in Medieval England, ed. Sue Sheridan Walker, pp. 141–64.

Barbara Hanawalt, The Ties that Bound: Peasant Families in Medieval England (Oxford: Oxford University Press, 1986).

Barbara Hanawalt, The Wealth of Wives: Women, Law and Economy in Late Medieval London (Oxford: Oxford University Press, 2007).

F. Harris-Stoertz, 'Pregnancy and childbirth in chivalric literature', Mediaevalia, 29 (2008), 25–36.

David J. Hay, The Military Leadership of Matilda of Canossa, 1046–1115 (Manchester: Manchester University Press, 2008).

Jennifer Wynne Hellwarth, The Reproductive Unconscious in Medieval and Early Modern England (London: Routledge, 2002).

R. H. Helmholz, Marriage Litigation in Medieval England (Cambridge: Cambridge University Press, 1974).

María del Carmen García Herrero, Del nacer y el vivir: fragmentos para una historia de la vida en la baja Edad Media, ed. Ángela Muñoz Fernández (Zaragoza: Institución Fernando el Catòlico, 2005).

María del Carmen García Herrero, Las mujeres en Zaragoza en el siglo XV, Vol. 2 (Zaragoza: Ayuntamiento de Zaragoza, 1990).

How the Good Wife Taught her Daughter, ed. T. Mustanoja (Helsinki: Suomalaisen Kirjallisuuden Scuran, 1948).

Diane Owen Hughes, 'From brideprice to dowry in Mediterranean Europe', Journal of Family History, 3 (1978), 262–96.

Diane Owen Hughes, 'Urban growth and family structure in medieval Genoa', Past and Present, 66 (1975), 3–28.

L. Huneycutt, Matilda of Scotland. A Study in Medieval Queenship (Woodbridge: Boydell, 2003).

R. F. Hunisett, The Medieval Coroner (Cambridge: Cambridge University Press, 1961, repr. 2008).

Susan Johns, Noblewomen, Aristocracy and Power in the Twelfth-Century Anglo-Norman Realm (Manchester: Manchester University Press, 2003).

Ruth Mazo Karras, From Boys to Men: Formations of Masculinity in Late Medieval Europe (Philadelphia: University of Pennsylvania Press, 2003).

Ruth Mazo Karras, 'The history of marriage and the myth of Friedelehe', Early Medieval Europe, 14 (2006), 119–51.

Richard Kieckhefer, Magic in the Middle Ages (Cambridge: Cambridge University Press, 1990).

Julius Kirshner, 'Wives' claims against insolvent husbands in late medieval Italy', in *Women of the Medieval World*, ed. Julius Kirshner and Suzanne Wemple (Oxford: Blackwell, 1985), pp. 256–303.

Ellen Kittell, 'Guardianship over women in medieval Flanders: A reappraisal', *Journal of Social History*, 31 (1998).

Rebecca Krug, *Reading Families: Women's Literate Practice in Late Medieval England* (Ithaca: Cornell University Press, 2002).

Thomas Kuehn, *Law, Family and Women: Toward a Legal Anthropology of Renaissance Italy* (Chicago: Chicago University Press, 1991).

Becky R. Lee, 'A company of women and men: Men's recollections of childbirth in medieval England', *Journal of Family History*, 27 (2002), 92–100.

Becky R. Lee, 'The purification of women after childbirth: A window onto medieval perceptions of women', *Florilegium*, 14 (1995–6), 43–55.

Helen Rodnite Lemay, 'Anthonius Guainerius and medieval gynecology', in *Women of the Medieval World*, ed. Julius Kirshner and Suzanne Wemple (Oxford: Blackwell, 1985), pp. 317–36.

D. Lett, *L'enfant des miracles: Enfance et société au moyen âge (XIIe–XIIIe siècle)* (Paris: Aubier, 1997).

Conrad Leyser, 'Long-haired kings and short-haired nuns: Writing on the body in Caesarius of Arles', *Studia Patristica*, 24 (1993), 143–50.

The Lombard Laws, tr. Katherine Fischer Drew (Philadelphia: University of Pennsylvania Press, 1973).

Christina Lutter, 'Ways of knowing and meanings of literacy in twelfth-century Admont', in *Strategies of Writing: Studies on Text and Trust in the Middle Ages: Papers from 'Trust in Writing in the Middle Ages' (Utrecht, 28–9 November 2002)*, ed. Petra Schulte, Marco Mostert and Irene van Renswoude, Utrecht Studies in Medieval Literacy, 13 (Turnhout: Brepols, 2008).

William F. MacLehose, *A Tender Age: Cultural Anxieties over the Child in the Twelfth and Thirteenth Centuries* (New York: Columbia University Press, 2008).

Ivan Marcus, *The Jewish Life Cycle: Rites of Passage from Biblical to Modern Times* (Washington: Washington University Press, 2004).

Masculinity in Medieval Europe, ed. D. M. Hadley (London: Longman, 1999).

June Hall McCash, *The Cultural Patronage of Medieval Women* (Athens, GA: University of Georgia Press, 1995).

Peggy McCracken, *The Curse of Eve and the Wound of the Hero: Blood, Gender and Medieval Literature* (Philadelphia: University of Pennsylvania Press, 2003).

Susan McDonough, 'Impoverished mothers and poor widows: Nego-
    tiating images of poverty in Marseille's courts', *Journal of Medi-
    eval History*, 34 (2008), 64–78.

Medieval London Widows, 1300–1500, ed. Caroline Barron and
    Anne Sutton (London: Hambledon, 1994).

Medieval Memories: Men, Women and the Past in Europe, 700–1300,
    ed. E. van Houts (Harlow: Longman, 2001).

Medieval Mothering, ed. John Carmi Parsons and Bonnie Wheeler
    (New York: Garland, 1999).

Medieval Women and the Law, ed. Noel James Menuge (Woodbridge:
    Boydell, 2000).

Medieval Writings on Female Spirituality, ed. Elizabeth Spearing
    (London and New York: Penguin Books, 2002).

Menstruation: A Cultural History, ed. Andrew Shail and Gillian
    Howie (Basingstoke: Palgrave Macmillan, 2005).

Irina Metzler, *Disability in Medieval Europe: Thinking about Physical
    Impairment in the High Middle Ages* (London: Routledge, 2006).

Mary Dockray Miller, *Motherhood and Mothering in Anglo-Saxon
    England* (New York: St Martins Press, 2000).

Narrative and History in the Early Medieval West, ed. Elizabeth M.
    Tyler and Ross Balzaretti (Turnhout: Brepols, 2006).

Carol Neel, *Medieval Families: Perspectives on Marriage, Household
    and Children* (Toronto: University of Toronto Press, 2004).

Janet L. Nelson, 'Gender and genre in women historians of the early
    middle ages', in *L'historiographie médievale en Europe*, ed. J.-P.
    Genet (Paris: Éditions du CNRS, 1991), pp. 149–63, reprinted in
    ead., The Frankish World, 750–900 (London: Hambledon, 1996),
    pp. 193–7.

Janet L. Nelson, 'Monks, secular men and masculinity', in *Masculinity
    in Medieval Europe*, ed. D. M. Hadley (London: Longman, 1998),
    pp. 121–42.

Janet L. Nelson, 'Queens as Jezebels: The careers of Brunhild and
    Bathild in Merovingian History', in *Medieval Women*, ed. Derek
    Baker (Oxford: Blackwell, 1978), pp. 31–77.

Janet Nelson, 'The wary widow', in *Property and Power in the Early
    Middle Ages*, ed. Wendy Davies and Paul Fouracre (Cambridge:
    Cambridge University Press, 1995), pp. 82–113.

*Old Age in the Middle Ages and the Renaissance: Interdisciplinary
    Approaches*, ed. Albrecht Classen (Berlin: Walter de Gruyter,
    2007).

Frederick Pedersen, *Marriage Disputes in Medieval England* (London:
    Hambledon Continuum, 2000).

Peter of Eboli, *De Rebus Siculis Carmen*, ed. E. Rota, Rerum Itali-
    carum Scriptores 31 (Città di Castello: S. Lapi, 1904).

Kim M. Phillips, *Medieval Maidens: Young Women and Gender in Eng-
    land, 1270–1540* (Manchester: Manchester University Press, 2003).

Eileen Power, *Medieval Women*, ed. M. M. Postan (Cambridge: Cam-
    bridge University Press, 1975).

Eileen Power, 'The position of women in the Middle Ages', in *The
    Legacy of the Middle Ages*, ed. C. G. Crump and E. F. Jacobs
    (Oxford: Clarendon Press, 1926), pp. 401–35.

Representing Rape in Medieval and Early Modern Literature, ed.
    Elizabeth A. Robinson and Christine A. Rose (London: Palgrave
    Macmillan, 2001).

Philip Lyndon Reynolds, *Marriage in the Western Church: The Chris-
    tianisation of Marriage during the Patristic and Early Medieval
    Periods* (Leiden: Brill, 1994).

J. M. Riddle, *Contraception and Abortion from the Ancient World to
    the Renaissance* (Cambridge: Harvard University Press, 1992).

Theodore J. Rivers, 'Widows' rights in Anglo-Saxon law', *The Ameri-
    can Journal of Legal History*, 19 (1975), 208–15.

J. T. Rosenthal, *Old Age in Late Medieval England* (Philadelphia:
    University of Pennsylvania Press, 1996).

Alwyn A. Ruddock, *Italian Merchants and Shipping in Southampton,
    1270–1600*, Vol. 1, Southampton Records Series (Southampton:
    University College, 1951).

Emmanuelle Santinelli, *Des femmes éplorées? Les veuves dans la
    société aristocratique du haut moyen âge* (Lille: Presses universi-
    taires du Septentrion, 2003).

B. Sawyer, *The Viking-Age Rune Stones Custom and Commemor-
    ation in Early Medieval Scandinavia* (Oxford: Oxford University
    Press, 2000).

Jane Tibbetts Schulenberg, *Forgetful of their Sex: Female Sanctity and
    Society, c.500–1100* (Chicago: University of Chicago Press, 1998).

Richard J. Shrader, *God's Handiwork: Images of Women in Early
    Germanic Literature* (Westport: Greenwood Press, 1983).

Elizabeth Sears, *The Ages of Man: Interpretations of the Life-cycle*
    (Princeton: Princeton University Press, 1986).

*Self and Society in Medieval France: The Memoirs of Abbot Guibert
    of Nogent*, ed. J. F. Benton (New York: Harper Torchbooks, 1970).

Shulamith Shahar, *Childhood in the Middle Ages* (London: Routledge,
    1992).

Shulamith Shahar, *Growing Old in the Middle Ages: 'Winter Clothes
    us in Shadow and Pain'* (London: Routledge, 1997).

Shulamith Shahar, 'Who were old in the Middle Ages?' *Social History of Medicine*, 6 (1993), 313–41.

Singlewomen in the European Past, 1250–1800, ed. Judith M. Bennett and Amy M. Froide (Philadelphia: Pennsylvania University Press, 1999).

W. Simons, *Cities of Ladies: Beguine Communities in the Medieval Low Countries, 1200–1565* (Philadelphia: University of Pennsylvania Press, 1999).

Sisters and Workers in the Middle Ages, ed. Judith Bennett, Elizabeth A. Clark, Jean F. O'Barr and B. Anne Vilen (Chicago: Chicago University Press, 1989).

Patricia Skinner, 'A cure for a sinner: Sickness and health care in medieval southern Italy', in *The Community, the Family and the Saint: Patterns of Power in Medieval Europe*, ed. Joyce Hill and Mary Swann (Turnhout: Brepols, 1998), pp. 297–309.

Patricia Skinner, 'Disputes and disparity: Women at court in medieval southern Italy', *Reading Medieval Studies*, 22 (1996), 85–105.

Patricia Skinner, 'Gender and poverty in the medieval community', in *Medieval Women in their Communities*, ed. Diane Watt (Cardiff: University of Wales Press, 1997), pp. 203–21.

Patricia Skinner, 'Gender and the sign languages of poverty', in *The Sign Languages of Poverty: International Round Table Discussion, Krems-an-der-Donau, October 10 and 11 2005*, ed. Gerhard Jaritz (Vienna: Verlag der Österreichischen Akademie der Wissenschaften, 2007), pp. 59–74.

Patricia Skinner, 'Gender, memory and Jewish identity: Reading a family history from medieval southern Italy', *Early Medieval Europe* 13, (2005), pp. 277–96.

Patricia Skinner, '"Halt! Be men!" Sikelgaita of Salerno, gender and the Norman conquest of southern Italy', *Gender and History*, 12 (2000), 622–41.

Patricia Skinner, *Health and Medicine in Early Medieval Southern Italy* (Leiden: Brill, 1997).

Patricia Skinner, 'Women, wills and wealth in medieval southern Italy', *Early Medieval Europe*, 3 (1993), 133–52.

Jennifer Smith, 'Unfamiliar territory: Women, land and law in Occitania, 1150–1250', in Menuge, ed., *Medieval Women and the Law*.

Richard M. Smith, 'Geographical diversity in the resort to marriage in later medieval Europe', in *Woman is a Worthy Wight: Women in English Society, 1200–1500*, ed. P. J. P. Goldberg (Stroud: Tempus, 1992), pp. 16–59.

Pauline Stafford, *Gender, Family and the Legitimation of Power:*

England from the Ninth to the Twelfth Century (Aldershot: Ashgate, 2006).

Pauline Stafford, *Queen Emma and Queen Edith: Queenship and Women's Power in Eleventh-Century England* (Oxford: Blackwell, 1997).

Pauline Stafford, 'Women and the Norman Conquest', *Transactions of the Royal Historical Society*, Sixth series, 4 (1994), 221–49.

Susan B. Steuer, 'Family strategies in medieval London: Financial planning and the urban widow', *Essays in Medieval Studies*, 12: *Children and Family in the Middle Ages*, ed. Nicole Clifton (Morgantown: West Virginia University Press, 1995), online edition at http://www.illinoismedieval.org/ems/VOL12/steuer.html (accessed 22/09/2009).

Brian Stock, *Listening for the Text: On the Uses of the Past* (Philadelphia: University of Pennsylvania Press, 1996).

Fiona Harris Stoertz, 'Young women in France and England, 1050–1300', *Journal of Women's History*, 12 (2001), 22–46.

S. Mosher Stuard, 'Ancillary evidence for the decline of medieval slavery', *Past and Present*, 149 (1995), 3–28.

Nathaniel L. Taylor, 'Women and wills: Sterility and testacy in Catalonia in the eleventh and twelfth centuries', *Medieval Encounters*, 12 (2006), 87–96.

The Treatise on the Laws and Customs of the Realm of England Commonly Called Glanvill, ed. G. D. G. Hall, with an introduction by M. T. Clanchy (Oxford: Clarendon Press, 1993).

The Trotula: A Medieval Compendium of Women's Medicine, ed. Monica H. Green (Philadelphia: University of Pennsylvania Press, 2001).

Upon My Husband's Death: Widows in the Literature and Histories of Medieval Europe, ed. Louise Mirrer (Ann Arbor: University of Michigan Press, 1992).

E. van Houts, 'Gender and authority of oral witnesses in Europe (800–1300)', *Transactions of the Royal Historical Society*, Sixth series., 9 (1999), 201–20.

E. van Houts, *History and Family Traditions in England and the Continent*, Variorum Collected Studies Series (Aldershot: Ashgate, 1999).

E. van Houts, *Memory and Gender in Medieval Europe 900–1200* (Basingstoke: Macmillan, 1999).

E. van Houts, 'Women and the Writing of History in the Early Middle Ages: The case of Abbess Matilda and Aethelweard,' *Early Medieval Europe*, 1 (1992), 53–68.

Veuves et veuvage dans le haut moyen âge, ed. M. Parisse (Paris: A. Picard et fils, 1993).

Violence against Women in Medieval Texts, ed. Anna Roberts (Gainsville: University Press of Florida, 1998).

Violence and Society in the Early Medieval West, ed. Guy Halsall (Woodbridge: Boydell, 1998).

Violence, Politics and Gender in Early Modern England, ed. J. P. Ward (London: Palgrave Macmillan, 2008).

The Voice of Silence: Women, Literacy and Gender in the Low Countries and Rhineland, 12th to 15th Centuries, ed. T. de Hemptinne and M. Gongora Diaz (Turnhout: Brepols, 2004).

Voices in Dialogue: Reading Women in the Middle Ages, ed. Linda Olson and Kathryn Kerby-Fulton (Notre Dame: University of Notre Dame Press, 2005).

Jennifer C. Ward, *Women in Medieval Europe, 1200–1500* (London: Longman, 2002).

Widowhood in Medieval and Early Modern Europe, ed. Sandra Cavallo and Lyndan Warner (London: Longman, 1999).

Wife and Widow in Medieval England, ed. Sue Sheridan Walker (Ann Arbor: University of Michigan Press, 1993).

Dudley Wilson, *Signs and Portents: Monstrous Births from the Middle Ages to the Enlightenment* (London: Routledge, 1993).

Rebecca Lynn Winer, 'Conscripting the breast: Lactation, slavery and salvation in the realms of Aragon and kingdom of Majorca, c.1250–1300', *Journal of Medieval History*, 34 (2008), 164–84.

Jocelyn Wogan-Browne, 'Powers of record, powers of example: Hagiography and women's history', in Erler and Kowaleski, eds., *Gendering the Master Narrative*, pp. 71–93.

Women and Gender in Medieval Europe: An Encyclopaedia, ed. Margaret Schaus (London: Routledge, 2006).

Women and Writing in Medieval Europe, ed. Carolyne Larrington (London: Routledge, 1995).

The Writings of Medieval Women, ed. Marcelle Thiebaux (New York: Garland, 1997).

Young Medieval Women, ed. Kim Phillips, Katherine Lewis and Noel James Menuge (Stroud: Alan Sutton, 1999).

Deborah Youngs, *The Life Cycle in Western Europe, c.1300–1500* (Manchester: Manchester University Press, 2006).